The Adams Test Preparation Guide for the PRAXIS I® and II® Tests

The Ultimate Test Prep Book for Teachers

Sandra Luna McCune, Ph.D.,
Vi Cain Alexander, Ph.D.,
Karen E. Jenlink, Ed.D.

Adams Media
Avon, Massachusetts

Published by
Adams Media, an F+W Publications Company
57 Littlefield Street, Avon, MA 02322. U.S.A.
www.adamsmedia.com

ISBN: 1-59337-115-2

Printed in the United States of America.

J   I   H   G   F   E   D   C   B   A

Library of Congress Cataloging-in-Publication Data
McCune, Sandra Luna.
The Adams test preparation guide for the PRAXIS I and II tests / Sandra Luna McCune,
Vi Cain Alexander, and Karen E. Jenlink.
p.   cm.
ISBN 1-59337-115-2
1. Pre-Professional Skills Tests—Study guides. 2. Principles of Learning and Teaching Test—Study guides. 3.
Teachers—Certification—United States. I. Alexander, Vi Cain. II. Jenlink, Karen E. III. Title.
LB2367.75.M33 2004
370'.76—dc22
2004022199

THE PRAXIS SERIES: PROFESSIONAL ASSESSMENTS FOR BEGINNING TEACHERS®
(with design [logo] or without), PRAXIS I®, PRAXIS II®, and PPST® are registered trademarks
of Educational Testing Service (ETS); PRAXIS™, PRAXIS III™, and THE PRAXIS SERIES™
are frequently used common law (non-registered trademarks) of ETS.

This publication is not endorsed or approved by ETS.

This publication is designed to provide accurate and authoritative information with regard to the subject matter covered. It is sold with the understanding that the publisher is not engaged in rendering legal, accounting, or other professional advice. If legal advice or other expert assistance is required, the services of a competent professional person should be sought.

—From a *Declaration of Principles* jointly adopted by a Committee of the
American Bar Association and a Committee of Publishers and Associations

Many of the designations used by manufacturers and sellers to distinguish their products are claimed as trademarks. Where those designations appear in this book and Adams Media was aware of a trademark claim, the designations have been printed in initial capital letters.

The questions included here represent a sample of possible types of questions you may expect to see on a PRAXIS® test. Not all types of test items that may appear on an actual test are illustrated in this publication. Actual test items are not necessarily identical to wording, format, or length in regard to the sample questions. The sample questions are designed to familiarize you with the nature of the PRAXIS® test; they are not designed to predict your performance on the test as a whole.

In settings that benefit learners' Student Retention Programs, permission is granted to freely copy, adapt, print, transmit, and distribute the "20 Memory Techniques" found on the Web at *http://students.uab.edu/services/show. asp?durki=54709.*

This book is available at quantity discounts for bulk purchases.
For information, call 1-800-872-5627.

Contents

Preface

The purpose of *The Adams Test Preparation Guide for the PRAXIS I® and II® Tests* is to serve as a preparation manual for teacher candidates taking the PRAXIS examination. This guide has been prepared to help test-takers apply their knowledge, improve test-taking skills, and build the confidence needed to earn successful qualifying scores. In addition, it will help to identify challenges, target areas that need reinforcement, and familiarize candidates with the PRAXIS examination format.

This book contains full-length multiple-choice diagnostic and practice tests with answers and explanations that cover reading, mathematics, and writing. The book's organization also includes an overview and sample questions for elementary education content knowledge. In addition, candidates will be provided with a Diagnostic Principles of Learning and Teaching examination and case study. Each of the tests is designed to enhance the teacher candidate's preparation effort.

When we planned this preparation guide, our aim was to provide teacher candidates with the tools necessary to master the PRAXIS examination. Our hope is that its organization, sample questions and explanations, and focus on content will facilitate the candidate's success in obtaining licensure.

Part 1

Overview

Chapter 1

Overview of the PRAXIS Exams

1.0

THE PRAXIS SERIES

The PRAXIS I and the PRAXIS II consist of a series of standardized exams, developed by Educational Testing Service (ETS), that are used by nearly 80 percent of states for certification (or licensure) of teachers. The way the exams are used varies from state to state. Commonly, the PRAXIS I exams, which are basic skills tests, are used in conjunction with other state criteria to determine eligibility for entry into a teacher education program. As candidates reach completion of their teacher education program, they take one or more exams from the PRAXIS II series.

The PRAXIS II series is designed for professional assessment of prospective teachers. Usually, a candidate for teacher certification must take and pass at least two types of exams: a pedagogy exam and a content exam. The pedagogy exam tests general knowledge about how to teach. The content exam tests candidates' knowledge of the subjects they will teach, as well as subject-specific pedagogical skills and knowledge. For states using the PRAXIS II series, the pedagogy exam is called the Principles of Learning and Teaching (PLT). Which of the PRAXIS II content tests will be required for the content exam depends on the certification field of study and state requirements.

Although about 80 percent of states require exams such as THE PRAXIS SERIES tests, the educational requirements, specific tests, and test scores needed to obtain certification vary widely. Due to this variation among the states and to the frequency with which the information changes, a list of state requirements is not included here.

However, if you want to become a teacher, we can offer you assistance in obtaining the certification information you need. There are several ways you can find out requirements for certification of teachers in a particular state. The teacher certification office at a university or college that offers a teacher education program in that state can tell you about state requirements, including which tests are required for your grade level and field of study. Web sites for state boards (departments) of education or state education agencies are reliable sources for current certification requirements. The National Association of State Directors of Teacher Education and Certification (NASDTEC) provides links to state Web sites at *www.nasdtec.org/state_info.tpl*. Finally, ETS maintains a listing by state of links to test requirements for those states that require THE PRAXIS SERIES exams for certification at *www.ets.org/praxis/prxstate.html*.

THE PRAXIS SERIES exams are given six times during an academic year (usually in September, November, January, March, April, and June). You can find information on fees, registration procedures, and policies in the current *Registration Bulletin,* available at *www.ets.org/praxis*. ETS charges a nonrefundable $35 registration fee per test date in addition to the fee or fees for the particular test or tests you are taking.

1.1

The PRAXIS I

The PRAXIS I exams are more commonly known as the Pre-Professional Skills Tests (PPST) of Reading, Mathematics, and Writing. The three tests comprising the PPST are designed to measure basic skills in the three areas of reading, mathematics, and writing.

The PPST Reading (Test Code 0710) will assess your ability to read, understand, and analyze written material. It contains forty multiple-choice questions that must be completed within sixty minutes. The test questions are matched to reading passages of 100 to 200 words each or to short statements. The reading material is from a variety of subject areas and is similar to what you have seen in your previous educational experience. You won't be asked to read something that is highly technical or that requires special prior knowledge to understand.

The PPST Mathematics (Test Code 0730) will assess your ability to perform the basic mathematics needed in everyday life—the math you learned in elementary school and your first year of high school. It contains forty multiple-choice questions that must be completed within sixty minutes.

The PPST Writing (Test Code 0720) will assess your ability to communicate clearly and effectively in writing. It consists of two sections: a set of forty-five multiple-choice questions and a writing sample, each of which has a thirty-minute time limit. The multiple-choice section is divided into two parts that assess your ability to recognize various elements of effective writing. For the writing sample, you are required to write an essay on an assigned topic. The writing sample section is designed to assess your ability to create, organize, and express ideas in writing. The writing prompt will be on a topic familiar to you and will not require that you have specialized knowledge in some subject area.

ETS allows you to take the PPST individually or in any combination. According to the *2003–2004 Registration Bulletin,* available online at *www.ets.org/praxis*, the current fee for each PPST is $25. You can always get up-to-date information about registration and fees by accessing the online *Registration Bulletin* or by calling ETS at (609) 771-7395 or sending an e-mail to *praxis@ets.org*.

1.2

The PRAXIS II

The PRAXIS II is not just one test—it is a series of tests designed to assess prospective teachers' general knowledge and skills about learning, teaching, assessment, and professionalism and to assess their knowledge and skills in their certification field of study.

The Principles of Learning and Teaching (PLT) tests are used to assess general knowledge and skills about learning, teaching, assessment, and professionalism. Each exam has a two-hour time limit and consists of two sections: a set of twenty-four multiple-choice questions and a set of twelve short-answer questions based on four case histories. Each case history describes a teaching situation and is followed by three short-answer questions related to the situation. ETS offers three levels for the PLT—the PLT: Grades K–6; the PLT: Grades 5–9; and the PLT: Grades 7–12. Your certification level will determine which of these three exams you should take. All of the PLT exams are based on the same set of broad topics that cover the knowledge and skills that beginning teachers should have in order to teach effectively. This book will help you prepare for any of the PLT tests. According to the *2003–2004 Registration Bulletin*, the current fee to take a PLT is $80.

The PRAXIS II series has over 100 subject-specific tests. For these tests you must demonstrate your knowledge and skills in your chosen field of study. Obviously, since there are 100 subject assessments, it is not feasible for this book to cover all of them. We have selected six that we feel may be of most interest to highlight in this publication. If your subject test is not featured in this book, you can find detailed information and sample questions by using the Tests at a Glance feature on the ETS Web site at *www.ets.org/praxis*.

Chapter 2

How to Use This Book

2.0

About This Book

This book focuses on test preparation for the PPST Reading, Mathematics, and Writing exams and for the Principles of Learning and Teaching (PLT) exam. Also included are overviews of the following:

- Elementary Education: Content Knowledge Test
- Elementary Education: Curriculum, Instruction, and Assessment Test
- Elementary Education: Content Area Exercises
- Fundamental Subjects: Content Knowledge Test
- English Language, Literature, and Composition: Content Knowledge Test
- Mathematics: Content Knowledge Test

2.1

PPST Preparation

The PPST assesses your basic skills in reading, mathematics, and writing. Use the following guidelines in preparing for the PPST:

1. To help you organize and budget your time, set up a specific schedule of study sessions. Try to set aside at least two hours per session. If your test date is coming up soon, you may need to extend the session length in order to be ready on your planned test date.

2. After reading over the general test-taking strategies in Chapter 3, take the diagnostic PPST in Chapter 4 before you begin your study program. Take the tests under the same conditions you expect for the real test, and be very careful to adhere to the time limits for each test. The diagnostic tests will help you pinpoint your strengths and weaknesses. When you finish taking the tests, carefully study

the answer explanations given in Chapter 5. For the multiple-choice questions, read the explanations for all the questions, not just the ones you missed, because you may have arrived at some of your correct answers incorrectly or by guessing. For the essay response, try to see where your answer might have failed to adequately address the given prompt. Of course, you will have to judge the quality of your response in comparison to the suggested response.

3. Plan your study program so that you work on your weakest area first. If you did fairly well in mathematics and writing but poorly in reading, then you may want to begin your PPST study with the reading review.

4. Work through the PPST reviews in Chapters 6 through 8, and read the study tips in Chapter 9. Take notes as you study, and put ideas in your own words. Make flashcards for concepts you had difficulty understanding. Review your cards periodically, and always carry a few with you to look over when you have spare minutes of idle time.

5. When you finish your review, take the practice PPST in Chapter 10. As before, take the tests under the same conditions you expect for the real test, and adhere to the time limits for each test. When you finish taking the tests, check your answers against those given in Chapter 11.

6. Review topics in which you are still weak.

7. Retake the diagnostic test for practice when you feel your PPST preparation is complete.

2.2

Principles of Learning and Teaching (PLT) Test Preparation

The PLT assesses your general knowledge about learning, teaching, and professionalism. As you will notice, the PLT guidelines for test preparation are very similar to the guidelines for preparing for the PPST. Keep in mind, though, that the PPST is a basic skills entry-level test while the PLT is an exit-level assessment. This means, of course, that the PLT tests your higher-order thinking skills much more than the PPST.

1. To help you organize and budget your time, set up a specific schedule of study sessions. Try to set aside at least two hours per session. If your test date is coming up soon, you may need to extend the session length in order to be ready on your planned test date.

2. After reading over the general test-taking strategies in Chapter 3, take the diagnostic PLT test in Chapter 12 before you begin your study program. Take the test under the same conditions you expect for the real test, and be very careful to adhere to the two-hour time limit. The diagnostic test will help you pinpoint

your strengths and weaknesses. When you finish taking the test, carefully study the answer explanations given in Chapter 13 for all the questions. For the multiple-choice responses, make sure you understand why the correct answer is correct. For the short-answer questions, try to see where your answer might have failed to adequately address the question. Of course, you will have to judge the quality of your response in comparison to the suggested response.

3. Plan your study program so that you work on those topics you didn't fully understand. Additionally, if you did fairly well on the multiple-choice questions but feel your responses on the short-answer questions were weak, then plan to concentrate more on how to respond to the short-answer questions.

4. Work through the PLT review in Chapter 14. Take notes as you study, and try to relate what you read to real teaching situations. Make flashcards for important ideas and terms. Review your cards periodically, and always carry a few with you to look over when you have spare minutes of idle time.

5. Review the "Tips for New Teachers" in the Appendix.

6. When you finish your review, take the practice PLT test in Chapter 15. As before, take the tests under the same conditions you expect for the real test and adhere to the two-hour time limit. When you finish taking the test, check your answers.

7. Review those topics that warrant additional study time.

8. Retake the diagnostic test for practice when you feel your PLT test preparation is complete.

Chapter 3

General Test-Taking Strategies

The following test-taking strategies should help you maximize your performance on the PRAXIS tests.

1. Arrive early, and take time to relax before the test begins. Mentally prepare yourself by visualizing yourself achieving your goal of performing successfully on the test.

2. When you receive your test, plan how you will use the time allotted for the test. Bring a watch so that you can keep track of the passing time. When half your time is up, check to see whether you have reached the halfway point in that section of the test. If not, you will need to speed up.

3. Follow all directions carefully, including the oral directions of the test administrator and the written directions in the test booklet.

4. Answer the test questions in order without skipping or jumping around. If a question is taking too long, make a guess and move on. Make a mark in the margin of the test booklet next to questions you are not sure of. Go back to these questions as time permits after all questions have been answered.

5. If a test section is made up of multiple-choice and short-answer questions, answer the multiple-choice questions first. However, be sure to leave enough time to organize your ideas and write adequate responses for the short-answer questions.

6. Read each question carefully and completely. Do not try to save time by skimming through the question; you may misread important words and select the wrong answer. To help you stay focused, circle or underline key information in the test booklet.

7. Be especially alert when the question stem contains negative wording such as *not* or *except*. Always reread these questions before answering.

8. Watch out for qualifying words such as *all, none, always,* and *never* in answer choices. These words often signal incorrect answers because they are too absolute. Be careful, though! Test-makers know you know about these words. They might try to trick you.

9. Read all the answer choices before deciding which one to choose because there might be two answers that sound good, but one is a better response to the question.

10. Eliminate as many wrong answers as you can. If two answer options say the same thing in different words, it means they both must be wrong. If two answers contradict each other, one of them must be wrong. After you've made your eliminations, go back and reread the question before you decide between the remaining choices. This will help you make the right choice.

11. If a question addresses a topic that you know you studied, but you can't recall the information you need in order to answer the question, try to think of something that is linked to the information you're trying to recall. Think of related facts and concepts. Also try to visualize where you were and what you were doing when you were studying the topic. These associations may trigger your memory. Even if you don't recall the information right away, your unconscious mind will still search and may give you the answer later. If that happens, stop immediately and jot down what you remembered because it might fade away again.

12. Try to answer all the test questions. You are not penalized for wrong answers on the PRAXIS tests (you merely score a zero for that question), so mark an answer for every multiple-choice question even if you don't have a clue what the correct answer is. For the essay and short-answer questions, do your best to write a response. You may get a passing score even if you think you wrote a poor answer.

13. Write in the test booklet. It's okay to do so. Take advantage of this by circling or underlining information, marking up graphs or figures, and working out mathematical computations in the test booklet. However, don't forget to mark your answers on the separate answer sheet.

14. Change an answer only if you have a good reason to do so. You shouldn't change an answer based on a hunch or whim. If you do change an answer, be sure to erase the old answer completely before marking the new one.

15. Take care in marking your answer sheet. The multiple-choice questions on the tests are scored electronically, so you must be very careful in recording your answer choices. Using a circular motion, fill in the answer space corresponding to your answer, starting in the middle of the answer space and working outwards. Be careful not to make stray marks outside the answer space because the scoring machine may misinterpret these.

16. Mark the answers on your answer sheet in bunches rather than one question at a time. As you proceed through the test booklet, circle the letters of your chosen answers in the test booklet. Then transfer those answers to the answer sheet in bunches of five or more (until the last minutes of the time allotted, when you should start marking answers one by one). That way there's less chance that you will accidentally mark the wrong answer.

Practice these tried-and-true strategies as you work through the diagnostic and practice tests provided in this test preparation book. They are good tips that you can use to get the most out of your knowledge. However, remember that studying and knowing the material well is the best insurance for success on a test! So don't rely solely on these strategies—study!

Part 2

Diagnostic PPST

Chapter 4

Diagnostic PPST

READING

40 Questions
Time—60 minutes

Directions: Each statement or passage in this test is followed by a question or questions based on its content. After reading each statement or passage, read each question that follows, and then choose the one best answer from the five choices given. Answer the questions based on what is stated or implied in the passage.

Mark your answer on the answer sheet. Fill in the space that has the same letter as the answer you have selected.

Questions 1–5

In the period following the Civil War, dishonesty of every sort crept into city and state governments. Public money was misused. Bribery was widespread. In their desire for wealth and power, some men in high places forfeited their honor for gold and silver.

1. Which of the following statements best summarizes the main idea of the passage?
   A. The Civil War led to corruption of city and state government officials.
   B. Following the Civil War, city and state government officials engaged in dishonest practices.
   C. Gold and silver are poor substitutes for honor.
   D. Prior to the Civil War, dishonesty of city and state officials was not a problem.
   E. Following the Civil War, dishonesty of public officials led to widespread demand for reform.

2. The author's primary purpose in this passage is to:
   A. inform
   B. entertain
   C. explain
   D. ridicule
   E. compare

3. The tone of the passage is:
   A. sarcastic
   B. inquiring
   C. amusing
   D. disapproving
   E. indifferent

4. Which of the following words, if substituted for the word *forfeited* in sentence 4, would introduce the LEAST change in the meaning of the sentence?
   A. desecrated
   B. procured
   C. relinquished
   D. foreswore
   E. perverted

5. Which of the following statements can be inferred from the passage?
   A. Following the Civil War, some government officials used public money inappropriately.
   B. Prior to the Civil War, city and state public officials acted honorably.
   C. Following the Civil War, there was a need for political reform in city and state governments.
   D. In the period after the Civil War, some men in high places forfeited wealth and power for gold and silver.
   E. After the Civil War, all public officials were corrupt and dishonest.

Questions 6–10

Comprehension of a continuous prose passage may be measured by various methods. Simplest and most common is that of reproduction. The child is required to relate viva voce, or to set down in writing from memory, the substance of the passage just read. The account may then be assessed either by reckoning the number of unit ideas correctly reproduced or, more simply, by crossing out erroneous words and phrases, and counting the total number of written words remaining. However the exercise must be marked, the procedure in itself is not very exact and, in any case, affords a test of memory rather than of comprehension. One child may precipitate, as it were, whole clauses, word for word, without ever having absorbed a particle of their meaning. Another may omit an entire block of sentences, not because the child has read them without grasping them, but because, through the relative unimportance of the contents, through the distraction of writing and spelling, or, it may be, through some inexplicable freak of recollection, the child fails for the moment to recall a paragraph that he or she fully comprehends.

6. What is the main idea of this passage?
   A. Comprehension is shown by what can be recalled at a given moment.
   B. One of the simplest and most common forms of measuring comprehension is reproduction.
   C. Comprehension can be taught by memory drills and repetition.
   D. Children use a variety of methods to comprehend a continuous prose passage.
   E. Testing memory is not a test of comprehension.

7. Being able to repeat long phrases word for word ensures that a student comprehends a continuous prose passage.
   A. This statement is true.
   B. This statement is false.
   C. It depends on the situation whether this statement is true or false.
   D. This statement cannot be evaluated from the passage.
   E. Comprehension can always be determined through testing memory.

8. What, according to the passage, is reproduction?
   A. being able to repeat word for word
   B. writing from memory what the passage said
   C. relating viva voce
   D. continuity
   E. repetition

9. What does the term viva voce mean?
   A. the ability to relate the text to the reader's own life
   B. analyzing the text
   C. reporting by mouth
   D. paraphrasing
   E. outlining the text

10. What does the term "erroneous" mean in this passage?
   A. not necessary
   B. misleading
   C. mistaken
   D. false
   E. distant

Questions 11–14

The Jews were tolerated in England because of the immense sums of money they possessed. Hence, they were frequently approached by the nobles for loans. Though put under various forms of taxation in order to wring their money from them, they seemed to regain it. The meanest serfs would not sit at the table with them. Even though they were persecuted, the Jews remained in England because they could collect from their debtors sums of money so large as to make the persecution seem worthwhile. Even the king borrowed sums of money from them. Some of the nobles tortured the Jews to force their money from them.

11. In the passage money was wrung from the Jews by all the following ways EXCEPT:
    A. taxes
    B. persecution
    C. torture
    D. resentment
    E. borrowing

12. According to the passage, why did the Jews remain in England and suffer heavy persecution?
    A. They were rich.
    B. They suffered and were persecuted.
    C. The king borrowed sums of money from them.
    D. Debt-collecting was worth it.
    E. They were poor.

13. "The meanest serfs would not sit at the table with them." This form of persecution is:
    A. heavy taxation
    B. asking for loans
    C. torture
    D. exclusion
    E. abandonment

14. According to the passage, the Jews were tolerated because:
    A. They were rich.
    B. They loaned money to nobles.
    C. They loaned the king sums of money.
    D. They were poor.
    E. They loaned money to the Jews.

Questions 15–20

In medieval and early modern times those articles only could be transported for any considerable distance which had great value in small bulk. Such were drugs, spices, fine clothes, rare silks and cottons, choice weapons, and armor. Chiefly the small circle of the rich used these; trading them did not affect the mass of the population. Where water transportation could be used there was indeed some possibility of trade and exchange in the bulkier commodities. For this reason, England, with her insular position and much-indented seacoast, was able at a comparatively early stage to export such commodities as wool, copper, and tin, and to develop in some degree the geographical division of labor. With the improvement and enlargement of some vessels, the greater security of the seas, and the use of the mariner's compass, trade by water gradually grew to greater and greater dimensions. A still further extension came in the latter part of the eighteenth century, when parts of the interior of the civilized countries were tapped by canals. But the most far-reaching development of the geographical division of labor came with the railway, for the railway can reach all parts of the land. The industry of almost every part of the world has been transformed by this mighty solvent.

—F.W. Taussig, *The Principles of Economics*

15. What is the main idea of the passage?
    A. The greatest achievement in the transformation of trade from medieval times to current times has been caused by the invention of the railway.
    B. Water was the primary choice of travel for trading in the medieval and early modern times.
    C. The geographical division of labor became more prevalent as methods of trade became more advanced.
    D. Trading, while previously only affecting the small circle of the rich, has come to affect the mass of population.
    E. With the improvement and enlargement of some vessels, the greater security of the seas, and the use of the mariner's compass, trade by water gradually grew to greater and greater dimensions.

16. To what does the "mighty solvent" in the last sentence refer?
    A. the geographical division of labor
    B. the invention of the railway
    C. the industry of almost every part of the world
    D. all parts of the land
    E. tapping the interior of civilized countries with canals

17. Which mode of transportation of trade helped to initially define the geographical division of labor?
    A. water
    B. canals
    C. railways
    D. cars
    E. buses

18. Why was the invention of the railway called most far-reaching?
    A. Trade became land-based.
    B. Railways can be laid anywhere.
    C. Waterways dried up, and they needed a new alternative.
    D. It promoted the geographical division of labor.
    E. It transformed industry in almost every part of the world.

19. Why was England considered more advanced in trading than other countries?
    A. It was first to be able to trade bulkier items such as wool, copper, and tin.
    B. It developed a geographical division of labor before other countries.
    C. It had an insular position and indented seacoast.
    D. It made improvements and enlargements to its vessels.
    E. The trade of water grew to greater dimensions.

20. It can be inferred from the passage that:
    A. Automobiles had not been invented yet.
    B. Airplanes had not been invented yet.
    C. The biggest achievement in trade transportation is that land-based trade barriers have been overcome.
    D. The geographical division of labor caused many advances in trade transportation.
    E. Industry of every part of the world has been transformed by the railway system.

Questions 21–25

Of course, there is a portion of reading quite indispensable to a wise man. History and exact science he must learn by laborious reading. Colleges, like in manner, have their indispensable office, to teach elements. But they can only highly serve us, when they aim not to drill, but to create; when they gather from far every ray of various genius to their hospitable halls, and, by the concentrated fires, set the hearts of their youth on flame. Thought and knowledge are natures in which apparatus and pretension avail nothing. Gowns and pecuniary foundations, though of towns of gold, can never countervail the least sentence or syllable of wit. Forget this, and our American colleges will recede in their public importance, whilst they grow richer every year.

—from "The American Scholar," a commencement address delivered by Ralph Waldo Emerson to the Phi Beta Kappa Society at Harvard in 1837

21. In the passage the author explicitly states that a purpose for reading is:
    A. to acquire wisdom
    B. to increase knowledge and thought
    C. to teach elements
    D. to broaden your horizons
    E. to learn history and exact science

22. The term *pecuniary foundations* in the sixth sentence means which of the following?
    A. financial institutions
    B. institution requiring high academic achievement
    C. military academies
    D. private colleges or universities
    E. state colleges or universities

23. According to the author, colleges can serve the public in the highest capacity by:
    A. drilling facts
    B. encouraging thought
    C. encouraging repetition and practice
    D. ignoring the hearts of youth
    E. reaching out to people of all ages

24. The term *gowns* in the sixth sentence means which of the following:
    A. administration of a university
    B. fancy dress that comes with a degree from a university
    C. bursar's office of a university
    D. full-time students of a university
    E. part-time students of a university

25. "Forget this, and our American colleges will recede in their public importance, whilst they grow richer every year." In the context of the passage, the author uses this statement to mean the following.
    A. American colleges can increase knowledge by increasing their own wealth.
    B. The expensive schools are the better schools in America.
    C. If American colleges ignore their calling to create great thinkers, they will only become rich institutions that have decreased in public importance.
    D. Cheaper schools offer a better education.
    E. American colleges are a better choice than studying abroad.

Questions 26–31

Could the young realize how soon they would become mere walking bundles of habits, they would give more heed to their conduct while in the plastic state. We are spinning our own fates, good or evil, and never to be undone. Every smallest stroke of virtue or of vice leaves its never-so-little scar. The drunken Rip Van Winkle, in Jefferson's play, excuses himself for every fresh dereliction by saying, "I won't count this time!" Well, he may not count it, and a kind of heaven may not count it; but it is being counted none the less. Down among his nerve-cells and fibres the molecules are counting it, registering and storing it up to be used against him when the next temptation comes. Nothing we ever do is, in strict scientific literalness, wiped out.

Of course, this has its good side as well as its bad one. As we become permanent drunkards by so many separate drinks, so we become saints in the moral, and authorities and experts in the practical and scientific spheres, by so many separate acts and hours of work. Let no youth have any anxiety about the upshot of his education, whatever the line of it may be. If he keeps faithfully busy each hour of the working day, he may safely leave the final result to itself. He can with perfect certainty count on waking up some fine morning to find himself one of the component ones of his generation, in whatever pursuit he may have singled out. Silently, between all the details of his business, the *power of judging* in all that class of matter will have built itself up within him as a possession that will never pass away. Young people should know this truth in advance. The ignorance of it has probably engendered more discouragement and faint-heartedness in youths embarking on arduous careers than all other causes put together.

—William James, *Talks to Teachers*

26. The main point of the first paragraph is which of the following?
    A. Nothing is ever "wiped out" completely.
    B. Just like drunkards that "don't count this one," our actions are always affected.
    C. Every smallest stroke of virtue or of vice leaves its never-so-little scar.
    D. We are spinning our own fates, good or evil, and never to be undone.
    E. Someone is always watching everything you do.

27. The main point of the second paragraph is which of the following?
    A. As we become permanent drunkards by so many separate drinks, so we become saints in the moral, and authorities and experts in the practical and scientific spheres, by so many separate acts and hours of work.
    B. He can with perfect certainty count on waking up some fine morning to find himself one of the component ones of his generation, in whatever pursuit he may have singled out.
    C. Young people should know this truth in advance.
    D. If he keeps faithfully busy each hour of the working day, he may safely leave the final result to itself.
    E. Let no youth have the anxiety about the upshot of his education, whatever it may be.

28. The term *plastic* in the first sentence refers to what?
    A. malleable
    B. durable
    C. changing
    D. impressionable
    E. easily influenced

29. "We are spinning our own fates, good or evil, and never to be undone." In this statement, the author means:
    A. We are good and evil characters, and that state never changes.
    B. Our beginning acts are practice for what later become habits that never change.
    C. We are condemned to a life of good or evil, which will never change.
    D. We choose our own fates by our actions, which can be changed later.
    E. You learn from your mistakes.

30. The example of Rip Van Winkle is used to illustrate which point?
    A. Actions have consequences.
    B. Drunkards always start with one drink that "doesn't count."
    C. Drunkards develop habits, which are impossible to break.
    D. Drinking causes nerve damage.
    E. Consequences, although invisible, are always present from our actions.

31. In the second paragraph, to what does "the power of judging" refer?
    A. a possession that will never pass away
    B. moral judgment
    C. gaining importance and expertise
    D. the result of many separate acts and hours of work
    E. all the details of his business

Questions 32–37

Experience is a continuous process of choice and comparison, selecting one thing and correlating that in the mind with another. I believe that choice and comparison are in some degree present every time that anyone is really conscious of anything. It is easy to show that choice is always present; you have only to go somewhere, and stand still, and reflect how many things there are about you, which you are not seeing. Existence is too full for you. You see only the things that your tastes and purposes determine, and of these you see sharply only such features as affect those tastes and purposes. Other persons will see other things, and other features of the same things.

Suppose that you are standing by the side of the road, and a horse and wagon jogs by. You see the horse and wagon, and you observe that it is picturesque. The horse is shaggy, a strawberry roan. But suppose that there is a farmer standing beside you, and he sees it too; he observes that the horse is lazy, ewe-necked, pot-bellied, has a ring-bone on the left hind foot, and other features which relate to the purposes of agriculture. How different is your perception from his, though you are looking the same way and standing almost in the same tracks! It might be, indeed, if you choose to look a different way, and if you happened to have that genius for concentrating yourself upon what you do see which is called absent-mindedness—it might be that you would never be aware there was a horse there at all, or so much as the noise of a wagon.

—Max Eastman, *The Enjoyment of Poetry*

32. The main idea of the passage is which of the following?
    A. You see only the things that your tastes and purposes determine, and of these you see sharply only such features that affect those tastes and purposes.
    B. Other persons will see other things, and other features of the same things.
    C. Experience is a continuous process of choice and comparison, selecting one thing and correlating that in the mind with another.
    D. Existence is too full for you.
    E. Choice and comparison are in some degree present every time that anyone is really conscious of anything.

33. Which of the following would be the best title for the passage?
    A. Perception and Reality
    B. Experience and Perception
    C. Perception Is Reality
    D. Perception Affects Experience
    E. Perception Depends Upon Experience

34. In the second paragraph and third sentence, the term *roan* is used to mean:
    A. ewe
    B. horse
    C. man
    D. farmer
    E. wagon

35. As it is used in the passage, absent-mindedness refers to which of the following?
    A. forgetfulness
    B. ability to concentrate on many aspects
    C. choosing to look in a different way
    D. unawareness
    E. conscientious

36. The example of the horse and wagon is used to illustrate which point?
    A. Two people can see the exact same thing and observe different aspects of it.
    B. Two people experiencing the same reality will experience the same perceptions.
    C. Two people that see a horse and wagon going by will see it as picturesque.
    D. A farmer that sees a horse and wagon going by sees the agricultural characteristics of the horse.
    E. Absent-minded people will not notice the presence of the horse or hear the noise of the wagon.

37. According to the author, which of the following is NOT true about choice?
    A. Choice is omnipresent.
    B. Choice is in every experience.
    C. It is easy to show that choice is present.
    D. Choice and comparison are affected by experience.
    E. There are good and bad choices in life.

Questions 38–40

In arithmetic, more than in other subjects, teachers are prepared to define, precisely and without hesitation, the attainments to be expected at successive ages. In arithmetic, graded tests would prove the easiest of all such tests to construct. They have proved the most arduous. In no subject are children so influenced by the range of instruction and so responsive to the degree of practice in the specific processes; and in no subject do those influences now so obstinately defy prediction. Teaching, instead of unifying the grading, renders it unstable.

38. According to the passage, what is different about arithmetic when compared to other subjects?
    A. Tests are easy to construct.
    B. Practicing discourages success.
    C. Children are influenced by the range of instruction.
    D. It is difficult to attain children's attention.
    E. Instructors are influential.

39. What is the main idea of the passage?
    A. Teaching is an important factor in math education.
    B. Students should achieve certain mathematical milestones at certain ages.
    C. Constructing arithmetic tests is an arduous process.
    D. Teaching makes grading mathematics unstable.
    E. Learning can be a fun experience.

40. The term *arduous* in the passage means:
    A. easy
    B. difficult
    C. laborious
    D. fun
    E. effortless

GO ON TO THE NEXT PAGE

MATHEMATICS

40 Questions
Time—60 minutes

Directions: Read each question that follows, and then choose the one best answer from the five choices given. Mark your answer on the answer sheet. Fill in the space that has the same letter as the answer you have selected.

1. Which of the following numbers is least?
   A.   15.72
   B.   15.4
   C.   15.20
   D.   15.49
   E.   15.5

2. A recipe calls for $2\frac{1}{2}$ cups of milk and $1\frac{3}{4}$ cups of water. The remaining ingredients are sugar, flour, and butter. How much liquid is called for in the recipe?

   A. $3\frac{1}{4}$ cups

   B. $4\frac{1}{4}$ cups

   C. $4\frac{1}{2}$ cups

   D. $4\frac{4}{6}$ cups

   E. $3\frac{1}{2}$ cups

3. The graph shows a budget for a monthly salary.

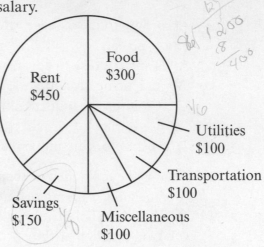

Monthly Budget

Which of the following is a reasonable conclusion from the information in the graph?

   A.   The combined amount budgeted for rent and food uses less than $\frac{1}{2}$ of the monthly salary.

   B.   The budget indicates $\frac{1}{8}$ of the monthly salary goes into savings.

   C.   The monthly salary is $1000.

   D.   The budget allows $\frac{1}{6}$ of the monthly salary for utilities.

   E.   The amount budgeted for rent is $250 more than the amount budgeted for miscellaneous expenses.

4. Once a week, a music store selects one name out of a box to win a free CD. This week, if there are 160 boys' names and 200 girls' names in the box, what is the probability that a boy will be selected as the winner?

  A. $\dfrac{4}{9}$

  B. $\dfrac{5}{9}$

  C. $\dfrac{4}{5}$

  D. $\dfrac{5}{4}$

  E. $\dfrac{9}{5}$

5. The scale on a map is 1 inch = 12 miles. What is the actual distance between two towns that are $8\dfrac{1}{2}$ inches apart on the map?
  A. 8.5 miles
  B. 12 miles
  C. 85 miles
  D. 96 miles
  E. 102 miles

6. In 1970, the tuition at a certain university was $4 per semester credit hour. In 2004, the tuition had increased to $50 per semester credit hour. What is the increase in tuition cost for a 15 semester-credit-hour course load?
  A. $46
  B. $60
  C. $690
  D. $750
  E. $810

7. A baseball team played 135 games and won 75 of those games. What is the ratio of the number of games lost to the number of games won?

A. 4 to 5
B. 5 to 4
C. 5 to 9
D. 9 to 5
E. 4 to 9

8. If 5 yards of cable costs $18.75, what is the cost per foot?
  A. $1.25
  B. $1.88
  C. $3.75
  D. $6.25
  E. $11.25

9. A runner runs 5 miles each day for 6 days and records the following running times: 30 minutes, 35 minutes, 34 minutes, 26 minutes, 32 minutes, 35 minutes. What is the median running time for the 6 days?
  A. 30 minutes
  B. 32 minutes
  C. 33 minutes
  D. 35 minutes
  E. 192 minutes

10. The wingspan of a particular airplane is 42 feet. A scale model of the airplane is $\dfrac{1}{12}$ of the plane's actual size. Which proportion should be used to find the measure, w, of the model's wingspan?

  A. $\dfrac{w}{42} = \dfrac{12}{1}$

  B. $\dfrac{42}{w} = \dfrac{1}{12}$

  C. $\dfrac{w}{42} = \dfrac{2}{12}$

  D. $\dfrac{42}{12} = \dfrac{1}{w}$

  E. $\dfrac{w}{1} = \dfrac{12}{42}$

11. A student needs an average of at least 80 on four tests to earn a grade of B in a college course. The student has grades of 78, 91, and 75 on the first three tests. What is the lowest grade the student can make on the fourth test and still receive a B in the course?
   A. 76
   B. 80
   C. 81
   D. 82
   E. 100

12. In a city election, 35% of the registered voters went to the polls and voted. If 14,700 people voted, how many registered voters are in the city?
   A. 4200
   B. 5145
   C. 9555
   D. 19,845
   E. 42,000

13. A farmer has a 750-acre farm. If the farmer plants corn on $\frac{1}{5}$ of the farm and wheat on $\frac{1}{6}$ of the farm, how many acres are planted in corn and wheat?
   A. 125 acres
   B. 136 acres
   C. 150 acres
   D. 275 acres
   E. 475 acres

14. A teacher needs 6 sheets of construction paper for each student in her class of 35 students. She has 24 sheets on hand. If the sheets cost $0.18 each, how much will it cost her to have enough construction paper for all the students?
   A. $1.08
   B. $4.32
   C. $6.30
   D. $33.48
   E. $37.80

15. An elementary school has an enrollment of 400 students. Each day, about 12 students forget to bring their lunch money to school. Approximately what percent of the students forget their lunch money daily?
   A. 0.03%
   B. 3%
   C. 30%
   D. 12%
   E. 0.12%

16. A punch recipe mixes 2 quarts of orange juice with 3 quarts of soda. How many quarts of orange juice will be needed to mix with 18 gallons of soda using this recipe?
   A. 12 quarts
   B. 24 quarts
   C. 36 quarts
   D. 48 quarts
   E. 108 quarts

17. Students in a nutrition class indicate their preference for certain juices by writing the initial of their first name inside the circles of the Venn diagram shown below.

   According to the diagram, what is the total number of students who like both apple and grape juice?

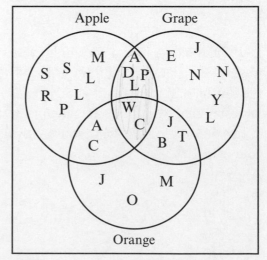

   A. 4
   B. 5
   C. 6
   D. 11
   E. 24

18. Of the following, the unit that would most likely be used to measure the height of a small house plant is the:
    A. millimeter
    B. centimeter
    C. meter
    D. kilometer
    E. liter

19. The graph below shows the number of students in a school district that participate in sports as extracurricular activities.

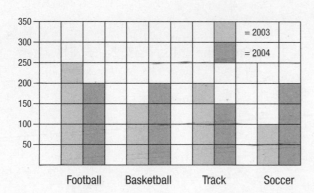

Number of Student Participants

In which extracurricular activity is the ratio of the number of student participants in 2003 to the number of student participants in 2004 approximately 4 to 3?
    A. Football
    B. Basketball
    C. Track
    D. Soccer
    E. It cannot be determined from the information given in the graph.

20. A new employee's starting salary at a part-time job is $10,000 per year. If the employee receives a 10% raise each year, what will be the employee's salary after receiving four raises?
    A. $12,101.00
    B. $14,000.00
    C. $14,641.00
    D. $16,105.10
    E. $40,000.00

21. A cab company charges $3 for the first mile and 75¢ for each additional one-half mile. A customer paid the cab company $20, which included a tip of $2, for a trip from the airport. How many miles was the trip?
    A. 9 miles
    B. 10 miles
    C. 11 miles
    D. 12 miles
    E. 13 miles

22. Which of the following rational numbers is least?
    A. $\dfrac{7}{8}$

    B. $\dfrac{11}{12}$

    C. $-\dfrac{4}{3}$

    D. $-\dfrac{1}{4}$

    E. 0

23. If $x - 10 = 28$, then $3x - 1$ equals:
    A. 17
    B. 37
    C. 38
    D. 113
    E. 114

24. Use the following table to answer the question that follows.

x	y
1	1
4	16
5	25
7	49
9	81

Which of the following formulas expresses the relationship between x and y in the table?

A. $y = x + x$
B. $y = x^2$
C. $y = \sqrt{x}$
D. $y = 4x$
E. $y = 15 + x$

25. A small jar contains a number of quarters and dimes. There are twice as many dimes as quarters in the jar. Which of the following is the best expression of the amount of money in cents if Q equals the number of quarters in the jar?

A. $Q + 2Q$
B. $10Q + 25(2Q)$
C. $25Q + 10(2Q)$
D. $35(2Q)$
E. $Q + 10(2Q)$

26. If L and F are related by the formula $L = \dfrac{2}{3} F + 10$, what value of F will yield L equal to 12?

A. 3
B. 12
C. 13
D. 28
E. 33

27. Which of the following mathematical statements is NOT true?

A. $0 < 5$
B. $3 < 10$
C. $-4 < 7$
D. $-6 < -7$
E. $-2 < 0$

28. A box contains tiles numbered 1 through 30. If one tile is drawn from the box, what is the probability that the number on the tile is a factor of 12?

A. $\dfrac{1}{15}$
B. $\dfrac{1}{10}$
C. $\dfrac{2}{15}$
D. $\dfrac{1}{6}$
E. $\dfrac{1}{5}$

29. What is the value of $3x^3 - x^2 + 5$ when $x = 2$?

A. 19
B. 25
C. 33
D. 217
E. 225

30. If $3x + 15 = 2x + 11$, which of these statements is NOT true?

A. $x < 0$
B. $5x = -20$
C. $-x > 0$
D. $x + x = 8$
E. $2x < 0$

31. Use the diagram below to answer the question that follows.

If the perimeter of the rectangle above is 34 units, what is its length?

A. 29 units
B. 24 units
C. 19 units
D. 12 units
E. 6 units

32. Use the figure below to answer the question that follows.

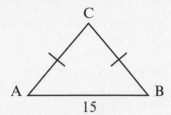

ΔABC is an isosceles triangle. If the perimeter of the triangle is 41 units, what is the length of side AC?

A. 11 units
B. 13 units
C. 15 units
D. 26 units
E. It cannot be determined from the information given in the figure.

$$\frac{41}{15}$$
$$26$$

33. The length of a rectangle is 5 inches greater than its width. The perimeter of the rectangle is 38 inches. The width is:

A. 7 inches
B. 12 inches
C. 26 inches
D. 28 inches
E. 33 inches

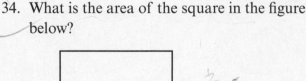

$2(w+5) + 2w = 38$

$2w + 10 + 2w = 38$

$4w = 28$

$w = 7$

34. What is the area of the square in the figure below?

2.5 meters

A. 5 square meters
B. 10 square meters
C. 6.25 square meters
D. 62.5 square meters
E. 625 square meters

35. Use the diagram below to answer the question that follows.

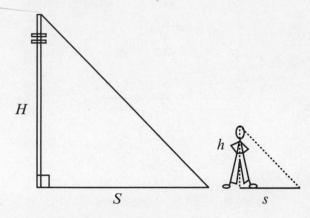

The diagram shows a method that is used to indirectly measure the height, H, of a telephone pole. A person measures his or her own height, h; the length of his or her shadow, s; and the length of the telephone pole's shadow, S. The measured values are inserted into a proportion, which is solved for H.

To calculate H, the height of the telephone pole, which of the following proportions would be correct to use?

A. $\dfrac{h}{s} = \dfrac{S}{H}$

B. $\dfrac{h}{H} = \dfrac{S}{s}$

C. $\dfrac{H}{h} = \dfrac{S}{s}$

D. $\dfrac{s}{H} = \dfrac{S}{h}$

E. $\dfrac{h}{S} = \dfrac{s}{H}$

$\dfrac{H}{S} = \dfrac{h}{s}$

$\dfrac{h}{H} = \dfrac{s}{S}$

$\dfrac{h}{s} = \dfrac{H}{S}$

36. What is the approximate area of the shaded part of the following figure?

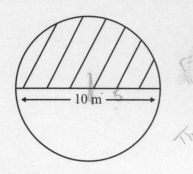

(Use π = 3.14)
A. 15.7 m²
B. 39.3 m²
C. 78.5 m²
D. 157.1 m²
E. 314.2 m²

37. One acre is 4840 square yards. Which of the following could be the dimensions, in feet, of a one-acre rectangular lot?
A. 40 feet × 363 feet
B. 120 feet × 363 feet
C. 120 feet × 484 feet
D. 420 feet × 2000 feet
E. 484 feet × 10 feet

38. If the weight of 10 cubic feet of water is approximately 625 pounds, what is the weight of the water in a box-shaped container measuring 9 feet by 15 feet by 2 feet that has been filled to capacity with water?
A. 6250 pounds
B. 16,875 pounds
C. 11,250 pounds
D. 56,250 pounds
E. 168,750 pounds

39. What conclusion logically can be drawn from the following statements?

All blond-haired contestants are winners.
All contestants from Norway have blond hair.

A. All winners are from Norway.
B. All contestants have blond hair.
C. All blond-haired contestants are from Norway.
D. All contestants from Norway are winners.
E. No winners have dark hair.

40. Which of the following statements is logically equivalent to the statement below. "If you eat rotten fruit, you will get sick."
A. If you get sick, then you have eaten rotten fruit.
B. If you don't get sick, then you have not eaten rotten fruit.
C. If you don't eat rotten fruit, then you won't get sick.
D. If you get sick, then you have not eaten rotten fruit.
E. If you eat rotten fruit, you won't get sick.

SECTION 1

WRITING

45 Questions
Time—30 minutes

PART A

25 Questions
Suggested Time—10 minutes

Directions: In the sentences below four parts are underlined and lettered. Read each sentence and decide whether any of the underlined parts contains an error. If so, on your answer sheet, mark the answer choice that is the same as the letter printed beneath the error in the sentence. If the sentence does not contain an error, mark choice E on your answer sheet. No sentence has more than one error.

1. When the temperature is below freezing outside you should wear heavy socks with your boots.
   A   B   C   D

   No error
   E

2. Cory felt badly about forgetting to bring a gift to his sister's birthday party. No error
              A   B   C   D   E

3. I see no reason for there to be animosity between you and I. No error
          A   B   C   D   E

4. Him talking on his cell phone during dinner bothers me. No error
   A   B   C   D   E

5. I was frightened, because I had never before given a speech in public. No error
      A   B   C   D   E

6. Portia's new song has very strange lyrics and the most unique melody. No error
                         A   B   C   D   E

7. My cousin, who is a basketball player, is taller than me. No error
              A   B C   D   E

8. The students invited whoever wanted to attend to their production of the controversial play.
       A   B   C   D

   No error
   E

9. After grading the two student's papers, the teacher commended them on their clever solutions
   A   B   C

   to the problems she had assigned. No error
   D   E

10. The test it was really hard, but I think I did all right on it. No error
         A   B   C   D   E

11. Your duties will consist of planning the menus, purchase of the food, preparing the meals,
                   A   B

    and keeping a check on the dining area. No error
                  C   D   E

12. Each of the children gave their account of what had caused the disturbance on the play
      A   B   C

    ground during recess. No error
           D   E

13. A chorus of shouts and cheers were heard as the team paraded triumphantly around the field.
                          A   B   C   D

    No error
     E

14. Keeping a positive attitude has a good affect on her performance in school. No error
      A   B   C   D   E

15. Through a survey of the county residents, we obtained data that show strong support for the
      A   B   C   D

    bond issue. No error
             E

16. The letter that was sent home to parents requested that children bring notebook paper,
             A   B   C

    pencils, and, a box of tissue to school on the first day. No error
            D   E

17. The reason the bride and groom decided to have an indoor reception at the last minute is
                                             A   B

    because it began to rain immediately after the church service was over. No error
        C   D   E

18. If a student interrupts another student who is talking, you must apologize to that student.
                 A   B   C D

    No error
     E

19. My children had too many toys, so I gave them to charity for distribution to needy children in
                A   B   C   D

    underdeveloped countries. No error
                       E

20. My grandfather's favorite poem was "Ozymandias", which he could recite from memory.
         A   B   C D

    No error
     E

21. The <u>principle</u> reason the club members are not supportive <u>of</u> raising the dues is <u>that</u> dues
       A   B   C

    <u>have been raised</u> three times in the last five years. <u>No error</u>
         D   E

22. The runner <u>found it</u> <u>real</u> hard to keep on going <u>when</u> the course became muddy and <u>slick</u>.
              A   B   C   D

    <u>No error</u>
     E

23. <u>Most</u> people from other states are surprised when they learn <u>that</u> the <u>capitol</u> of Texas is Austin,
     A   B   C

    <u>rather than</u> Houston or Dallas. <u>No error</u>
       D   E

24. <u>After</u> the recreation center was destroyed by fire, a fundraising project was <u>began</u> in early <u>spring</u>.
      A   B   C   D

    <u>No error</u>
     E

25. The tourists <u>would sit</u> for hours <u>beside</u> the fountain, <u>watching</u> the goldfish playing was <u>their</u>
            A   B   C   D

    only amusement. <u>No error</u>
                    E

PART B

20 Questions
Suggested Time—20 minutes

Directions: In the sentences below, part or all of the sentence is underlined. The five answer choices offer five ways of writing the underlined part—with choice A being the same as the original. Select the answer choice that is best in terms of correctness and effectiveness.

1. When a child helps their mother unload the dishwasher, they are showing autonomy and initiative.

   A. When a child helps their mother unload the dishwasher, they are showing autonomy and initiative.
   B. When a child helps her mother unload the dishwasher, they are showing autonomy and initiative.
   C. When a child helps his mother unload the dishwasher, he is showing autonomy and initiative.
   D. When children help their mother unload the dishwasher, they are showing autonomy and initiative.
   E. When a child helps their mother unload the dishwasher, he or she is showing autonomy and initiative.

2. Michelle and I watched as the ballerinas twirled gracefully through the air.

   A. Michelle and I watched as the ballerinas twirled gracefully through the air.
   B. Michelle and I watched, as the ballerinas twirled gracefully through the air.
   C. Michelle and I watched as the ballerinas twirled, gracefully through the air.
   D. Michelle and I watched, as the ballerinas twirl gracefully through the air.
   E. Michelle and I watched as the ballerinas twirled gracefully, through the air.

3. The bride was not young nor was she very pretty.

   A. The bride was not young nor was she very pretty.
   B. The bride was not young, nor was she very pretty.
   C. The bride was not young either was she very pretty.
   D. The bride, was not young nor was she very pretty.
   E. The bride was not young or was she very pretty.

4. A string orchestra has five sections, but four instruments: the chello, the violin, the viola, and the double bass.

   A. A string orchestra has five sections, but four instruments: the chello, the violin, the viola, and the double bass.

   B. A string orchestra has five sections but four instruments: the cello, the violin, the viola, and the double bass.

   C. A string orchestra has five sections, but four instruments. The cello, the violin, the viola, and the double bass.

   D. A string orchestra is made up of five sections, but four instruments: the cello, the violin, the viola, and the double bass.

   E. A string orchestra contains five sections, but four instruments: the cello; the violin; the viola; and the double bass.

5. While my mom was cooking for me, I worked on my paper that was due in three hours. I was definately rushing to get it finished on time.

   A. I was definately rushing to get it finished on time.

   B. I was definitely rushing to get it finished on time.

   C. I was definately rushed to get it finished on time.

   D. I definitely rushed to get it finished on time.

   E. To get it finished on time, I definitely had to rush.

6. Caffeine, which is highly addictive, can deteriorate calcium in your body, making your bones more susceptible to fracture.

   A. Caffeine, which is highly addictive, can deteriorate calcium in your body, making your bones more susceptible to fracture.

   B. Caffeine which is highly addictive, can deteriorate the amount of calcium in your body making your bones more susceptible to fracture.

   C. Caffeine which is highly addictive can deteriorate calcium in your body, making your bones more susceptible to fracture.

   D. Caffeine, which is highly addictive can deteriorate calcium in your body, making your bones more susceptible to fracture.

   E. Caffeine, which is highly addictive. can deteriorate calcium in your body making your bones more susceptible to fracture.

7. They're mom is a workaholic; however, she pays attention to them when she has time.

   A. They're mom is a workaholic; however,

   B. Their mom is a workaholic; however,

   C. There mom is a workaholic; however,

   D. They're mom is a workaholic: however

   E. Their mom is a workaholic. However

8. A jury does not judge a mediation. A civil suit could be tried in front of a jury.

   A.   A jury does not judge a mediation. A civil suit is tried in front of a jury.
   B.   A jury does not judge a mediation, and a civil suit is tried in front of a jury.
   C.   A jury does not judge a mediation, so a civil suit is tried in front of a jury.
   D.   A jury does not judge a mediation, but a civil suit is tried in front of a jury.
   E.   A jury does not judge a mediation, or, a civil suit is tried in front of a jury.

9. The movie *Apollo 13* was based on a true story about Jim Lovell's last trip in space.

   A.   The movie *Apollo 13* was based on a true story about Jim Lovell's last trip in space.
   B.   The movie, *Apollo 13,* was based on the true story about Jim Lovell's last trip in space.
   C.   The movie *Apollo 13* was based on a true story, about Jim Lovell's last trip in space.
   D.   The movie, *Apollo 13,* was based on the true story, about Jim Lovell's last trip in space.
   E.   The movie. *Apollo 13* was based on the true story about Jim Lovell's last trip in space.

10. When it gets below 40 degrees, I bring my bluebonnets in so they won't freeze.

   A.   When it gets below 40 degrees, I bring my bluebonnets in so they won't freeze.
   B.   When the temperature gets below 40 degrees, I bring my bluebonnets in so they won't freeze.
   C.   When it gets below 40 degrees, I bring my bluebonnets inside, so they won't freeze.
   D.   When the temperature gets below 40 degrees, I bring my bluebonnets inside so they won't freeze.
   E.   When the temperature gets below 40 degrees, I bring my bluebonnets inside, so they won't freeze.

11. It is farther from El Paso, Texas to Orange, Texas than it is from El Paso to the Pacific ocean.

   A.   It is farther from El Paso, Texas to Orange, Texas than it is from El Paso to the Pacific ocean.
   B.   It is farther from El Paso, Texas to Orange, Texas than it is from El Paso to the Pacific Ocean.
   C.   It is further from El Paso, Texas to Orange, Texas than it is from El Paso to the Pacific ocean.
   D.   It is further from El Paso, Texas to Orange, Texas than it is from El Paso to the Pacific Ocean.
   E.   It is further from El Paso, Texas to Orange, Texas, than it is from El Paso to the Pacific Ocean.

12. My great-grandmother came to the United States from Germany in 1898. She did not have hardly anything but the clothes she wore on the ship.

   A.   She did not have hardly anything
   B.   She didn't have hardly anything
   C.   She had hardly anything
   D.   She hardly had anything
   E.   She did not have hardly nothing

13. In the days of the Great Depression, <u>many people became ill from the dust storms that blew frequently.</u>

   A. many people became ill from the dust storms that blew frequently.
   B. many people became ill from the dust storms, that blew frequently.
   C. many people became ill from the dust storms that, blew consistently.
   D. many people became ill from the dust storms, which blew frequently.
   E. many people became ill from the dust storms which blew frequently.

14. <u>With the increasing dependence of humans on computers,</u> our world will likely become disabled if we were to lose access to them.

   A. With the increasing dependence of humans on computers,
   B. With the increase in depending upon computers by humans,
   C. With humans depending more on computers,
   D. With humans becoming increasingly dependent upon computers,
   E. As humans become increasingly dependent upon computers,

15. <u>Unlike many states,</u> Texas has many different landscapes, including mountains, prairies, desert, hills, shorelines, and forests.

   A. Unlike many states,
   B. Not like in other states,
   C. Contrary to other states,
   D. Unlike all other states,
   E. Contrary to states,

16. The practice of discriminating against <u>someone on the basis of the color of skin</u> is known as racism.

   A. someone on the basis of the color of skin
   B. someone on the basic of the color of skin
   C. someone because of the color of their skin
   D. someone on the reason of skin color
   E. someone on the basis of their skin color

17. <u>Despite</u> how strong the cold air was blowing, I ran four miles this morning before getting ready for work.

   A. Despite
   B. Irregardless of
   C. Disregarding of
   D. Even though
   E. However

18. My brother loves football and baseball <u>equally as well</u>.

    A. equally as well
    B. equally
    C. equal
    D. well and equally
    E. equally as well as the other

19. <u>Desparate is the feeling that I have</u> when I have a lot of work that needs to get done.

    A. Desparate is the feeling that I have
    B. I have a feeling of desparation
    C. Desparation is the feeling that I have
    D. I have a feeling of desperation
    E. I am desparate

20. In the <u>desert—</u>many cacti bloom and grow to become six or seven feet tall.

    A. desert—
    B. dessert,
    C. desert
    D. desert:
    E. desert;

SECTION 2

ESSAY

Time—30 minutes

1 Topic

Directions: Write an essay on the topic presented on the next page. You have 30 minutes to complete this portion of the test. BE SURE TO WRITE ON THE ASSIGNED TOPIC. No credit will be given for essays that are off-topic.

Write your entire essay below. Keep in mind that when you take the test, only what you write on the answer sheet will be scored.

GO ON TO THE NEXT PAGE

Chapter 5

Answer Explanations for Diagnostic PPST

READING

1. Choice B is the best response because it summarizes the points the passage makes about the dishonesty of city and state government officials following the Civil War.

2. Choice A is the best response. The passage is intended to inform the reader about an event in history. Although the reader may find entertainment in reading about a scandalous period in American history, to entertain (choice B) is clearly not the primary purpose of the passage. No attempt is made to explain (choice C) the events described, to ridicule them (choice D), or to compare the events to another situation (choice E).

3. Choice D is the best response. The author reports the situation in a disapproving manner. The choice of words ("forfeited their honor for gold and silver") in the last line of the paragraph most clearly shows the author's disapproval. The author does not use a mocking, sarcastic tone (choice A); a questioning, inquiring tone (choice B); an amusing, humorous tone (choice C); or a detached, indifferent tone (choice E).

4. Choice C is the best response. Forfeited and relinquished both mean "to give up." Yielded means "giving way under pressure," not giving up something. Foreswore means "renounced or repudiated under oath." Perverted means "corrupted." Relinquished best retains the original meaning of the sentence.

5. Choice C is the best response. The author's description of the situation clearly indicates a need for reform in city and state governments after the Civil War. The information in choice A is given in the passage, so choice A is not an inference. There is not enough information given to support choices B, D, or E.

6. Choice D is the best response. The introductory sentence to the passage gives the correct answer (D). Choices A and C are false; therefore, they are incorrect. Choices B and E, subtopics of answer D, are too specific to be main ideas.

7. Choice B is the best response. The following sentence makes this clear: "However the exercise be marked, the procedure in itself is not very exact; and, in any case, affords a test of memory rather than of comprehension."

8. Choice E is the best response. It is clear from the third and sixth sentences of the passage, which indicates the act of repeating words and phrases correctly is a measurement of comprehension.

9. Choice C is the best response. Voce is the Latin word for "voice," so choice C is most logical. The passage discusses comprehension of text, not analyzing it; therefore, choices A and B are incorrect.

10. Choice C is the best response. Erroneous, meaning "in error," refers to the words or phrases that the student mistakenly remembered.

11. Choice D is the best response. The paragraph lists A, B, C, and E as ways the British tried to wring money from the Jews.

12. Choice D is the best response. While all of the other choices are true, the fourth sentence states this was the reason Jews remained in England.

13. Choice D is the best response. Exclusion is a form of persecution, and the third sentence says that "the meanest serfs" refused to sit with them.

14. Choice A is the best response. While the other choices are true, the first sentence states that the Jews were tolerated because of "the immense sums of money they possessed."

15. Choice C is the best response because it summarizes the points the passage makes about the development of the geographical division of labor. Choice A only refers to the last two sentences of the passage, not the entire passage. Choices B and E are only specific to the ways of water trade and do not apply to the whole passage. Choice D does not discuss how or why trade has come to affect the mass of population.

16. Choice B is the best response. The last two sentences discuss the importance of the invention of the railway. The geographical division of labor (choice A) is incorrect because this had been slowly occurring before the invention of the railway. Choice C is incorrect because it does not make sense to say that industry of almost every part of the world has transformed itself. Choice D is incorrect because land cannot transform industry. Choice E is incorrect because the passage states that railways were the major cause of the geographical division of labor.

17. Choice A is the best response. The question asks which mode initially helped to define the geographical division of labor. Although each of the other answers contributed, the fifth sentence states that water transportation was able to "develop in some degree the geographical division of labor."

18. Choice B is the best response. Choice A does not discuss how the railway was able to reach more people. Choice C is not supported by the passage. Choice D

does not make sense. Choice E does not explain how the railway was far-reaching by transforming industry. The second half of the eighth sentence states that the railway was able to reach all parts of the land.

19. Choice A is the best response. Choice B, while true, is a result of the advances in water transportation and trade and not a reason that England was considered more advanced. Choice C does not make sense because a coastline does not make one country more advanced than another. Choice D is incorrect because the passage did not state that it was England that made improvements and enlargements to vessels. Choice E is incorrect because the passage discusses trade *over* water rather than *of* water.

20. Choice E is the best response. Choices A and B are incorrect because the passage does not discuss the invention of automobiles or airplanes. Choice C is incorrect because the passage does not state that the overcoming of land-based trade barriers is the biggest achievement in trade transportation. Choice D is incorrect because the passage does not explicitly state this point.

21. Choice E is the best response because it is directly stated in the second sentence of the passage. None of the other choices are explicitly stated.

22. Choice A is the best response. *Pecuniary* in this context means "financial" with *pecuniary foundations* therefore meaning "financial institutions."

23. Choice B is the best response. The third sentence supports choice B as the correct answer. The second sentence excludes choices A and C, and the third sentence makes choice D incorrect.

24. Choice B is the best response. The term *gowns* refers to the fancy dress that comes with a degree, rather than knowledge or wisdom.

25. Choice C is the best response. Choices A, B, and D incorrectly interpret the statement to mean that the wealth of a school is associated with the quality of education it offers. Choice E is completely off-topic.

26. Choice C is the best response. Choice A does not discuss the point that every action has a consequence or result. Choice B limits the actions to those that "are not counted." Like A, choice D does not discuss the results of actions.

27. Choice A is the best response. Choice B is too specific to be the main point of the paragraph. Choice C is too vague to be the main point. Choice D discusses the hard work that is put into each day, but it does not connect the theme of the second paragraph to the first, that habits formed early become our ways of life.

28. Choice A is the best response. Choices B, C, D, and E refer to capacity for change and does not imply that change is happening.

29. Choice B is the best response. Choices A and C are untrue and not supported by the passage. Choice D is unclear as to whether it is the action or the fate that cannot be undone.

30. Choice A is the best response. Choices B, C, and D are too specific to drinking to illustrate the main point. Choice E is incorrect because consequences of our actions are not always invisible, which is what choice E implies.

31. Choice C is the best response. Choice B is incorrect because the topic is not that of moral judgment. The paragraph is about work practices in youth that later become adult habits. Choice A is incorrect because the "possession that will never pass away" refers to the "power of judging." Choice D makes sense, but it does not reflect a characteristic of the person in the same way that choice C does. Choice E does not make any sense.

32. Choice B is the best response. Choice A is too specific to the first paragraph. Choice C is also too specific to the first paragraph. Choice D is too vague to be a main point of the passage. Choice E does not address the idea of perception, which is what the passage is about.

33. Choice E is the best response. Choices A and C are incorrect because the passage never discusses "reality." Choice B is incorrect because it does not show the relationship between perception and experience. Choice D is incorrect because it is backwards—"Experience Affects Perception" would make it correct.

34. Choice B is the best response. "Roan" means a horse with a solid color coat (of many possible colors) with white hairs distributed throughout.

35. Choice D is the best response. Choice A is incorrect because the passage does not discuss forgetfulness. Choice B is incorrect because the passage states that it is concentrating on what you see, not necessarily on many different aspects. Choice C is incorrect because it includes the concept of choice, which the passage does not discuss.

36. Choice A is the best response. Choice B is incorrect because the second paragraph illustrates the opposite point. Choice C is incorrect because the second paragraph shows that it is untrue. Choices D and E are examples, but not a main point of the paragraph.

37. Choice E is the best response. All of the other choices are true and stated in the first paragraph.

38. Choice C is the best response because it is clearly supported by the fourth sentence in the passage. The passage does not support the statements in choices A, B, D, and E.

39. Choice A is the best response. Choices B and D are supportive statements of the main idea, and C is an extraneous comment.

40. Choice B is the best response. Choices A, D, and E are incorrect. While arduous can mean "laborious" (choice C), but in this context, the word *difficult* (choice B) best fits the meaning.

MATHEMATICS

1. Choice C is the correct response. To compare two decimal numbers, start at the left and compare corresponding digits until you get to two digits that differ. The smaller digit belongs to the smaller number. In the answer choices, the first two digits on the left are the same for all the answer choices. The next digit is a 2 in choice C, which is smaller than the corresponding digits in the other answer choices.

2. Choice B is the correct response. You need to find the total amount of liquid, so add the two amounts given.

$$2\frac{1}{2} \text{ cups} + 1\frac{3}{4} \text{ cups} =$$
total amount of liquid in the recipe

Since you are adding fractions, find a common denominator. (Hint: you can omit the units until the final step after you determine that the units work out correctly.)

$$2\frac{1}{2} + 1\frac{3}{4} = 2\frac{2}{4} + 1\frac{3}{4} = 3 + \frac{5}{4} = 3 + 1\frac{1}{4} = 4\frac{1}{4}$$

Therefore, $4\frac{1}{4}$ cups = total amount of liquid in the recipe. The other answer choices result when the two fractions are added incorrectly.

3. Choice B is the correct response. Reading choice B, you see that you need to first determine the monthly salary by adding up the amounts in the pie graph:

$$\$450 + \$300 + \$100 + \$100 + \$100 + \$150 = \$1200$$

Then you must find $\frac{1}{8}$ of $\$1200 = \dfrac{\$1200}{8} = \$150$, which is the amount budgeted for savings.

Choice A is incorrect because as you can see from the graph, the combined costs of rent and food account for more than half of the pie. Now that you know the monthly salary is $1200, you can work out choice A like this: $450 + $300 = $750, which is greater than $600 ($\frac{1}{2}$ of $1200, the monthly salary).

Choice C is incorrect because the monthly salary is $1200, not $1000. Choice D is incorrect because $\frac{1}{6}$ of $1200 is $200, not $100. Choice E is incorrect because $450 – $100 is $350, not $250.

4. Choice A is the correct response. First, determine the total number of entries in the box: $160 + 200 = 360$ entries. Of those 360 entries, 160 are boys' names. Therefore, the probability that a boy's name is drawn is

$$\frac{\text{number of entries with a boy's name}}{\text{total number of entries}} = \frac{160}{360} = \frac{4}{9}$$

Choice B is the answer you get if you determine the probability that a girl's name is drawn. Choice C is the answer you get if you compute the ratio of boys' names to girls' names. Choices D and E are incorrect because probabilities (unlike other ratios) cannot be expressed in terms that exceed 1.

5. Choice E is the correct response. Solve this problem by using a proportion. The first sentence gives you the first ratio:

$$\frac{1 \text{ inch}}{12 \text{ miles}}$$

If you let x = the actual distance between the two towns, the second sentence gives you the second ratio:

$$\frac{8.5 \text{ inches}}{\text{x (miles)}}$$

Set the two ratios equal to each other:

$$\frac{1 \text{ inch}}{12 \text{ miles}} = \frac{8.5 \text{ inches}}{\text{x (miles)}}$$

For convenience, omit the units while you solve the proportion:

$$\frac{1}{12} = \frac{8.5}{\text{x}}$$

Multiply 12 by 8.5 and then divide by 1:
$$(12)(8.5) = 102 \text{ miles}$$

You should eliminate choices A and B right away because these answers are not reasonable. If 1 inch is 12 miles, 8 inches must be greater than 12 miles. Choices C and D result if you make a computation error when figuring the proportion.

6. Choice C is the correct response. Three steps are needed to solve the problem:
Step 1. Find the cost for a 15 semester-credit-hour (s.c.h.) course load in 1970:

$$\frac{\$4}{\text{s.c.h.}} \times 15 \text{ s.c.h.} = \$60 \text{ in } 1970$$

(Hint: Quantities following the word *per* should be written in the denominator of a fraction.)

Step 2. Find the cost for a 15 semester-credit-hour (s.c.h.) course load in 2004:

$$\frac{\$50}{\text{s.c.h.}} \times 15 \text{ s.c.h.} = \$750 \text{ in } 2004$$

Step 3. Find the difference in cost between the two years:

$$\$750 - \$60 = \$690$$

Choice A is the difference in tuition for one semester credit hour, not 15 semester credit hours. Choice B is the tuition for 15 semester credit hours in 1970, not the difference between the two years. Choice D is the tuition for 15 semester credit hours in 2004, not the difference between the two years. Choice E is the sum of the two tuitions, not the difference.

7. Choice A is the correct response. First, find the number of games lost: $135 - 75 = 60$. Next, find the ratio of the number of games lost to the number of games won:

$$\frac{\text{no. games lost}}{\text{no. games won}} = \frac{60}{75} = \frac{4}{5}$$

(which is read as "4 to 5"). Choice B is the ratio of the number of games won to the number of games lost. Order makes a difference, so read carefully!

Choice C is the ratio of the number of games won to the number of games played. Choice D is the ratio of the number of games played to the number of games won, and choice E is the ratio of the number of games lost to the number of games played.

8. Choice A is the correct response. Notice that the question gives the cost per yard but asks for the "cost per foot." First, find the number of feet in 5 yards:

$$5 \text{ yd} \times \frac{3 \text{ ft}}{\text{yd}} = 15 \text{ ft}$$

Find the cost per foot:

$$\frac{\$18.75}{15 \text{ ft}} = \frac{\$1.25}{\text{ft}} = \$1.25 \text{ per foot}$$

(Hint: Quantities following the word *per* go in the denominator of a fraction.)

Choice B results if you use the wrong conversion factor of 2 feet per yard; that is,

$$\frac{2 \text{ ft}}{\text{yd}}$$

Choice C results if you fail to change yards to feet. Choice D results if you overlook that the price is for 5 yards, not one yard. Choice E occurs if you convert yards to feet by dividing by 3 instead of multiplying by 3 and you fail to carry the units through the calculations correctly.

9. Choice C is the correct response. In an ordered set of numbers, the median is the middle number if there is a middle number; otherwise, the median is the arithmetic average of the two middle numbers. First, put the running times in order from smallest to largest:

    26 min. 30 min. 32 min. 34 min. 35 min. 35 min.

    Average the two middle numbers:

    $$\frac{32 \text{ min.} + 34 \text{ min.}}{2} = \frac{66 \text{ min.}}{2} = 33 \text{ minutes}$$

    Choice A results if you forget to put the running times in order first.
    Choice B is the mean running time.
    Choice D is the mode running time.
    Choice E is the sum of the running times.

10. Choice C is the correct response. The model is built on a scale of 1 to 12. This means:

    $$\frac{\text{wingspan of model}}{\text{wingspan of "real" airplane}} = \frac{w}{42} = \frac{1}{12}$$

    Choice C correctly expresses the relationship of the model's size to its scale.

11. Choice A is the correct response. A quick way to work this problem is to check the answer choices—a good test-taking strategy for multiple-choice math tests. Checking A, you obtain:

    $$\frac{\text{sum of 4 test grades}}{4} = \frac{78 + 91 + 75 + 76}{4} = \frac{320}{4} = 80$$

    which means 76 works. Since 76 is the smallest of all the choices, you do not have to check further. (If you do check the remaining choices, you'll find that choice B gives an average of 81, choice C gives an average of 81.25, choice D gives an average of 81.5, and choice E gives an average of 86.)

12. Choice E is the correct response. To solve this problem, you need to answer the question: 14,700 is 35% of what number? You should eliminate choices A, B, and C right away because these answers are not reasonable: 35% is less than 100%, so it is clear that the answer to this question must be greater than 14,700. Let x = the number of registered voters. Set up a proportion, and solve it:

    $$\frac{35}{100} = \frac{14,700 \text{ ("is")}}{x \text{ ("of")}}$$

    Multiply 14,700 by 100 and then divide by 35:

    $$\frac{14,700 \times 100}{35} = 42,000 \text{ registered voters}$$

Choice D is the result if you solve the problem by incorrectly deciding to calculate 135% of 14,700.

13. Choice D is the correct response. Three steps are needed to solve the problem:
Step 1. Find the number of acres planted in wheat:

$$\frac{1}{5} \text{ of } 750 \text{ acres} = \frac{750 \text{ acres}}{5} = 150 \text{ acres}$$

Step 2. Find the number of acres planted in corn:

$$\frac{1}{6} \text{ of } 750 \text{ acres} = \frac{750 \text{ acres}}{6} = 125 \text{ acres}$$

Step 3. Add to find the total number of acres planted in corn and wheat:

$$150 \text{ acres} + 125 \text{ acres} = 275 \text{ acres}$$

Choice A is the number of acres planted in wheat, not the total. Choice C is the number of acres planted in corn, not the total. Choices B and E are the result of calculation errors.

14. Choice D is the correct response. Three steps are needed to solve the problem:
Step 1. Find the total number of sheets needed:

$$\frac{6 \text{ sheets}}{\text{student}} \times 35 \text{ students} = 210 \text{ sheets needed in all}$$

Step 2. Subtract from the total the number of sheets on hand:

$$210 \text{ sheets} - 24 \text{ sheets} = 186 \text{ additional sheets needed}$$

Step 3. Find the cost for the number of additional sheets needed:

$$186 \text{ sheets} \times \frac{\$0.18}{\text{sheet}} = \$33.48$$

The incorrect answer choices are the results of calculating the cost of the wrong number of sheets of construction paper. Choice A is the cost of 6 sheets of construction paper. Choice B is the cost of 24 sheets of construction paper. Choice C is the cost of 35 sheets of construction paper. Choice E is the cost of 210 sheets of construction paper.

15. Choice B is the correct response. To solve this problem, you need to answer the question: 12 is what percent of 400?

Set up a proportion and solve it:

$$\frac{?}{100} = \frac{12 \text{ ("is")}}{400 \text{ ("of")}}$$

Multiply 12 by 100 and then divide by 400:

$$\frac{12 \times 100}{400} = 3, \text{ so } 3\% \text{ is the answer.}$$

Choices B and C are the results of calculation errors. Choices D and E are the results of misinterpreting the problem.

16. Choice D is the correct response. Solve the problem by using a proportion. The first sentence gives you the first ratio:

$$\frac{2 \text{ quarts of orange juice}}{3 \text{ quarts of soda}}$$

The second sentence gives you the second ratio:

$$\frac{x \text{ (quarts) of orange juice}}{18 \text{ gallons of soda}}$$

Notice that you have a problem because the denominator for the first ratio is in quarts, but the denominator of the second ratio is in gallons. You will need to change 18 gallons to quarts before going on:

$$18 \text{ gallons} \times \frac{4 \text{ quarts}}{\text{gallon}} = 72 \text{ quarts}$$

Set the two ratios equal to each other:

$$\frac{2 \text{ quarts of orange juice}}{3 \text{ quarts of soda}} = \frac{x \text{ (quarts) of orange juice}}{72 \text{ quarts of soda}}$$

For convenience omit the units, then solve the proportion:

$$\frac{2}{3} = \frac{x}{72}$$

Multiply 2 by 72 and then divide by 3:

$$\frac{2 \times 72}{3} = 48 \text{ quarts of orange juice}$$

Choice A results if you fail to change gallons to quarts. Choices B and C result if you convert gallons to quarts incorrectly. Choice E results if you set up the proportion incorrectly.

17. Choice C is the correct response. The word *and* means you need to count the initials in the intersection of the apple and grape circles. The intersection looks like a football. There are 6 initials inside this intersection. Choice A results if you mistakenly leave out the 2 initials in the overlapping portion from the orange

circle. You are looking for the number of students who like apple and grape juice, regardless of whether they like orange juice, too. Choice B is the number of initials in the intersection of the grape and orange circles. Choice D is the number of initials in all the overlapping intersections (that is, the number of students who like more than one kind of juice, not just apple and grape). Choice E is the sum of initials in the apple and grape circles.

18. Choice B is the correct response. A small houseplant would most likely be measured in centimeters. A centimeter is about the width of a large paper clip. For instance, a 12-inch ruler is about 30 centimeters in length. One centimeter equals about 0.4 inch. Millimeters (choice A) would be too small. Meters (choice C) and kilometers (choice D) would be too large. Liters (choice E) are used to measure volume, not length or height.

19. Choice C is the correct response. You want to find an activity in which the ratio of participants in 2003 to those in 2004 is 4 to 3. Since 4 is greater than 3, look for activities in which the lighter-shaded bar is "taller" than the darker-shaded bar. This eliminates basketball (choice B) and soccer (choice D). For football (choice A), the participation was 250 in 2003 and 200 in 2004. This gives a ratio of

$$\frac{250}{200} = \frac{5}{4}$$

or 5 to 4, not 4 to 3. For track (choice C), the participation was 200 in 2003 and 150 in 2004, giving a ratio of

$$\frac{200}{150} = \frac{4}{3}$$

or 4 to 3, making choice C the correct response.

20. Choice C is the correct response. Find the salary after each raise:

$$\$10,000 + 10\% \text{ of } \$10,000 =$$
$$\$10,000 + \$1000 = \$11,000 =$$
salary after raise 1

$$\$11,000 + 10\% \text{ of } \$11,000 =$$
$$\$11,000 + \$1100 = \$12,100 =$$
salary after raise 2

$$\$12,100 + 10\% \text{ of } \$12,100 =$$
$$\$12,100 + \$1210 = \$13,310 =$$
salary after raise 3

$$\$13,310 + 10\% \text{ of } \$13,310 =$$
$$\$13,310 + \$1331 = \$14,641 =$$
salary after raise 4

Choice A is the salary after raise 2. Choice B is the result of multiplying a 10% raise ($1000) by 4 and adding that amount to the original salary of $10,000, which does not take into account that new raises are based on the *new* salary, not the original salary. Choice D is the salary after raise 5. Choice E is the result of multiplying $10,000 by 4.

21. Choice C is the correct response. A good strategy for this problem is to check the answer choices. From the problem, you can see that the mileage has to be broken into a one-mile portion plus a portion of one-half mile segments.

For choice A, 9 miles breaks into 1 mile plus 8 miles = 1 mile plus 16 half miles.

Cost of the trip =
$3 for 1 mile plus $0.75 × 16 plus $2 (tip) =
$3 + $12 + $2 = $17, not $20. Eliminate A.

For choice B, 10 miles breaks into 1 mile plus 9 miles = 1 mile plus 18 half miles.

Cost of the trip =
$3 for 1 mile plus $0.75 × 18 plus $2 (tip) =
$3 + $13.50 + $2 = $18.50, not $20. Eliminate B.

For choice C, 11 miles breaks into 1 mile plus 10 miles = 1 mile plus 20 half miles.

Cost of the trip
= $3 for 1 mile plus $0.75 × 20 plus $2 (tip) = $3 + $15 + $2 = $20,
making choice C the correct response.

You would not have to check choices D and E; but FYI, choice D gives $21.50 and choice E gives $23, both of which are too high.

22. Choice C is the correct response. Since positive numbers and zero are greater than negative numbers, eliminate choices A, B, and E. To decide which negative number is less, pick the one that would be farthest to the left on a number line:

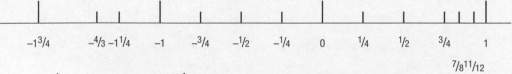

Since $-\dfrac{4}{3}$ is to the left of $-\dfrac{1}{4}$, it is the *least* of the numbers given.

23. Choice D is the correct response. This is a two-step problem.
Step 1. Solve the first equation for x:

$x - 10 = 28$. To find x, add 10 to both sides.
$x - 10 + 10 = 28 + 10$
$x = 38$

Step 2. Substitute 38 for x in the expression $3x - 1$:

$$3(38) - 1 = 114 - 1 = 113$$

Choices A and B are the results of an error in step 1.
Choice C occurs if you stop after step 1.
Choice E occurs if you forget to subtract 1 in step 2.

24. Choice B is the correct response. Look for a pattern from left to right. Notice that every number in the right-hand column is the square of its partner in the left-hand column. Choice B is the only one that expresses this relationship. Another way to work the problem is to check the answers using the values in the table.

    For choice A, using the first pair, $x = 1$ and $y = 1$, you ask, "Does $1 = 1 + 1$?" The answer is no, so eliminate A.

    For choice B, every set of pairs works.

    For choice C, the first pair works, but the second pair doesn't: $16 \neq \sqrt{4}$.

    For choices D and E, the first pair, $x = 1$ and $y = 1$, doesn't work.

25. Choice C is the correct response. You are finding the amount of money in cents, so you will have to multiply the number of quarters by 25 (cents) and the number of dimes by 10 (cents):

    $$\text{Amount of money in cents} =$$
    $$25(\text{no. of quarters}) + 10(\text{no. of dimes}).$$

    Q is the number of quarters. The number of dimes is twice (2 times) the number of quarters = 2Q. Substituting, you get:

    $$25(\text{no. of quarters}) + 10(\text{no. of dimes})$$
    $$= 25Q + 10(2Q).$$

    Choice A simply gives you the total number of coins, not their value. Choice B results if you use the same number of dimes and quarters. Choice D results if you combine terms incorrectly. Choice E results if you forget to multiply Q by 25.

26. Choice A is the correct response. A good strategy for this problem is to check the answer choices. To check choice A, substitute 3 for F in the formula:

    $L = \dfrac{2}{3}(3) + 10 = 2 + 10 = 12$, correct. You do not have to check further.

    FYI, choice B gives $L = 14$, Choice C gives $L = \dfrac{56}{3}$, Choice D gives $L = \dfrac{76}{3}$,

    and choice E gives $L = 32$, all of which are incorrect.

27. Choice D is the correct response. Check each statement as follows.

    Choice A, $0 < 5$:
    True. 0 is to the left of 5 on the number line.

    Choice B, $3 < 10$:
    True. 3 is to the left of 10 on the number line.

    Choice C, $-4 < 7$:
    True. -4 is to the left of 7 on the number line.

    Choice D, $-6 < -7$:
    False. -6 is to the right of -7 on the number line.

    Choice E, $-2 < 0$:
    True. -2 is to the left of 0 on the number line. (Of course, it is not necessary to check this one since you know D is the correct response.)

28. Choice E is the correct response. This is a two-step problem.

    Step 1: Determine the factors of 12: 1, 2, 3, 4, 6, 12

    Step 2: Determine the probability of drawing a tile with one of these 6 numbers on it from the 30 tiles:

    Probability of drawing 1, 2, 3, 4, 6, or $12 = \dfrac{6}{30 \text{ (the total number of tiles)}} = \dfrac{1}{5}$

    Choices A, B, C, and D occur if you make a mistake in Step 1.

29. Choice B is the correct response. First, rewrite the expression putting parentheses in place of x: $3(\ )^3 - (\ )^2 + 5$. Put 2 inside the parentheses and evaluate, being sure to follow the order of operations PE(MD)(AS): $3(2)^3 - (2)^2 + 5 = 3(8) - 4 + 5 = 24 - 4 + 5 = 25$.

    Choice A results if you evaluate $(2)^3$ as 6. Choice C results if you square the $-$ sign before $(2)^2$; that is, if you think $-(2)^2 = +(-2)^2$. Choice D results if you mistakenly multiply 2 by its coefficient (3) before you apply the exponent. Choice E results if you combine errors from choices C and D.

30. Choice D is the correct response. This is a two-step problem.
    Step 1. Find out the value of x by solving the equation:

    $$3x + 15 = 2x + 11$$
    $$3x - 2x + 15 = 2x - 2x + 11 \qquad \text{Subtract } 2x \text{ from both sides.}$$
    $$x + 15 = 11$$
    $$x + 15 - 15 = 11 - 15 \qquad \text{Subtract 15 from both sides.}$$
    $$x = -4$$

Step 2. Check each of the statements:

Choice A, $x < 0$: True. $-4 < 0$.

Choice B, $5x = -20$: True. $5(-4) = -20$.

Choice C, $-x > 0$: True.$-(-4) = 4$, and $4 > 0$.

Choice D, $x + x = 8$: False.$-4 + -4 = -8$.

Choice E, $2x < 0$: True. $2(-4) = -8$, and $-8 < 0$.

31. Choice D is the correct response. The perimeter of a rectangle is given by the formula: $P = 2L + 2W$, where L is the length of the rectangle and W is its width. You know the perimeter is 34, and you can see from the figure that the width is 5. Substitute these values into the formula: $34 = 2L + 2(5)$, so $34 = 2L + 10$. Now check the answers to see which one works in this equation:

    Choice A: For $L = 29$, $34 = 2(29) + 10 = 58 + 10 = 68$, doesn't work.

    Choice B: For $L = 24$, $34 = 2(24) + 10 = 48 + 10 = 58$, doesn't work.

    Choice C: For $L = 19$, $34 = 2(19) + 10 = 38 + 10 = 48$, doesn't work.

    Choice D: For $L = 12$, $34 = 2(12) + 10 = 24 + 10 = 34$, works.

    You do not have to check choice E, but FYI: using $L = 6$ gives a perimeter of 22, not 34.

32. Choice B is the correct response. The perimeter of a triangle equals the sum of the lengths of its sides. For convenience, let $x =$ the length of side AC. Notice the single slash marks on sides AC and BC of the triangle. In geometry, this means line segments AC and BC are congruent, so these two sides have the same length. You know from the figure that the other side (AB) has length 15. Thus, the perimeter of the triangle (omitting the units) = (length of side AB) + (length of side AC) + (length of side BC) = $15 + x + x = 15 + 2x$. You are told the perimeter is 41, so you can write: $41 = 15 + 2x$. Now check the answers to see which one works in this equation.

    Choice A: For $x = 11$, $41 = 15 + 2(11) = 15 + 22 = 37$, doesn't work.

    Choice B: For $x = 23$, $41 = 15 + 2(13) = 15 + 26 = 41$, works.

    You do not have to check further, but FYI: Choice C using $x = 15$ gives a perimeter of 45, not 41; and choice E using $x = 26$ gives a perimeter of 67, not 41.

33. Choice A is the correct response. The perimeter of a rectangle is given by the formula: $P = 2L + 2W$, where L is the length of the rectangle and W is its width. For this problem you are told the length is 5 inches greater than its width. Since the length is described in terms of the width, let $W =$ the width. Then you can write that the length $L = 5 + W$. You know the perimeter is 38 inches, so now you can substitute that value into the formula:

$$38 = 2L + 2W$$
$$38 = 2(5 + W) + 2W$$

Now check the answers to see which one works in this equation.

Choice A: For $W = 7$, $38 = 2(5 + 7) + 2(7) = 2(12) + 14 = 38$, works.

You do not have to check further, but FYI: choice B using $W = 12$ gives a perimeter of 58, not 38; choice C using $W = 26$ gives a perimeter of 114, not 38; choice D using $W = 28$ gives a perimeter of 122, not 38; and choice E using $W = 33$ gives a perimeter of 142, not 38. You might have eliminated C, D, and E from the start as being unreasonable answers just by looking at them.

34. Choice C is the correct response. The formula for the area of a square is $A = s^2$, where s is the length of one side of the square. From the figure, you can see that the length of the side of the square is 2.5 meters. Substitute this value into the formula:

$$A = (2.5m)^2 = 6.25 \text{ m}^2$$

Choice A results if you add the two sides instead of multiplying them together. Choice B results if you confuse the formula for perimeter with the formula for area. Choices D and E are the results of calculation errors.

35. Choice C is the correct response. The triangle created at the telephone pole and the triangle with the person standing are two similar triangles. Similar triangles have the same shape. Their corresponding angles are equal, and their corresponding sides are proportional. Looking at the triangle, you can see that side H and side h are corresponding sides, and side S and side s are corresponding sides. The proportion that expresses this relationship is: $\dfrac{H}{h} = \dfrac{S}{s}$, which is choice C.

The other answer choices do not show the correct proportion.

36. Choice B is the correct response. The shaded part of the circle is one-half the area of the circle. The formula for the area of a circle is $A = \pi r^2$, where r is the radius of the circle. You can see by the figure that the diameter of the circle is 10 m. The diameter is twice the radius, so the radius of the circle is 5 m. Therefore, the area of the shaded part of the circle =

$$\frac{1}{2} \pi (5 \text{ m})^2$$

Using $\pi = 3.14$ gives $\frac{1}{2}(3.14)(25 \text{ m}^2) = 39.25 \text{ m}^2$, which rounds off to 39.3 m².

Choices A results if you evaluate $(5 \text{ m})^2$ as 10 m². Choice C results if you forget to take half the area of the whole circle. Choice D results if you use 10 m as the radius.

Choice E results if you use 10 m as the radius and you forget to take half the area of the whole circle.

37. Choice B is the correct response. The area of the rectangular lot is 4840 square yards. The formula for the area of a rectangle is $A = L \times W$. You are looking for the answer choice in which the two quantities multiply to give 4840 square yards. Find the number of square feet (ft^2) in 4840 square yards (yd^2). Do this by multiplying by $\dfrac{9 \ ft^2}{yd^2}$, then checking the answers. (Notice that the conversion factor is $\dfrac{9 \ ft^2}{yd^2}$, not $\dfrac{3 \ ft^2}{yd^2}$ because a square yard is a square that is 3 ft by 3 ft):

$$\frac{4840 \ yd^2}{1} \times \frac{9 \ ft^2}{yd^2} = 43{,}560 \ ft^2.$$

Now check the answers to see which one works.

Choice A: 40 feet $\times$ 363 feet = 14,520 ft^2, doesn't work.

Choice B: 120 feet $\times$ 363 feet = 43,560 ft^2, works.

You do not have to check further, but FYI:

Choice C: 120 feet $\times$ 484 feet = 58,080 ft^2, doesn't work.

Choice C: 420 feet $\times$ 2000 feet = 840,000 ft^2, doesn't work.

Choice C: 484 feet $\times$ 10 feet = 4,840 ft^2, doesn't work.

38. Choice B is the correct response. This is a two-step problem:

Step 1. Find the volume of the water in the box in cubic feet.

The formula for the volume of a rectangular prism (a box) is $V = L \times W \times H$, where L is the length, W is the width, and H is the height of the box. Substituting in the formula gives: $V = (9 \ ft)(15 \ ft)(2 \ ft) = 270 \ ft^3$.

Step 2. Let x = weight in pounds of the water in the box. Write a proportion.

$$\frac{x \ (lb)}{270 \ ft^3} = \frac{625 \ lb}{10 \ ft^3}$$

Omit the units and solve the proportion:

$$\frac{x}{270} = \frac{625}{10}$$

Multiply 270 by 625 and then divide by 10:

$$\frac{270 \times 625}{10} = \frac{168750}{10} = 16{,}875 \ lbs. \ of \ water$$

Choice A results if you multiply 625 by 10. Choices C, D, and E occur if you calculate the volume incorrectly.

39. Choice D is the correct response. You can draw a Venn diagram to illustrate the problem. The largest circle, circle W, contains all the winners. The next

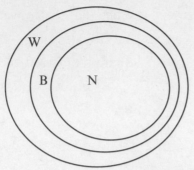

largest circle, circle B, contains all blond-haired contestants. That circle is completely contained in circle W because the first statement says, "All blond-haired contestants are winners." The smallest circle, circle N, is the circle containing contestants from Norway. That circle is completely contained in circle B because the second statement says, "All contestants from Norway have blond hair."

From the diagram you can see that circle N is completely contained in circle W, so you can logically conclude the statement in choice D: "All contestants from Norway are winners."

Choice A is incorrect because you could have a blond-haired contestant from another country and that contestant would be a winner according to the first statement. Choice B is incorrect because there could be contestants without blond hair. Choice C is incorrect because you could have a blond-haired contestant from another country. Choice E is incorrect because there is no statement ruling out that a contestant could have dark hair.

40. Choice B is the correct response. The statement "If you eat rotten fruit, you will get sick" has the form if p, then q, where p = "you eat rotten fruit" and q = "you will get sick." The form if p, then q is called a conditional statement and is used frequently in reasoning. Logically, the statement that is equivalent to if p, then q, is the statement called its contrapositive: If not q, then not p. Look at the answer choices. You want to find one where the part after the word "if" is the opposite of "you will get sick" and the part after the word "then" is the opposite of "you did eat rotten fruit." Choice B comes closest to this. It makes sense, too. Knowing that you didn't get sick does imply that you did not eat rotten fruit. You can check the other choices to convince yourself that they are not logically equivalent to the original statement:

Choice A: Not logically equivalent because you could get sick for other reasons besides that you ate rotten fruit.

Choice C: Not logically equivalent because not eating rotten fruit is no guarantee that you won't get sick.

Choice D: Not logically equivalent because there are other reasons for getting sick besides not eating rotten fruit; furthermore, logically this statement would imply that eating rotten fruit would keep you from getting sick.

Choice E: Not logically equivalent because this implies that eating rotten fruit keeps you from getting sick.

SECTION 1

WRITING

PART A

1. Choice C is the correct response. A comma is needed following the introductory subordinate clause.

2. Choice A is the correct response. In this sentence, the word following the verb *felt* modifies the subject (a noun). The word *badly* is an adverb. It should not be used to modify a noun. The adjective *bad* should be used instead. Change *badly* to *bad* to make the sentence grammatically correct.

3. Choice D is the correct response. The word *between* is a preposition. The object of a preposition should be in the objective case. Change *I* to *me* to make the sentence grammatically correct.

4. Choice A is the correct response. A pronoun modifying a gerund should be in the possessive case. The word *Him* should be changed to *His*.

5. Choice B is the correct response. No comma is needed before the subordinate clause.

6. Choice D is the correct response. The adjective *unique* is absolute in its meaning and thus does not have degrees of comparison. Something is either unique or it isn't. Change *the most unique* to *a unique* to make the sentence grammatically correct.

7. Choice D is the correct response. The word at D is the subject of the verb *am* (which is understood) and thus should be in the nominative case. Change *me* to *I* to make the sentence grammatically correct.

8. Choice E is the correct response. This sentence is correct as written. (The word *whoever* at B is correct because it is the subject of the verb *wanted*.)

9. Choice B is the correct response. To form the possessive of a plural noun ending in *s*, put an apostrophe after the *s*. Change *student's* to *students'* to make the sentence grammatically correct.

10. Choice A is the correct response. Delete the word *it* to make the sentence grammatically correct.

11. Choice B is the correct response. To make the sentence grammatically correct, change *purchase* to *purchasing* so that the construction is parallel, with all verbs in the same tense: planning, purchasing, preparing, and keeping.

12. Choice B is the correct response. The word *Each* is the singular antecedent of the pronoun at B. Do not use the plural pronoun *their* to refer to a singular noun.

13. Choice A is the correct response. The singular subject *chorus* requires a singular verb. Change *were* at A to *was* to make the sentence grammatically correct.

14. Choice C is the correct response. The word *affect* is a verb. Replace *affect* with the noun *effect* to make the sentence grammatically correct.

15. Choice E is the correct response. This sentence is correct as written. The plural verb *show* at C is correct because the word *data* is a plural noun.

16. Choice D is the correct response. Delete the comma at D to correct the error.

17. Choice C is the correct response. The sentence contains a redundant construction; the word *because* means "for the reason that." Change *because* to *that* to make the sentence grammatically correct.

18. Choice D is the correct response. The pronoun *you* at D does not agree with its antecedent (student).

19. Choice C is the correct response. Does *them* refer to *children* or *toys*? Change *them* at C to *the toys* to avoid ambiguity.

20. Choice C is the correct response. The comma should be placed inside the quotation marks, not outside.

21. Choice A is the correct response. The word at A should be an adjective. The word *principle* is a noun. Change *principle* to *principal* to make the sentence grammatically correct.

22. Choice B is the correct response. The word at B should be an adverb. The word *real* is an adjective. Replace *real* with an adverb like *really* or *very*.

23. Choice C is the correct response. The word *capitol* refers to a building, not to a city. Change *capitol* to *capital* to make the sentence grammatically correct.

24. Choice C is the correct response. Change *began* to *begun* to make the sentence grammatically correct.

25. Choice C is the correct response. This sentence is an example of a comma splice, in which two independent clauses are joined by a comma without a coordinating conjunction. It can be made grammatically correct by substituting a semicolon for the comma at C.

PART B

1. Choice C is the best response. When referring to a singular antecedent, you must use a singular pronoun.

2. Choice A is grammatically and structurally correct. There are no words or phrases that need to be set off with commas.

3. Choice B is the best response. A comma is used to form a compound sentence by linking two independent clauses with a coordinating conjunction. Therefore, answers A and D are incorrect. The conjunctions used in choices C and E do not correlate.

4. Choice B is the best response. A colon is used to introduce a list of items that completes a sentence. In choice A the word cello is misspelled. Choice C contains a sentence fragment. Choice D is an awkward way of expressing the sentence. Choice E uses incorrect punctuation for the items in series.

5. Choice D is the best response. *Definitely* is misspelled in A and C. In choice D, past tense (*rushed*) is used to indicate the task had been completed.

6. Choice A is the best response. The sentence contains a nonrestrictive clause that must be set off by commas, and a comma is needed to separate the participial phrase from the rest of the sentence; thus, choices B, C, D, and E are incorrect.

7. Choice B is the best response. The possessive pronoun *Their* should be used instead of the contraction *They're*. A semicolon is needed between the two independent clauses that are joined by the conjunctive adverb *however*. A comma should be placed after the conjunctive adverb.

8. Choice D is the best response. Joining the two independent clauses contrasting *mediation* and *civil suits* with the coordinating conjunction *but* is a more effective way to express the intent of the two sentences. A comma is needed before the coordinating conjunction. Choice D is the only answer that meets these criteria.

9. Choice A is the best response. The appositive phrase is necessary for the meaning of the sentence and should not be separated by commas.

10. Choice D is the best response. A and C have pronouns without an antecedent and also use the more ambiguous preposition *in*. D uses the preposition *inside* for precision.

11. Choice B is the best response. The word *farther* is properly restricted to measurable distances. A is incorrect because *ocean* is not capitalized.

12. Choice C is the best response. *Hardly* is an adverb modifying the verb *had* that tells to what extent.

13. Choice D is the best response. In choices A, B, and C the relative pronoun *that* is incorrectly used to introduce a nonrestrictive clause. *Which* is a better choice in nonrestrictive clauses. Choice E omits the comma needed before the nonrestrictive clause. Choices A, B, and C use the relative pronoun *that,* but *which* is the better choice in nonrestrictive clauses.

14. Choice A is correct and free from grammar, logic, or structure errors.

15. Choice A is the best response. The phrase "unlike many states" makes a comparison with other states.

16. Choice E is the best response. The possessive pronoun *their* is needed for clarity.

17. Choice A indicates the best word usage and is the correct answer.

18. Choice B is the best response. The word *well* is not necessary to the sentence.

19. Choice D is the best response. *Desperation* is misspelled in all other choices.

20. Choice C is the best response. The sentence begins with a short prepositional phrase, which does not need to be followed by punctuation. Answer B contains an incorrect spelling of *desert*.

SECTION 2

ESSAY

A Well-Written Sample Response

The way children view themselves affects their experience in school. If a child comes into a classroom with the belief that he or she is not capable of performing successfully, then that child probably will be reluctant to participate fully in class. Having a negative self-concept likely will make the child unsure of himself or herself. The child may be afraid to raise his or her hand to answer a question because the child thinks his or her answer will be wrong—even if it is correct. As this behavior continues day after day, the child gradually gives up, loses interest in school, and, ultimately, gets poor grades.

On the other hand, if a child believes that he or she is capable, then the child is usually more willing to try new things and take risks. This child probably will try harder and will be less likely to become frustrated when faced with obstacles. A positive self-concept helps the child believe that he or she can learn—even when the subject matter is challenging. This attitude helps the child perform better and leads to a successful experience in school.

ESSAY CHECKLIST

My essay:
- ✓ Addresses the topic
- ✓ Is well organized and coherent
- ✓ Has key ideas clearly explained and illustrated
- ✓ Has varied sentence structure
- ✓ Shows command of the language
- ✓ Follows rules of standard English

Part 3

Review

Chapter 6

Review for the PPST Reading

The passages contained within the PRAXIS Preparation Book have been constructed with various types of reading matter. These different kinds of reading matter vary in the way paragraphs are written and therefore in the way they present the facts. Textbooks are not written in the same style as novels or short stories and consequently cannot be read the same way. For the reading of the passages to be more effective, attention must be paid to the characteristics of these different writing styles. Textbook and literary materials are read differently not only because they differ in construction but also because we read them for different purposes.

Textbooks have a relatively formal style. Each major paragraph may open with a topic sentence giving the main idea to be presented in the paragraph. Or if several paragraphs cover the same idea, the reader may be carried along from the end of one to the next by a transitional sentence. This may be the closing sentence of the first paragraph or the opening sentence of the next paragraph. Thus most of the main ideas of a textbook paragraph are presented in the opening sentence or two. These ideas are enlarged upon, and supporting facts or details are given in the body of the paragraph. Another characteristic of formal textbook writing is the use of summary closing sentences which give the thoughts of the paragraph. The conclusions that may be drawn from the main idea and its supporting details are often restated in these summary sentences. Major ideas are often presented in the opening sentences of a paragraph and the minor facts or details are contained within the body of the paragraph.

Many literary, nontechnical materials are not written in the formal style described above. There are often as many main ideas, details, and conclusions in a novel as in any average textbook. But they are deliberately presented differently. The literary author is not so concerned about teaching facts as he is in creating moods, impressions, and emotions. Certainly he may be teaching us something, but does it more subtly. He gives us ideas and feelings by the words he chooses rather than enumerating the facts.

Literary and textbook materials are read differently not only because they differ in construction but also because we read them for different purposes. For the most part, we read literary materials for moods and impressions, for ideas about people, places, or times, for comparing another man's ideas with our own, and similar reasons.

Reading is a purposeful activity comprised of several literal, critical, and inferential comprehension skills. The Reading questions contained within this preparation manual assess the following skills:

Main Idea

Identifying the main idea involves determining the focus of the passage. This requires being able to understand how the details of the passage work together to support one idea. Identifying the main idea is an essential skill of comprehension and, therefore, of understanding the message of the text. Main ideas can be stated or implied. Stated main ideas are topic sentences that usually appear as the first or last sentence in a reading selection. Implied main ideas are not presented in topic sentences but can be identified by adding up the details in the selection. A main idea question can be asked in the following ways:

Which of the following expresses the main idea of this selection?
The main idea of the passage is which of the following?
Which of the following statements best summarizes the main idea of the passage?
What is the main idea of the passage?
The main point of the first paragraph is which of the following?

Recognizing the main idea is a matter of adding up the separate facts into a broad statement or generalization. Each paragraph contains one or several major concepts. To support, illustrate, or prove these ideas, the writer usually offers a number of facts or statements. It is the task of the reader to decide whether each statement or sentence prevents a supporting fact. As he reads, the person mentally enumerates the facts presented, recognizing that some are new while others are merely repetitions of earlier statements. He decides whether there is one really unified, related group of facts and how all of these could be summed up in one broad statement. Or he may discover that there are actually two or more groups of facts, or several main ideas, that must be summarized separately. This process of identifying the ideas is therefore more or less an additive process with the reader grouping the facts into one or more summarizing sentences.

Main ideas are somewhat easier to identify in a formal, textbook style of writing. There the main ideas are commonly presented in the opening sentence or two, which is called a topic sentence. In the body of the paragraph, the details supporting the main idea usually appear. Then the conclusions possible from the facts presented, or perhaps a restatement of the main idea, may often be found in the concluding or summary sentence.

Of course, not all writers of textbooks follow this plan of writing. Or even when they do for the most part, many of their paragraphs are not arranged exactly in this fashion. Many paragraphs are simply repetitions or elaborations of an idea presented previously. Thus a writer may devote three or four paragraphs to the enlargement of a single main topic. When he does so, the reader still may not find the idea presented in a topic sentence each time, then the details, and then the conclusions.

A whole paragraph may be nothing but details, or a paragraph may consist entirely of conclusions. Or paragraphs may be tied together by transitional sentences at the end of the first paragraph or the beginning of the second paragraph. Although the reader may be aware of the characteristics of formal style and use his knowledge to facilitate analysis of ideas, he still must be alert to recognize deviations in style.

Recognizing paragraph types and structures will improve the reader's comprehension by providing a clearer focus on what the author is saying. There are six major types of paragraph structure or organization often found in textbooks. They are as follows:

Definition   *Compare-Contrast*
Sequence   *Analysis or Description*
Cause-Effect   *Thesis statement and support*

Definition paragraphs serve to define. Some are obvious because they use the term define or definition; however, they function the same whether or not these words are stated.

Sequence paragraphs present the steps in a process in a chronological manner which is clear to the reader. The paragraph could involve time order or events.

Cause and effect paragraphs involve result or consequence. They may be presented as the cause or causes and then the resultant condition, or the effect may be stated first followed by the cause.

Compare-contrast paragraphs are looking at two or more things in a relationship. They are compared to show similarities and contrasted to show differences.

Analysis or descriptive paragraphs show some concept being broken down so the reader can understand it more clearly. Description is more often found in narrative material.

Thesis statement and support paragraphs are usually presented early to the reader. They are then defended or supported. Many kinds of logic and argument can be used.

A reader has two useful references for finding the structure or organizational pattern of a paragraph—the main idea or signal words. Certain signal words can indicate the paragraph type.

WORD OR PHRASE	PARAGRAPH TYPE
on the other hand	contrast
however	contrasts
similarly	compare
as a result	cause and effect
therefore	cause and effect
	thesis and supporting statement
afterward	sequence
	cause and effect
is made up of	analysis or description

Here is a typical textbook paragraph in which you may identify the ideas. In the paragraph, decide which of the facts can be combined into a meaningful, complete idea.

> *With the spread of grazing and farming many hunting and fishing people have either disappeared from the earth or have become herders or tillers of the soil. The struggles of many tribes of ancient man through the centuries in Eurasia confirm this thesis. Comparatively recently, the hunting people of Australasia coming in contact with the white man have largely vanished; with them have gone many animals with furnished food, meager articles of raiment, shelter, and artifacts. Of the once numerous Bushmen who were pre-eminent hunters of southern Africa, only a miserable remnant of inferior character lingers in the inhospitable Kalahari Desert. In southeastern South America, plains Indians, who were primarily people of the chase even when they had European horses and cattle, finally vanished in face of the onslaught of Spanish cattlemen and farmers. In the great plains of North America, from the northern forest to the Rio Grande, the hunter-trapper, cattlemen, and farmer replaced during the last century several hunting tribes of Indians.*

Clarence F. Jones, *Economics Geography*, New York: Macmillan, 1949, p. 21.

Choose the main idea of this selection:

1. Hunting and fishing have ceased to function as means of subsistence for large groups of people.
2. People dependent upon hunting or fishing for their subsistence have largely disappeared from the earth.
3. The spread of farming and grazing makes it impossible for primitive people to exist by hunting and fishing.
4. Agricultural pursuits cannot exist in the same area with hunting and fishing.

All of these statements of the ideas of the paragraph are essentially correct. But they do not all satisfy as complete summaries of the paragraph. The first choice is incomplete because it does not explain why hunting and fishing as a means of subsistence have disappeared. Choice two also fails to support its assertion. Choice four implies that agricultural pursuits will be driven out by hunting and fishing, which is the essence of the paragraph in reverse. The third choice is probably the best statement of the main idea. It carries the implication intended by the writer, that farming and grazing drive out hunting and fishing, and that those who live by hunting and fishing may change their means of livelihood or disappear.

Phrases or signal words will help you locate certain types of materials or let you know what the author considers important. The following are examples of signal words that may indicate a main idea:

In summary…
All of this leads to…
The main point here is…
This section tells how…

Author's Purpose

There are many purposes for writing. Some are listed here:

- to inform
- to entertain
- to perform a task
- to follow instructions
- to sell
- to inspire

- to correct a misunderstanding
- to change a reader's opinion
- to show differing points of view
- to communicate ideas
- to review a film
- to review a book

Knowing the author's purpose helps readers in several ways. It helps prepare your mind for the type of information in the reading. Also, it makes the article easier to summarize. In addition, it makes it easier for the reader to determine the article's main idea and important details. Author's purpose questions can be asked in several ways. The following questions are examples of those ways:

According to the passage, what is the author's purpose?
What is the purpose of the passage?

The mark of an efficient reader is flexibility in reading methods and reading speeds. The reader decides what he wishes to accomplish in a reading, chooses a method suited to this purpose and to the difficulty of the material, and reads accordingly. The ability to read at widely different rates, chosen deliberately according to the purpose of the reading and the degree of comprehension desired, is one of the outstanding characteristics of a truly efficient reader.

Supporting Ideas

When authors write, they have an idea in mind that they are trying to get across. This is especially true as authors compose paragraphs. An author organizes each paragraph's main idea and supporting details in support of the topic or central theme, and each paragraph supports the paragraph preceding it.

The first thing you must be able to do to get at the main idea is to identify the topic—the subject of the paragraph. Think of the passage as a wheel with the topic being the hub—the central core around which the whole wheel (or passage) spins. Your strategy for topic identification is simply to ask yourself the question, "What is this about?" The bulk of the passage is made up of supporting sentences (major and minor details), which help to explain or prove the main idea. These sentences present facts, reasons, examples, definitions, comparisons, contrasts, and other pertinent details. These sentences are most important because they sell the main idea. "Support idea" questions can be asked in the following ways:

> *What does the passage state about the immediate aims of high school*
> *In the first sentence, the "fire o'nights" refers to which of the following?*
> *The author compares a person's recollections to which of the following?*
> *According to the passage, the rule between oral and written communication is which of the following?*

Once you have identified the main idea in the passage, the remaining material is made up of mostly details, transitions, introductions, conclusions, and fillers. Being able to pick out significant details will help the reader retain more of what he or she read.

Details provide different functions according to their relationship to the main idea.

They may:
Explain
Elaborate
Illustrate
Give specific examples
Define

They may also:
Sidetrack
Confuse
Entertain

Details that sidetrack or are irrelevant should not be considered. Details that confuse need to be investigated further. In other words, you may find a detail confusing because you misunderstood the main idea, or because the writer has included something that really doesn't fit in. Details that entertain can help the reader retain the information.

As with main idea, signal words can help the reader identify details or a set of details in a passage. The following are examples of signal words for a detail:

First . . .
Furthermore . . .
As a result . . .
However . . .
For example . . .
On the other hand . . .
In addition . . .
As a result . . .
This illustrates the preceding point.
There are three reasons why . . . . These are . . .

Some signal words actually let the reader know what to expect. For example, *on the other hand* or *however* signals a change of viewpoint or opinion. Signals like *addition to* or *furthermore* do the opposite. They indicate that a continuation of a point is ahead.

Organization

The use of sentences and paragraphs is crucial to the organization of the passage. Each sentence should convey a specific idea, and the sentences should be organized into paragraphs, each of which has a central theme. In other words, how is the passage put together to achieve the author's purpose. The following are a few considerations of authors as they organize their writing:

- developing and focusing on a topic, then refining the writing
- author's audience, purpose, arguments, and assumptions
- framing a thesis, main idea, or "big picture"
- presenting appropriate evidence to support ideas
- describing, analyzing, and synthesizing readings; recognizing analogies and metaphoric or figurative connections among ideas
- locating, evaluating, and analyzing potential sources from the library, the Internet, and printed and other media, and integrating them in your writing
- quoting, paraphrasing and summarizing sources, including when to do each of these and how to do so properly
- generating and organizing ideas and arguments, and then revising, editing, and proofreading
- well-defined purpose (describing, analyzing, and persuasion) and with some level of investment in a topic
- using description, narration, and analysis, and deciding when each approach is most effective
- choices about content, rhetoric, structure, vocabulary, style, and format
- organizing writing to unify and focus ideas and to knit ideas together coherently

Some examples of questions regarding organization can include:

The author's primary purpose in the passage is to
According to the author, colleges can only serve us by
In the second paragraph and third sentence, the term "roan" is used by the author to mean
According to the author, which of the following is true about choice?

Vocabulary in Context

Many times authors give the meaning of words in a phrase or clause following the word so that no real analysis is necessary. But, if they do not, determining the meaning of words using context is a favorite technique of readers. The reader tries to sense the word meaning implied by the rest of the sentence or paragraph. Here are helpful ideas in deciphering the meaning of the word:

- Look for other words in the sentence that clearly have a similar meaning to the unknown word.
- Look for nearby words or phrases that might describe the cause of the unknown word.
- Look for words that make the unknown word part of a group of recognizable things.
- Look for clues to a word's opposite meaning.
- Vocabulary in context questions can be asked in the following ways:
  - The term "slovenly" in the sixth sentence means __?
  - To what does the term "passage" refer in the second paragraph?

Possibly the most important of the skills of reading that must be acquired is the ability to recognize and use appropriately a great many words. Basically, of course, a person cannot read on a higher level than his vocabulary skills. Words are the tools of accurate thought.

The average adult reader has one favorite technique for determining the meanings of unknown words—the guess. This technique is formally known as finding words in context. It may be sheer guesswork in which the reader tries to sense the meaning implied by the rest of the sentence or paragraph. This hit or miss technique fails half the time.

The most common way of finding meaning from the context is by inference, or trying to reason out the meaning from the sense of the sentence. Most readers do this so unconsciously that often they are not even aware of the process.

Try to choose the correct definition from the two words that follow. Then read the sentences to see how easily, and perhaps unconsciously, you discover their true meanings.

1. *gauntlet* means
   A. a heavy glove with a deep flaring cuff
   B. the upper edge of a tower or battlement
   C. a tropical American lizard
   D. a long, high steep face of rock

2. *contiguous* means
   A. liable or likely to occur
   B. occurring in uninterrupted succession
   C. self-restraining; exercising self-control
   D. touching or being in contact

On his right hand, the gentleman wore a gauntlet of heavy leather with an embroidered cuff.
The pillars were almost immediately contiguous, with scarcely space enough between for a hand to enter, much less a human.

These sentences actually tell you what the meanings of gauntlet and contiguous are. The first sentence describes a gauntlet and tells where it is worn. The second sentence explains how close pillars were and, in doing so, explains the meaning of contiguous. The meanings of the new words are explained so obviously that the reader may not have been aware of the explanation if they were reading rapidly.

Meanings can also be derived from structural clues, figures of speech, and tone or mood. Many times the meaning of a difficult word is given in a phrase or clause following the word closely, or by comparing or contrasting the unknown word with a simpler one.

Figures of speech are often clues to the meaning of difficult words. The figure of speech known as a simile includes the word *like* or *as*. A metaphor may serve to show meaning by using a colorful word that has common ideas associated with it.

Fact and Opinion

Distinguishing fact from opinion is not always an easy task. Many writings contain both fact and opinion. The following may help make the determination:

- A statement of fact makes this implied claim: "This is true. You can check it out for yourself if you want. You can ask other people. Everybody will agree with me about this."
- A statement of opinion makes this implied claim: "This is true because I have thought about it and I believe it is true. People who disagree with me about this are wrong. Take my word for it."
- Fact vs. opinion questions usually don't require you to go back and look at the selection to choose your answer.
- Opinion statements tend to use words that mean different things to different people. Fact statements often use words that mean the same thing to everyone.

Fact and opinion questions may be asked in the following way:

Is the author's accounting of the event in the passage considered fact or opinion?

It is easy to establish fact from opinion by asking can the statement be proved right or wrong with verifiable evidence. Otherwise the statement is an opinion. The fact may not always be accurate or correct. A reader could be receiving incorrect information that was presented as a fact.

Inferences

Some questions test your understanding of information that is directly stated in a passage. Other questions, however, require you to think about the ideas discussed in the passage. The answers to some reading questions are not directly stated in the passage.

You must arrive at the answers by making inferences, drawing conclusions, formulating judgments, or evaluating ideas. Some examples of this type of question are:

It can be inferred from the passage that _____.
Which of the following can be inferred from the passage?

Inference can be explained as reading between the lines. The inference is not stated but perceived by the reader. Inferred material may be informational or it may relate to mood, tone, or slant of a message. Sometimes an author's purpose may have to be inferred.

Predictions

Prediction activates thought about the content before reading. The reader must rely on what he or she knows through previous study and experience to make educated guesses about the material to be read. Readers generally have a prior purpose or expectation of what they might find in the text. Readers predict within the most likely range of alternatives. Prediction questions may be worded as follows:

According to the last paragraph, what will most likely happen to the gold?
After leaving Spain, where might the travelers journey next?

Readers should be aware of what they think and how they interact with the author while they read. Being proactive will allow them to assume responsibility for their comprehension. The strategies of setting a purpose and predicting are applications of metacognition to reading comprehension.

Affixes and Roots

Use of affixes and roots strongly promote vocabulary growth, since literally thousands of English words can be quickly recognized and understood if the reader knows only a relatively few base word parts. Readers who learn to use affixes and roots skillfully are more fluent and successful readers than those lacking this type of approach.

PREFIX	MEANING	CURRENT WORDS
re-	back	recall, recede, repay, reflect, retract, rebate
sub-	under, below	submarine, subzero, submerge, subordinate, subhuman
super-	above, beyond	superman, supernatural, superior, superpower, supervise
tele-	distant	telephone, telescope, television, telegram, telepathy
trans-	across	transport, transfer, translate, transatlantic, transcribe
un-	not	unhappy, unable, uncomfortable, uncertain, unbeaten
under-	below, less than	underpaid, undercover, underground, underneath, underage

Additional Common Prefixes

PREFIX	MEANING	CURRENT WORDS
after-	after	afternoon, afterward, aftershock, aftereffect, afterthought
ambi-, amphi-	both, around	ambidextrous, ambiguous, ambivalent, ambiance amphibian, amphitheater, amphora
auto-	self	automobile, automatic, autograph, autobiography, autonomy
be-	make	befriend, bewitch, beguile, bejewel, becalm
bene-	good	benefit, benefactor, benediction, beneficial, benevolent
bi-	two	bicycle, binocular, bifocal, biannual, bimonthly
centi-	hundred, hundredth	century, centigrade, centimeter, centennial
circu-	around	circulate, circumference, circus, circumspect, circumstance
co-	together	cooperate, collaborate, coordinate, coincide, cochair
com-, con-	with	combine, commune, combat, compare, command, concert, concur, connect, confer, concede, confident
contra-	against, opposite	contrary, contradict, contrast, contraband, contraception
counter-	against, opposite	counteract, countermand, counterproposal, counteroffensive
de-	down, away	deduct, descend, decrease, degrade, depart
de-	not, opposite	deform, deplete, deactivate, defuse, dehumidify
dec-	ten	decathlon, December, decennial, decade
	tenth	decimeter, decimate, decibel, decile, decimal
di-	two, double	dilemma, dioxide, dichotomy, diplomas, digraph
dia-	through, across	diameter, dialogue, diagonal, diagnose, dialect
du-, duo-	two	duotone, duet, dual, duplex, duplicate
dys-	bad	dysfunctional, dysentery, dysphasia, dystrophy
e-	out, away	evict, eject, erupt, emigrate, edict, emancipate
equi-	equal	equator, equation, equilibrium, equidistant, equinox
eu-	good	eulogy, euphoria, euphemism, Eucharist, euthanasia
giga-	billion	gigawatt, gigahertz, gigabyte
hemi-	half	hemisphere, hemistich, hemiplegia, hemicycle
hept-	seven	heptagon, heptameter, heptarchy
hetero-	different	heteronym, heterodoz, heterogenous, heterosexual
hex-	six	hexagon, hexameter, hexagram, hexadecimal
homo-	same	homogeneous, homogenize, homosexual, homophone
hyper-	excessive	hyperactive, hypersensitive, hyperbole, hypercritical
hypo-	under, too little	hypodermic, hypothesis, hypothermia, hypoxia
il-	not	illegal, illegible, illiterate, illogical, illegitimate
ir-	not	irregular, irreconcilable, irrevocable, irresponsible
kilo-	thousand	kilometer, kilogram, kilobyte, kilowatt, kiloliter
macro-	large, long	macroeconomics, macron, macrobiotic, macrocosm
magni-	great, large	magnify, magnificent, magnitude, magnanimous
mal-	bad	maladjusted, malfunction, malice, malevolent
mega-	large, million	megaphone, megalith, megacycle, megawatt, megaton, megabuck, megahertz
meta-	change	metamorphosis, metaphor, metastasis
mid-	middle	midnight, midway, midsummer, midyear, midshipman
milli-	thousand	million, milligram, millimeter, millennium, millibar
mon-, mono-	one	monk, monarch, monocular, monorail, monogamy
neo-	new	neoclassical, neologism, neonatal, neophyte, neon
omni-	all	omnibus, omnificent, omnipotent, omnivorous, omniscient

(continued)

Additional Common Prefixes (continued)

PREFIX	MEANING	CURRENT WORDS
pan-	all	panorama, panacea, pandemonium, pandemic, Pan-American
para-	almost	paramedic, paralegal, paraprofessional, parasail
per-	through	perennial, permeate, permit, pervade, percolate
peri-	around	perimeter, periscope, peripatetic, periphery, periodontist
poly-	many	polysyllabic, polyglot, polyester, polyandry, polygamy
prot-	first, chief	protagonist, proton, prototype, protocol, protoplasm
pseudo-	false	pseudonym, pseudoclassical, pseudointellectual
quadr-	four	quadrangle, quadrant, quadriplegic, quadruple
quint-	five	quintuplet, quintet, quintessential, quintuple
self-	self	selfish, self-denial, self-respect, self-taught
semi-	half	semiannual, semicircle, semiconscious, semiautomatic
sept-	seven	September, septet, septuagenarian
syn-	together	synchronize, syndrome, synergy, synonym, synthesis
tri-	three	triangle, tricycle, trillion, triplet, tripartite, triumvirate
ultra-	beyond	ultramodern, ultraconservative, ultranationalist
uni-	one	unicorn, uniform, unite, universe, unique, unison

Number Prefixes

PREFIX	MEANING	CURRENT WORDS
deci-	tenth	decimeter
centi-	hundredth	centimeter
milli-	thousandth	millimeter
micro-	millionth	micrometer
nano-	billionth	nanometer
pico-	trillionth	picometer
femto-	quadrillionth	femtometer
atto-	quintillionth	attometer
demi-	half	demigod, demitasse
hemi-	half	hemisphere, hemicycle
semi-	half	semiannual, semicircle, semiclassic
prot-	first	protagonist, protein, proton, prototype
mon-, mono-	one	monk, monarch, monocular, monogamy
uni-	one	unicorn, unicycle, uniform, unify, unite
di-	two	digraph, dioxide, diphthong
tri-	three	triangle, tricycle, trillion, triplet
quadr-	four	quadrangle, quadrant, quadruple
tetra-	four	tetrahedron, tetrameter
pent-	five	pentagon, pentathalon, Pentecost
quint	-five	quintet, quintuplets
hex-	six	hexagon, hexameter
sex-	six	sextant, sextet, sextuple
hept-	seven	heptagon, heptameter
sept-	seven	September, septuagenarian
oct-	eight	October, octagon, octane, octopus
ennea-	nine	enneagon, enneahedron, ennead
non-	nine	nonagenarian

(continued)

Number Prefixes (continued)

PREFIX	MEANING	CURRENT WORDS
nove-	nine	November, novena
deca-, dec-	ten	December, decade, decathlon, decameter
cent-	hundred	century (note: cent- is a shortened form of centi, which usually means one hundredth)
hect-	hundred	hectogram, hectometer, hectare
milli-	thousand	million, millipede (note: in metric system, milli- means thousandth)
kilo-	thousand	kilometer, kilogram, kilowatt, kiloliter
myria-	ten thousand	myriameter
mega-	million	megawatt, megabyte
giga-	billion	gigabyte
tera-	trillion	terameter
peta-	quadrillion	petameter
exa-	quintillion	exameter

Prefixes That Indicate Size

PREFIX	MEANING	CURRENT WORDS
macro-	large, long	macrocosm, macron, macroscopic
magni-	great	magnify, magnitude, magnificent
mega-	large	megacycle, megalith, megalomania
micro-	small, short	microbe, microphone, microcosm

Prefixes That Indicate When

PREFIX	MEANING	CURRENT WORDS
after-	after	afterglow, afternoon, aftertaste, afterward
ante-	before	antebellum, antecedent, antedate, antediluvian
epi-	after	epilogue, epitaph, epidermis
post-	after	postdate, postdoctoral, posterior, postpone, postscript
pre-	before	preamble, precaution, prefix, prejudice
pro-	before	prognosis, progeny, program, prologue

Prefixes That Indicate Where

PREFIX	MEANING	CURRENT WORDS
a-	on	aboard, afire, afoot, ashore, atop
ab-	from	abnormal, abhor, abolish, abstain
ac-	to	accent, accept, access, accident, acquire
ad-	to	adapt, add, addict, adhere, admit
af-, ag-	to	affair, affect, affiliate, affirm, afflict, agglomeration, aggrandize, aggravate
an-, as-	to	annex, annihilate, annotate, announce, ascend, ascertain, aspect, aspire, assert
by-	to	bypass, byplay, bystander, byway
circu-	to	circulate, circumference, circumspect

(continued)

Prefixes That Indicate Where (continued)

PREFIX	MEANING	CURRENT WORDS
de-	to	debate, decay, deceive, decide, deform
dia-	through, across	diagnose, diagonal, dialogue, diameter
e-	out, out of, from	effect, effort, eject
em-, en-	put into	emigrate, erupt, embalm, embed, embezzle, embrace, enchant, enclose, encounter, encourage
enter-	between, among	enterprise, entertain
epi-	upon	epicenter, epidemic, epidermis, epithet
ex-	out	excel, exalt, exceed, exhaust, exit
extra-	outside	extracurricular, extraordinary
hypo-	under	hypochondria, hypodermic, hypothesis
im-, in-	into	immediate, immerse, immigrate, implant, incision, include, induce, inhale, infect
inter-	among, between	intercede, interpret, interrupt
intra-	within	intramural, intrastate, intravenous
intro-	inside	introduce, introspect, introject, introvert
mid-	middle	midriff, midshipman, midsummer
off-	from	offset, offshoot, offshore, offspring
on-	on	oncoming, ongoing, onrush, onshore
para-	beside	paradigm, paragraph, parallel, paraphrase
per-	throughout	perceive, percolate, perfect, perform
peri-	all around	perimeter, periscope, peripatetic
pro-	forward	proceed, produce, proficient, progress
pro-	in front	proclaim, profane, profess
re-	back	recall, recede, reflect, repay, retract
retro-	back	retroactive, retrogress, retro-rocket
sub-	under	subcontract, subject, submerge
super-	over	superimpose, superscript, supersede
tele-	distant	telegram, telekinesis, telephone
thorough-	through	thoroughbred, thoroughfare
trans-	across	transatlantic, transcend, transcribe
under-	below	undercover, underground, underneath
with-	back, away	withdraw, withhold, within, without

Prefixes That Indicate Extent

PREFIX	MEANING	CURRENT WORDS
equi-	equal	equal, equilibrium, equidistant, equator
extra-	beyond	extraordinary, extravagant
hyper-	excessive	hyperactive, hyperbole, hypercritical
hypo-	too little	hypoactive, hypoglycemic
is-	equal	isometric, isomorph, isosceles, isotope
multi-	many, much	multicolored, multifarious, multiply
olig-	few	oligarchy, oligopoly, oligophagous
omni-	all	omnibus, omnificent, omnipotent
out-	surpassing	outbid, outclass, outdo, outlive
over-	too much	overactive, overbearing, overblown
pan-	all	panacea, pandemonium, Pandora

(continued)

Prefixes That Indicate Extent (continued)

PREFIX	MEANING	CURRENT WORDS
pene-	almost	peneplain, peninsula, penultimate
poly-	many	polyandry, polyester, polygamy, polyglot
super-	more	superfine, superhuman, supernatural
ultra-	beyond	ultraconservative, ultramodern
under-	less than	underage, underdone, underripe

Prefixes That Indicate Together/Apart

PREFIX	MEANING	CURRENT WORDS
ab-	away from	abdicate, abduct, aberrant, absent
co-	together	coauthor, cognate, coincide, cooperate
col-	with	collaborate, collateral, colleague, collect
com-	with	combat, combine, comfort, commune
con-	with	concede, concur, concert, confident
syl-	together	syllable, syllogism
sym-	together	symbiosis, symbol, symmetry, sympathy
syn-	together	synchronize, syndrome, synergy

Prefixes That Indicate Not or Opposite

PREFIX	MEANING	CURRENT WORDS
a-	not	apathy, atheist, atrophy, atypical
an-	not	anarchy, anesthesia, anorexia
counter-	opposite	counteract, countermand
de-	opposite	deactivate, deform, degrade, deplete
for-	prohibit	forbid, forget, forgo, forsake, forswear
ill-	not	illegal, illegible, illegitimate, illiterate
im-	not	imbalance, immaculate, immature
in-	not	inaccurate, inactive, inadvertent
ir-	not	irrational, irreconcilable, irredeemable
ne-	not	nefarious, never
neg-	not	negative, neglect, negotiate
non-	not	nonchalant, nonconformist, nondescript
un-	opposite	unable, undo, unbeaten, uncertain

Prefixes That Indicate For/Against

PREFIX	MEANING	CURRENT WORDS
anti-	against	antinuclear, antisocial, antislavery
bene-	good	benediction, benefactor, beneficial
contra-	against	contraband, contraception, contradict
dys-	bad	dysentery, dysfunction, dyspepsia
eu-	good	Eucharist, eugenic, euphoria, eulogy
mal-	bad	maladjusted, malaise, malevolent
mis-	bad	misanthrope, misbehave, miscarriage
pro-	for	pro-American, pro-education

Other Prefixes

PREFIX	MEANING	CURRENT WORDS
ambi-	both, around	ambidextrous, ambiance, ambiguous
amphi-	both, around	amphibian, amphitheater, amphora
auto-	self	autobiography, autocratic, autograph
be-	make	becalm, befriend, beguile, bewitch
hetero-	different	heterodox, heteronym, heterosexual
homo-	same	homogeneous, homogenize, homograph
meta-	change	metabolism, metamorphosis, metaphor
neo-	new	neoclassic, neologism, neon, neonatal
para-	almost	paralegal, paramedic
pseudo-	false	pseudoclassic, pseudonym, pseudopod
re-	again	reappear, reclassify, recopy, redo, repaint
self-	self	self-denial, self-respect, selfish

Vocabulary-Building Through Suffixes

A suffix is a syllable or syllables placed after a word to qualify its meaning. For example, measure means dimension, size, or quantity while measurable means capable of being measured. The meanings of measurable has been modified by adding to measure the suffix "able" meaning capable of being measured. Note that the suffix does not change the meaning of the word as drastically as does the prefix, but it does change the grammatical function. Avocation and vocation are nouns, but the noun *measure,* because of the addition of the suffix, has become an adjective, *measurable.* Likewise the adjective *loose* becomes an adverb when the suffix "ly" is added (*loosely*) and the verb *commit* becomes a noun when the suffix "sion" is added (*commission*). Certain minor changes in spelling frequently occur. These are intended to make pronunciation easier. Here is a list of selected suffixes.

Suffixes

SUFFIX	MEANING	CURRENT WORDS
-able, -ible	is, can be	comfortable, learnable, walkable, climbable, perishable, durable, gullible, combustible
-ar, -er, -or	one who	beggar, liar, teacher, painter, seller, shipper, doctor, actor, editor
-en	to make	strengthen, fasten, lengthen, frighten, weaken
-er	more	smarter, closer, lighter, quicker, softer, luckier
-ess	one who (female)	princess, waitress, countess, hostess, actress
-est	most	smartest, closest, lightest, quickest, softest, luckiest
-ette	small	dinette, diskette, majorette, barrette
-ful	full of	joyful, fearful, careful, thoughtful, cheerful
-ish	relating to	childish, fiftyish, bookish, selfish
-less	without	thoughtless, tireless, joyless, ageless, careless
-like	resembling	lifelike, homelike, childlike, computerlike
-ly	resembling	fatherly, scholarly, motherly, sisterly, brotherly
-ment	action or process	government, development, experiment
-ness	state or quality of	kindness, happiness, goodness, darkness, fullness
-ship	state or quality of	friendship, hardship, citizenship, internship

Other Suffixes

SUFFIX	MEANING	CURRENT WORDS
-a, -ae	plural	data, criteria, memoranda, alumnae, algae, formulae
-acious	inclined to action	loquacious, mendacious, audacious, fallacious
-ade, -age	or process action	blockade, promenade, escapade
	or process	marriage, voyage, pilgrimage, blockage, rummage
-an	relating to	urban, American, veteran, Hawaiian, metropolitan
-ance, -ence	state or quality of	repentance, annoyance, resistance, violence, absence, reticence
-aney, -eney	state or quality of	buoyancy, truancy, vacancy, vagrancy, frequency, clemency, expediency, consistency
-ant, -ent	one who	servant, immigrant, assistant, merchant, regent, superintendent, resident
-ant	inclined to	vigilant, pleasant, defiant, buoyant, observant
-arian	one who	librarian, humanitarian, libertarian
-arium, -orium	place for	aquarium, planetarium, solarium, auditorium
-ary, -ory	place for	library, mortuary, sanctuary, infirmary, laboratory, conservatory
-ation, -ion, -sion, -tion	state or quality of	desperation, starvation, inspiration, tension, caution, suspicion, attention, fascination, companion
-ative, -ble	inclined to repeated	demonstrative, pejorative, talkative, stumble, squabble, mumble, tumble, fumble
-dom	action state or quality	freedom, boredom, martyrdom, wisdom
-ectomy	of surgical removal of object	tonsillectomy, appendectomy, mastectomy
-ee	of action	payee, lessee, employee
-ence	state or quality of	violence, absence, reticence, abstinence
-ency	state or quality of	frequency, clemency, expediency, consistency
-enne	female	comedienne, equestrienne, tragedienne
-er	action or process	murder, plunder, waiver, flounder, thunder
-ern	direction	eastern, western, northern, postern
-ery	state or quality of	bravery, savagery, forgery, slavery
-ese	relating to	Japanese, Chinese, Portuguese, Siamese
-esque	relating to	statuesque, picturesque, Romanesque
-etic	relating to	alphabetic, dietetic, frenetic, athletic, sympathetic
-hood	state or quality of	childhood, adulthood, falsehood, nationhood
-ial, -ian	relating to	filial, commercial, remedial, barbarian, Christian
-ic, -ical	relating to	comic, historic, poetic, public, rhetorical, economical
-ics	scientific or social	physics, economics, politics, statistics, system demographics
-ide, -ine	chemical compound	fluoride, peroxide, sulfide, iodine, chlorine, quinine

(continued)

Other Suffixes (continued)

SUFFIX	MEANING	CURRENT WORDS
-ify	to make	satisfy, terrify, falsify, beautify, vilify
-ina, -ine	female	czarina, ballerina, Wilhelmina, heroine, Josephine
-ious	state or quality of	gracious, ambitious, religious, nutritious, delicious
-ism	doctrine of	capitalism, socialism, communism, patriotism
-ist	one who practices	biologist, capitalist, communist, philanthropist
-itis	inflammation of	laryngitis, arthritis, bronchitis, appendicitis
-ity, -ty	state or quality of	necessity, civility, parity, loyalty, honesty, amnesty, unity
-ive	inclined to	active, passive, negative, restive, positive
-ization	state or quality of	civilization, standardization, organization
-ize	to make	standardize, computerize, popularize, pulverize, pasteurize
-ling	small	duckling, yearling, suckling, fledgling
-most	most	utmost, westernmost, innermost, foremost
-oid	resembling	humanoid, asteroid, paranoid, planetoid
-ose	sugars	glucose, sucrose, fructose, dextrose
-ous	full of	joyous, virtuous, nervous, wondrous
-phobia	fear of	claustrophobia
-some	inclined to	meddlesome, awesome, tiresome, fulsome
-th, -eth	numbers	fifth, twelfth, twentieth, fiftieth
-ulent	full of	turbulent, corpulent, fraudulent, truculent
-und, -uous	state or quality of	rotund, fecund, moribund, jocund, contemptuous, tempestuous, sensuous, vacuous
-ure	action or process	censure, procure, endure, inure, secure
-ward	direction	forward, backward, eastward, upward, onward
-ways	manner	sideways, longways, crossways
-wise	manner, direction	clockwise, lengthwise, counterclockwise
-y	being or having	fruity, sunny, rainy, funny, gooey, chewy

Inflectional suffixes denote the change in spelling that a word undergoes to show a change in its meaning. To derive nouns from verbs, add the suffixes -tion, -ion, -sion, and -ation (denounce/denunciation, compile/compilation, transpose/transposition). To derive adjectives from nouns, add the suffixes -ful, -less,-ious, -ous, or -y (hope/hopeful, end/endless, ambition/ambitious). To derive nouns from adjectives, add the suffixes -ness, -ity, -ce, or -cy (happy/happiness, loquacious/loquacity, fragrant/fragrance). To derive verbs from adjectives, add the suffixes -ize, -en, or -fy (fertile/fertilize, liquid/liquefy, solid/solidify). To derive adjectives from verbs, add the suffixes -able, -ible, or -ive (reverse/reversible, evade/evasive, repair/reparable). To derive adverbs from adjectives, add the suffix -ly (handy/handily, excitable/excitably, false/falsely).

English has relatively few suffixes that form verbs and adverbs. A large number of suffixes, however, form nouns and adjectives. Knowing the most common ones can help to identify several words from a single base word. The only regular suffix for adverbs is -ly, as in slowly, wisely, and casually.

Noun Suffixes

SUFFIX	MEANING	CURRENT WORDS
-a	plural	data, criteria, memoranda
-ade	action or process	blockade, escapade, parade, promenade
-ade	product or thing	lemonade, marmalade
-ae	plural (feminine)	alumnae, formulae, larvae, algae
-age	action or process	marriage, voyage, pilgrimage
-ance	state or quality of	repentance, annoyance, resistance
-ancy	state or quality of	buoyancy, truancy, vacancy, vagrancy
-ant	one who	servant, immigrant, assistant, merchant
-ar	one who	beggar, liar
-ard	one who	drunkard, steward, coward, wizard
-arian	one who	librarian, humanitarian, libertarian
-arium	place for	aquarium, planetarium, solarium
-ary	place for	library, mortuary, sanctuary, infirmary
-ation	state or quality of	desperation, starvation, inspiration
-ation	action or process	emancipation, narration, computation
-cle	small	corpuscle, particle, icicle, cubicle
-crat	person of power	democrat, autocrat
-cule	small	minuscule, molecule
-cy	state or quality of	accuracy, bankruptcy, conspiracy
-cy	action or process	truancy, diplomacy, vagrancy, piracy
-dom	state or quality of	freedom, boredom, martyrdom, wisdom
-ectomy	surgical removal of	tonsillectomy, appendectomy, mastectomy
-ee	object of action	payee, lessee, employee
-ence	state or quality of	violence, absence, reticence, abstinence
-ency	state or quality of	frequency, clemency, expediency, consistency
-enne	female	comedienne, equestrienne, tragedienne
-ent	one who	superintendent, resident, regent
-er	one who	teacher, painter, seller, shipper
-er	action or process	murder, thunder, plunder, waiver
-ery, -ry	trade or occupation	surgery, archery, sorcery, dentistry
-ery	establishment	bakery, grocery, fishery, nunnery
-ery, -ry,	goods or products	pottery, jewelry, cutlery
-ess -ry,	state or quality of	bravery, savagery, forgery, butchery, waitress
-et, -ette	one who (female)	actress, countess, hostess
	small	midget, sonnet, bassinet, cygnet
	small (female)	dinette, cigarette, majorette
-eur	one who	chauffeur, connoisseur, masseur
	state or quality of	hauteur, grandeur
-fy	cause to be	beautify, solidify
-hood	state or quality of	childhood, adulthood, falsehood
-i	plural	alumni, foci
-ics	scientific or social system	physics, economics, politics, statistics
-ide	chemical	fluoride, bromide, peroxide compound
-ier, -yer	one who	cashier, financier, gondolier, lawyer
-ina	female	czarina, Wilhelmina, ballerina
-ine	chemical or basic substance	iodine, chlorine, caffeine, quinine
-ine	female	heroine, Josephine, Pauline
-ing	material	bedding, roofing, frosting, stuffing

(continued)

Noun Suffixes (continued)

SUFFIX	MEANING	CURRENT WORDS
-ion	state or quality of	champion, companion, ambition, suspicion
-ish	near or like	pinkish, sevenish
-ism	state or quality of	baptism, heroism, racism
	doctrine of	despotism, capitalism, socialism, hedonism
-ist	one who practices	biologist, capitalist, communist
-ite	mineral or rock	granite, anthracite, bauxite
-itis	inflammation	laryngitis, arthritis, bronchitis
-ity, -ty	state or quality of	necessity, felicity, civility, parity
-ization	state or quality of	civilization, standardization, organization
-kin	small	lambkin, napkin, manikin, Munchkin
-let	small	owlet, rivulet, starlet, leaflet, islet
-ling	small	duckling, yearling, suckling, fledgling
-man	one who works with	cameraman, mailman, doorman
-mat	automatic machine	laundromat, vendomat
-ment	action or process	embezzlement, development, government
	state or quality of	amusement, predicament, amazement
	product or thing	instrument, ornament, fragment
-mony	product or thing	testimony, matrimony, ceremony, alimony
-ness	state or quality of	happiness, kindness, goodness, darkness
-ol	alcohols	methanol, ethanol, glycol
-ology	study or science of	biology, psychology
-or	one who	actor, doctor, donor, auditor
-or	state or quality of	error, stupor, candor, fervor, pallor
-orium	place for	auditorium, emporium
-ory	place for	laboratory, conservatory, purgatory
-ose	sugars	glucose, sucrose, fructose, dextrose
-osis	abnormal increase	tuberculosis, fibrosis
-phobia	fear of	claustrophobia, acrophobia
-s, -es	plural	pens, books, foxes, parentheses
-'s	possession	John's, dog's
-ship	skill or art of	penmanship, showmanship, horsemanship
-ship	state or quality of	friendship, hardship, citizenship
-sion	state or quality of	tension, compulsion
-th	state or quality of	strength, warmth, filth, depth, length
-tion	state or quality of	attention, caution, fascination
-trix	female	aviatrix, executrix
-tude	state or quality of	gratitude, fortitude, beatitude
-ty	state or quality of	loyalty, honesty, amnesty, unity
-ure	action or process	censure, failure, enclosure, exposure
-wright	one who works with	playwright, shipwright, wheelwright

Adjective Suffixes

SUFFIX	MEANING	CURRENT WORDS
-acious	inclined to	loquacious, mendacious, audacious, fallacious
-al	relating to	natural, royal, maternal, suicidal
-an	relating to	urban, American, Alaskan, veteran

(continued)

Adjective Suffixes (continued)

SUFFIX	MEANING	CURRENT WORDS
-ant	inclined to	vigilant, pleasant, defiant, buoyant
-ary	relating to	honorary, military, literary, ordinary
-ate	state or quality of	fortunate, desperate, passionate
-ative	inclined to	demonstrative, pejorative, talkative
-ble	inclined to	gullible, perishable, voluble, durable
-en	relating to	golden, ashen, wooden, earthen
-ent	inclined to	competent, different, excellent
-er	more (comparative)	fatter, smaller, crazier, smarter
-ern	direction	eastern, western, northern, postern
-ese	state or quality of	Japanese, Portuguese, Chinese, Siamese
-esque	relating to	statuesque, picturesque, Romanesque
-est	most (comparative)	fattest, smallest, smartest, fastest
-etic	relating to	alphabetic, dietetic, frenetic
-ful	full of	thoughtful, joyful, careful, fearful
-ial	relating to	filial, commercial, remedial
-ian	relating to	barbarian, physician, Christian
-ic	relating to	comic, historic, poetic, public
-ical	relating to	comical, rhetorical, economical
-id	state or quality of	candid, sordid, lucid, splendid, rigid
-ile	state or quality of	virile, agile, volatile, docile, fragile
-ine	relating to	feminine, bovine, feline, marine
-ious	state or quality of	gracious, ambitious, religious
-ish	relating to	childish, whitish, fiftyish, Scottish
-ive	inclined to	active, passive, negative, affirmative
-less	without	thoughtless, tireless, ageless, careless
-like	resembling	childlike, homelike, lifelike, boylike
-ly	resembling	fatherly, motherly, scholarly
-ly	every	daily, weekly, monthly, yearly
-most	most	utmost, westernmost, innermost
-oid	resembling	humanoid, asteroid, paranoid, planetoid
-ose	full of	verbose, morose, bellicose, comatose
-ous	full of	joyous, virtuous, nervous, wondrous
-some	inclined to	meddlesome, awesome, tiresome
-th, -eth	numbers	fifth, twelfth, twentieth, fiftieth
-ular	relating to	granular, cellular, circular, popular
-ulent	full of	turbulent, corpulent, fraudulent
-und	state or quality of	fecund, moribund, jocund
-uous	state or quality of	contemptuous, tempestuous, sensuous
-ward	direction	backward, eastward, upward
-y	state or quality of	fruity, sunny, rainy, funny, gooey

Verb Suffixes

SUFFIX	MEANING	CURRENT WORDS
-ade	action or process	blockade, promenade, parade
-age	action or process	ravage, pillage
-ate	to make	activate, fascinate, annihilate, liberate

(continued)

Verb Suffixes (continued)

SUFFIX	MEANING	CURRENT WORDS
-ble	repeated action	stumble, squabble, mumble, tumble, fumble
-ed, -d	past tense	talked, walked, baked, raised
-en	past completed action	taken, eaten, proven, stolen
-en	to make	strengthen, fasten, lengthen, frighten, weaken
-er	action or process	discover, murder, conquer, deliver
-fy	to make	satisfy, terrify, falsify, beautify
-ing	continuous action	singing, talking, jumping, eating
-ish	actin or process	finish, flourish, nourish, punish
-ize	to make	standardize, computerize, popularize
-s, -es	form third person	runs, finishes
-ure	action or process	censure, procure, endure, inure

Adverb Suffixes

SUFFIX	MEANING	CURRENT WORDS
-ly	forms adverb from adjective	slowly, beautifully, happily, largely
-ways	manner	sideways, always, longways, crossways
-wise	manner, direction	clockwise, lengthwise

Synonyms

Synonyms are words that have the same or nearly the same meanings. Thus, word pairs like gift-donation, woman-lady, intelligent-wise, are essentially similar in denotative meaning. Careful readers must note, however, that despite similarities, no two words are exactly alike. Usage, connotation, and idiom give to words special meanings which discriminate them from one another.

Average-mean: both words denote "a middle point between extremes." Nevertheless, whether in a specifically mathematical context or in more general usage, they differ slightly but significantly.

We swam, played tennis, and relaxed—in brief, we had an average vacation. Here average suggests what is typical or ordinary.

The ancient Greeks set the model behavior pattern for pursuing the golden mean. Here mean suggests a middle road, a moderate course between extremes. Neither word would be effectively substituted for the other in these contexts.

Sometimes a writer will restate or define an unfamiliar word. If you know the meaning of the synonym given in the restatement or definition, you can figure out the meaning of the unknown word.

Over the centuries, the English language has incorporated words from many other languages. As a result, English has a large vocabulary, rich in synonyms. Because English language contains so many synonyms, dictionaries often list synonyms for an entry word and explain their connotations.

The following is a list of synonyms provided to improve the reader's vocabulary:

able-capable-competent	defect-flaw-blemish
abrupt-sudden-hasty	delay-postpone-procrastinate
achieve-accomplish-attain	different-varied-diverse
add-total-sum up	disaster-calamity-catastrophe
after-following-subsequent	divide-separate-split
aim-purpose-goal	during-while-at the same time
all-every-entire	dwell-live-reside
allow-permit-grant	eat-consume-devour
anger-rage-fury	effort-exertion-endeavor
answer-response-reply	end-finish-complete
arrive-reach-get to	energy-power-strength
ask-question-interrogate	enough-adequate-sufficient
astonish-surprise-amaze	error-mistake-fallacy
back-rear-behind	explain-expound-elucidate
bear-endure-tolerate	faith-trust-reliance
before-prior to-in front of	fat-plump-stout
begin-start-initiate	fetch-bring-retrieve
below-under-beneath	find-locate-discover
birth-origin-genesis	fix-repair-mend
border-edge-margin	flat-level-flush
bother-annoy-pester	food-nourishment-sustenance
boy-lad-youth	form-shape-make up
brave-courageous-daring	fragile-delicate-breakable
bulge-swell-protrude	freedom-independence-liberty
busy-occupied-engaged	frequent-often-many times
call-shout-yell	gay-lively-vivacious
calm-composed-serene	gift-present-donation
car-auto-vehicle	give-grant-hand over
careful-cautious-prudent	glum-morose-sullen
carry-tote-lug	go-leave-depart
change-vary-alter	grateful-appreciative-thankful
charm-fascinate-enchant	great-grand-large
cheat-deceive-swindle	grow-mature-develop
children-youngsters-tots	happy-glad-joyous
city-borough-town	hard-difficult-troublesome
close-shut-seal	hate-detest-despise
consent-agree-acquiesce	have-own-possess
continue-persevere-persist	heal-mend-cure
country-nation-state	help-aid-assist
cure-heal-restore	hide-conceal-secrete
danger-peril-hazard	high-tall-lofty
decrease-lessen-diminish	hold-grasp-clutch

hurry-rush-accelerate
idea-thought-concept
ill-sick-indisposed
income-revenue-earnings
injure-wound-hurt
job-work-occupation
junk-rubbish-waste
just-fair-right
keep-hold-retain
key-answer-solution
kill-slaughter-murder
kind-considerate-helpful
large-big-enormous
last-endure-persist
late-tardy-delayed
learn-acquire-understand
leave-depart-go away
like-enjoy-be fond of
listen-hear-attend
little-small-petite
long-lengthy-drawn out
look-glance-see
mad-crazy-insane
make-build-construct
many-multitudinous-numerous
marvelous-wonderful-extraordinary
mean-stand for-denote
mend-repair-restore
method-way-manner
might-may-perhaps
mistake-error-blunder
move-transport-propel
name-title-designation
near-close by-in the vicinity
need-require-want
new-fresh-recent
noise-uproar-clamor
novice-beginner-learner
occur-happen-take place
often-frequently-repeatedly
old-aged-ancient
omit-delete-remove
one-single-unit

open-unlock-unseal
ornament-decoration-adornment
outlive-survive-outlast
page-sheet-leaf
pain-ache-hurt
pair-couple-duo
pardon-forgive-excuse
part-portion-piece
peak-summit-top
people-public-populace
play-frolic-romp
praise-acclaim-applaud
primary-chief-principal   *note spelling*
prohibit-forbid-restrict
put-place-locate
raid-attack-invade
reckless-careless-rash
remote-distant-secluded
renew-restore-revive
respect-honor-revere
revise-alter-correct
right-correct-proper
say-state-remark
seem-appear-look
sell-vend-market
shame-humiliation-mortification
show-demonstrate-display
sorry-regretful-penitent
speed-haste-hurry
start-begin-commence
still-unmoving-silent
stop-halt-end
story-tale-account
strength-power-energy
supply-provide-furnish
surpass-exceed-outdo
take-grab-seize
tense-taut-rigid
terrify-frighten-alarm
thanks-gratitude-appreciation
thaw-melt-dissolve
thief-robber-crook
thin-slender-slim

think-reflect-contemplate
time-period-season
timid-fearful-cowardly
tiny-small-diminutive
trial-test-experiment
true-faithful-loyal
try-attempt-endeavor
turn-revolve-pivot
ugly-homely-plain
understand-comprehend-discern
unify-consolidate-combine
uproar-tumult-pandemonium
urge-press-exhort
use-operate-employ
vacant-empty-unoccupied

value-worth-price
vast-huge-immense
verify-confirm-substantiate
victor-winner-champion
walk-stroll-saunter
want-desire-crave
waver-fluctuate-vacillate
weak-feeble-impotent
wealth-riches-fortune
word-term-expression
work-labor-toil
world-globe-earth
write-record-draft

Chapter 7

Review for the PPST Mathematics

7.0

About the PPST Mathematics Test (Test Code: 0730)

The PPST Mathematics test consists of forty multiple-choice questions, which you must complete in sixty minutes. Each test question requires that you choose among five answer choices labeled A, B, C, D, or E. You must bubble in your answer choice on a separate answer sheet. You are not allowed to use a calculator, protractor, ruler, or other such math aid when taking the test. Don't be concerned by this restriction because the test is designed so that you can achieve a satisfactory score without the aid of such devices. According to *The PPST Guide: An Official Publication of Educational Testing Service* (2002), the test covers five topics:

   I. Conceptual Knowledge—6 questions (about 15%)
  II. Procedural Knowledge—12 questions (about 30%)
 III. Representations of Quantitative Information—12 questions (about 30%)
  IV. Measurement and Informal Geometry—6 questions (about 15%)
   V. Formal Mathematical Reasoning—4 questions (about 10%)

This chapter provides a general review of these math topics with examples and explanations.

7.1

Conceptual Knowledge

Conceptual knowledge is an understanding of the concepts and ideas of mathematics.

Rational Numbers

The **rational numbers** are the numbers that you use in everyday life. Rational numbers include the whole numbers, integers, positive and negative fractions and decimals, and percents.

The **whole numbers** are the counting numbers and zero:

0, 1, 2, 3, …

The three dots to the right of the number 3 indicate that you are to continue in the same manner. Whole numbers that are greater than 1 are either *prime* or *composite*. A **prime number** is a whole number greater than 1 that is divisible (divides without a remainder) only by itself and by 1. Thus, the primes are:

2, 3, 5, 7, 11, 13, 17, 19, …

The whole numbers greater than 1 that are *not* prime are called the **composite numbers**. They are:

4, 6, 8, 9, 10, 12, 14, 15, …

The whole numbers 0 and 1 are neither prime nor composite.

The integers are the positive and negative whole numbers and zero:

…,–3, –2, –1, 0, 1, 2, 3, …

A negative number is indicated by a small horizontal line (–) written to the left of the number. Notice that we have adopted the common practice of omitting the + sign on positive numbers. If no sign is written with a number, then you know that it is a positive number. The number zero is neither positive nor negative.

Besides classifying the integers as positive (1, 2, 3, …), negative (…, –3, –2, –1), or zero, the integers can be subdivided as either *even* or *odd*. Integers that are divisible by 2 are called **even integers.** The **even integers** are:

…,–8, –6, –4, –2, 0, 2, 4, 6, 8, …

Notice that zero is an even integer because 0 divided by 2 is 0 (no remainder).

Integers that are *not* divisible by 2 are called **odd integers.** The **odd integers** are:

…, –9, –7, –5, –3, –1, 1, 3, 5, 7, 9, …

The **rational numbers** are all the numbers that can be written as a quotient of an integer divided by a *nonzero* integer. In other words, the rational numbers include zero plus the numbers that can be written as positive or negative fractions. All the whole numbers and integers are rational numbers because you can write them as fractions whose denominator is 1. For instance:

$$…, -3 = -\frac{3}{1}, -2 = -\frac{2}{1}, -1 = -\frac{1}{1}, 0 = \frac{0}{1}, 1 = \frac{1}{1}, 2 = \frac{2}{1}, 3 = \frac{3}{1}, …$$

Rational numbers can be expressed as **decimals** or **fractions**.

Decimals

Decimals are written using a place-value system. The whole system is based on the placement of the decimal point as shown in Figure 7.1.

9	9	9	9	9	9	9	.	9	9	9
Millions	100-Thousands	10-Thousands	Thousands	Hundreds	Tens	Ones	Decimal Point	Tenths	Hundredths	Thousandths

Figure 7.1

You can obtain the decimal representation of a fractional number by dividing the numerator by the denominator. (Hint: To remember which way to divide, think of the fraction as falling over to the right and collapsing into a long-division symbol like this: $\frac{3}{4}$ $4\overline{)3}$). For example, $\frac{3}{4} = 0.75$ because $4\overline{)3.00}$ $^{.75}$. In this case, the decimal **terminates** (eventually has a zero remainder). For some rational numbers, the decimal keeps going in a block of one or more digits that repeats over and over again.

These decimals are **repeating**. An example of a repeating decimal is $\frac{1}{3} = 3\overline{)1.000}..$ $^{.333..}$. No matter how long you continue to add zeroes and divide, the 3s in the quotient continue without end. Put a bar over the repeating digit (or digits when more than one digit repeats) to indicate the repetition. Thus, $\frac{1}{3} = 0.\overline{3}$.

Number Line

You can show rational numbers on a **number line** (Figure 7.2). The integers are represented by equally spaced points to the left and right of zero.

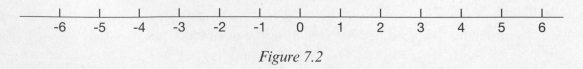

Figure 7.2

The number zero is called the **origin** of the number line. The arrows on the ends of the line indicate that the number line extends indefinitely in both directions. Numbers get larger as you move to the right on the number line. When you stop at a number, that number is greater than all the numbers to the left of it. For instance, you can see from the number line in Figure 7.2 that zero is greater than all the negative numbers and less than all the positive numbers.

Fractions

Equivalent fractions are fractions that have the same value. For example, $\frac{4}{8} = \frac{1}{2}$, so $\frac{4}{8}$ and $\frac{1}{2}$ are equivalent fractions. If the numerator and denominator of a fraction can be divided by the same number, you can **reduce** the fraction to an equivalent fraction in **lowest terms** by doing the division, as in $\frac{4}{8} = \frac{4 \div 4}{8 \div 4} = \frac{1}{2}$. Conversely, in working with fractions, you may need to write a fraction as an equivalent fraction with a larger denominator. You can accomplish this by multiplying the numerator and denominator by the same whole number (greater than 1). For example, $\frac{3}{4} = \frac{3 \times 2}{4 \times 2} = \frac{6}{8}$.

Fractions like $\frac{1}{2}$, $\frac{3}{4}$, and $\frac{9}{10}$, in which the numerator is smaller than the denominator, are called **proper fractions**. Fractions like $\frac{3}{2}$, $\frac{7}{4}$, and $\frac{10}{10}$, in which the numerator is greater than or equal to the denominator, are called **improper fractions**. Any improper fraction has a value greater than or equal to one. A **mixed number** is the sum of a whole number and a fraction, written together like this: $1\frac{1}{2}$, $5\frac{3}{4}$, and $3\frac{9}{10}$. Although a mixed number is a sum, you don't put a plus sign in it, but you do say the word "and" in between the whole number and the fraction when you read it. For instance, $1\frac{1}{2}$ is read "1 and $\frac{1}{2}$."

An improper fraction can be changed to a mixed number or a whole number by dividing the numerator by the denominator and writing the remainder like this: $\frac{\text{remainder}}{\text{denominator}}$. For example, $\frac{7}{4} = 4\overline{)7}^{\,1\ R\ 3} = 1\frac{3}{4}$

Comparing Rational Numbers

For the PPST, you will need to know how to compare two or more rational numbers to determine which is greater and which is less. For these questions, it is important that you understand inequality symbols. Table 7.1 summarizes commonly used inequality symbols.

TABLE 7.1: COMMON INEQUALITY SYMBOLS

INEQUITY SYMBOL	READ AS	EXAMPLE
<	"is less than"	$\frac{3}{4} < 1$
>	"is greater than"	$20 > 11$
≤	"is less than or equal to"	$5 \leq 5$
≥	"is greater than or equal to"	$3\frac{1}{2} \geq 3$
≠	"is not equal to"	$0 \neq 2$

When comparing rational numbers, think of their relative placement on the number line. The number that is farthest to the right is the larger number. For example, $-5 < -1$ because as you can see on the number line in Figure 7.3, -1 lies to the right of -5 on the number line.

Figure 7.3

When you compare fractions, you may find it helpful to write the fractions as equivalent fractions using a common denominator. The equivalent fraction with the larger numerator is the larger fraction. For example, $\frac{3}{4} > \frac{2}{3}$ because $\frac{9}{12} > \frac{8}{12}$.

When you compare decimals, you will find it helpful to write them with the same number of decimal places and compare the numbers place value by place value. Remember, inserting or deleting zeros at the *end* of a decimal fraction does not change its value: $0.5 = 0.50 = 0.500 = 0.5000$ and so on. Thus, $0.45 < 0.5$ because $0.45 < 0.50$. When you are instructed to **order** a list of numbers, you put them in order from **least to greatest** or from **greatest to least**, depending on how the question is stated.

Arithmetic Operations

Addition, subtraction, multiplication, and **division** are the four basic arithmetic operations. Table 7.2 shows the terminology related to these operations.

TABLE 7.2: TERMINOLOGY FOR THE FOUR BASIC ARITHMETIC OPERATIONS

OPERATION	SYMBOL(S) USED	NAME OF PARTS
Addition	+ (plus sign)	addend + addend = sum
Subtraction	− (minus sign)	minuend − subtrahend = difference
Multiplication	× (times sign)	factor × factor = product
	• (raised dot)	factor • factor = product
	( ) parentheses	(factor)(factor) = product
Division	÷ (division sign)	dividend ÷ divisor = quotient
	$\overline{)}$ (long division)	divisor $\overline{)\text{dividend}}$
	/ (slash or fraction bar)	dividend/divisor = $\frac{\text{dividend}}{\text{divisor}}$ = quotient

Addition and subtraction are **inverses** of each other; that is, one operation "undoes" the other. Similarly, multiplication and division are **inverses** of each other; they "undo" each other, *as long as division by zero is not involved.* A summary of division involving zero is given in Section 7.2.

Exponents

You can use **exponential notation** to write a shortened version of a product in which the same number is repeated as a factor. The shortened version for a product such as $2 \times 2 \times 2$ is 2^3. The 3, which is written as a small number to the upper right, is called the **exponent**. It tells how many times the 2, called the **base**, is used as a factor. Here are other examples:

$5 \times 5 \times 5 \times 5 = 5^4$

$(3)(3)(3)(3)(3) = 3^5$

$10 \times 10 = 10^2$

$2 \times 2 \times 2 \times 10 \times 10 = 2^3 \times 10^2$

Negative exponents are used to show reciprocals. For example, $2^{-3} = \dfrac{1}{2^3} = \dfrac{1}{8} = 0.125$. Similarly, $10^{-4} = \dfrac{1}{10^4} = \dfrac{1}{1000} = 0.0001$. A word of caution: Do *not* make the mistake of putting a negative sign in front of your answer. The negative part of the exponent is telling you to write a reciprocal; it is not telling you to make your answer negative.

Squares and Square Roots

Exponential expressions that use a 2 for the exponent, such as 2^2, 3^2, and 10^2, are called **squares**. The factor that is repeated is called the **square root** of the product. Thus, $2^2 = 4$, so 2 is the square root of 4; $3^2 = 9$, so 3 is the square root of 9; and $10^2 = 100$, so 10 is the square root of 100. Usually, the **square root symbol** ($\sqrt{}$) is used to show a square root. Thus, $\sqrt{4} = 2$; $\sqrt{9} = 3$; and $\sqrt{100} = 10$. When you want to find the square root of a number, try to find a factor that you can multiply by itself to give the number. Since you will not be allowed to use a calculator on the PPST, you should memorize the following fifteen square roots:

$\sqrt{1} = 1$	$\sqrt{36} = 6$	$\sqrt{121} = 11$
$\sqrt{4} = 2$	$\sqrt{49} = 7$	$\sqrt{144} = 12$
$\sqrt{9} = 3$	$\sqrt{64} = 8$	$\sqrt{169} = 13$
$\sqrt{16} = 4$	$\sqrt{81} = 9$	$\sqrt{225} = 15$
$\sqrt{25} = 5$	$\sqrt{100} = 10$	$\sqrt{625} = 25$

Scientific Notation

Very large numbers and very small numbers are often written in a shortened form called **scientific notation**. A number written in scientific notation is written as a product of two factors: a number that is greater than or equal to 1, but less than 10, and a power of 10. Any decimal number can be written in scientific notation. Follow these steps to write a number in scientific notation:

1. Move the decimal point to the immediate right of the first nonzero digit of the number.
2. Indicate multiplication by the proper power of 10.

If you moved the decimal point to the *left* in step 1, count the number of places you moved it and use that number as the exponent for 10 in step 2. For example, to write 34,016 in scientific notation, you would move the decimal point four places to the left (to get 3.4016), which would make the exponent 4: 3.4016×10^4.

If you moved the decimal point to the *right* in step 1, the *negative* of the number of places you moved it is the value of the exponent for 10 in step 2. For example, to write 0.00908 in scientific notation, you would move the decimal 3 places to the right (to get 9.08). This means the exponent would be –3: 9.08×10^{-3}.

You can always check to see if you did it right by multiplying out your answer to see if you get your original number back:

$$3.4016 \times 10^4 = 3.4016 \times 10 \times 10 \times 10 \times 10 =$$
$$3.4016 \times 10,000 = 34,016 \checkmark$$
$$9.08 \times 10^{-3} = 9.08 \times \frac{1}{10^3} = \frac{9.08}{1000} = 0.00908 \checkmark$$

Percents

Rational numbers may also be written as **percents**. A percent is another way of writing a fraction in which the denominator is 100. Thus, $25\% = \frac{25}{100} = 0.25$. You can think of percents as "fancy ways" to write ordinary decimals or fractions. For instance, 100% is just a fancy way to write the number 1—because $100\% = \frac{100}{100} = 1$. If you have 100% of something, you have all of it. A percent that is less than 100% is less than 1. A percent that is greater than 100% is greater than 1.

Any percent can be written as an equivalent fraction by writing the number in front of the percent sign as the numerator of a fraction in which the denominator is 100. The resulting fraction may then be reduced to lowest terms. For example,

$$75\% = \frac{75}{100} = \frac{75 \div 25}{100 \div 25} = \frac{3}{4}$$

A percent can be written as an equivalent decimal by changing it to an equivalent fraction in which the denominator is 100, then dividing by 100. For example, $75\% = \dfrac{75}{100} = 100\overline{)75.00}^{\,.75}$. (Hint: a shortcut for dividing by 100 is to move the decimal point 2 places to the left.) To write a decimal in percent form, move the decimal point two places to the right, and attach the percent sign (%) at the end. Look at these examples:

$0.45 = 45\%$

$0.01 = 1\%$

$0.125 = 12.5\%$

$2 = 2.00 = 200\%$

$0.0025 = 0.25\%$

To write a fraction in percent form, first convert the fraction to a decimal by performing the indicated division, then change the resulting decimal to a percent. When the quotient is a repeating decimal, carry the decimal to 2 places, then write the remainder as a fraction like this: $\dfrac{\text{remainder}}{\text{denominator}}$.

Look at these examples:

$\dfrac{1}{4} = 4\overline{)1.00}^{\,0.25} = 25\%$

$\dfrac{3}{5} = 5\overline{)3.00}^{\,0.60} = 60\%$

$\dfrac{1}{3} = 3\overline{)1.00}^{\,0.33R1} = 0.33\tfrac{1}{3} = 33\tfrac{1}{3}\%$

Here is a list of common percents with their fraction and decimal equivalents that you should memorize before you take the PPST:

$100\% = 1.00 = 1$	$33\tfrac{1}{3}\% = 0.33\tfrac{1}{3} = \dfrac{1}{3}$
$80\% = 0.80 = \dfrac{4}{5}$	$25\% = 0.25 = \dfrac{1}{4}$
$75\% = 0.75 = \dfrac{3}{4}$	$20\% = .20 = \dfrac{1}{5}$
$60\% = 0.60 = \dfrac{3}{5}$	$10\% = 0.1 = \dfrac{1}{10}$
$50\% = 0.50 = \dfrac{1}{2}$	$5\% = 0.05 = \dfrac{1}{20}$
$40\% = 0.40 = \dfrac{2}{5}$	

7.2

Procedural Knowledge

Procedural knowledge of mathematics means knowing the rules and procedures for doing mathematical tasks.

Operations with Signed Numbers

In Section 7.1, you learned that the rational numbers consist of the whole numbers, integers, positive and negative fractions and decimals, and percents. Rational numbers are sometimes called **signed numbers** because they may be positive (+), negative (–), or zero (no sign). On the PPST, you will need to know how to perform addition, subtraction, multiplication, and division with signed numbers.

Table 7.3 summarizes the rules for addition of two signed numbers.

TABLE 7.3: RULES FOR ADDITION OF TWO SIGNED NUMBERS

IF THE SIGNS ARE:	THE RULE IS:	IN SYMBOLS:
1. The same—both positive or both negative	Ignore the signs, add the two numbers like you would nonsigned numbers, and use the common sign as the sign for the answer	+ + + = + – + – = –
2. Different—one positive and one negative	Ignore the signs, subtract the two numbers like you would nonsigned numbers, and use the sign of the larger nonsigned number as the sign for the answer.	+ + – = + or – – + + = + or – depending on which non-signed number is greater

Look at these examples:

$4 + 6 = 10$	Same signs, both positive, sum is positive (Remember, you can omit the positive sign for positive numbers.)
$-4 + -6 = -10$	Same signs, both negative, sum is negative.
$4 + -6 = -2$	Different signs. –6 is larger nonsigned number, so sum is negative.
$-4 + 6 = 2$	Different signs. 6 is larger nonsigned number, so sum is positive.

If you have three or more signed numbers to add together, you may find it convenient to take the operation in steps. First, add up all the positive numbers; second, add up all the negative numbers; third, add the resulting two answers. For example: $14 + -35 + 6 + -25 = (14 + 6) + (-35 + -25) = 20 + -60 = -40$. Signs are different, and 60 is larger unsigned number, so sum is negative.

Good news. You do not have to memorize a set of new rules for subtraction of signed numbers! Instead, what you do when you want to subtract two signed numbers is to change the problem so that the rules in Table 7.3 will apply. Here's how you do it.

To subtract two signed numbers, first, change the sign of the number to the right of the minus sign. If it's positive, make it negative; if it's negative, make it positive. Next, change the minus sign to a plus sign, then add using the rules already laid out in Table 7.3. Think of the minus sign as "plus the opposite."

Look at these examples:

9 − 16: Think of this as "9 plus the opposite of 16," or 9 + −16 = −7. Different signs, and 16 is larger nonsigned number, so sum is negative.

24 − 15: Think of this as "24 plus the opposite of 15," or 24 + −15 = 9. Different signs, and 24 is larger nonsigned number, so sum is positive.

−8 − 20: Think of this as "−8 plus the opposite of 20," or −8 + −20 = −28. Same signs, both negative, so sum is negative.

3 − (−6): Think of this as "3 plus the opposite of −6," or 3 + 6 = 9. Same signs, both positive, so sum is positive.

−4 − 6: Think of this as "−4 plus the opposite of 6," or −4 + −6 = −10. Same signs, both negative, so sum is negative.

−18 − (−4): Think of this as "−18 plus the opposite of −4," or −18 + 4 = −14. Different signs, and 18 is larger nonsigned number, so sum is negative.

Multiplication and division of signed numbers share the same pattern. Table 7.4 summarizes the rules for multiplication or division of two signed numbers.

TABLE 7.4: RULES FOR MULTIPLICATION OF TWO SIGNED NUMBERS

IF THE SIGNS ARE:	THE RULE IS:	IN SYMBOLS:
1. The same—both positive or both negative	Ignore the signs, multiply or divide the two numbers like you would nonsigned numbers, and use a positive sign as the sign for the answer.	+ **x** + = + + ÷ + = +
2. Different—one positive and one negative	Ignore the signs, multiply or divide the two numbers like you would nonsigned numbers, and use a negative sign as the sign for the answer.	+ **x** − = − − **x** + = − + ÷ − = − − ÷ + = −

Look at these examples:

2 × 6 = 12   Same signs, so product is positive.

−2 × −6 = 12   Same signs, so product is positive.

32 ÷ 4 = 8   Same signs, so quotient is positive.

−32 ÷ −4 = 8 Same signs, so quotient is positive.

Notice that for multiplication/division when the signs are the same, it doesn't matter what the common sign is, the product/quotient is positive no matter what.

5 × −8 = −40   Different signs, so product is negative.

(−7)(4) = −28   Different signs, so product is negative.

36 ÷ −4 = −9   Different signs, so quotient is negative.

$\dfrac{-56}{8} = -7$ Different signs, so quotient is negative.

Notice that for multiplication/division when the signs are different, it doesn't matter which number is the larger unsigned number—the product/quotient is negative no matter what.

Operations with Fractions

Operations with signed numbers that are fractions follow the same rules as given in Tables 7.3 and 7.4. Table 7.5 summarizes additional rules for operations with non-signed fractions that will be helpful as you perform calculations.

The process of multiplying or dividing fractions can be simplified by dividing out common factors, if any, before any multiplication is performed. For example:

$$1\frac{1}{2} \times 2\frac{1}{3} = \frac{\cancel{3}^{1}}{2} \times \frac{7}{\cancel{3}_{1}} = \frac{7}{2} \text{ or } 3\frac{1}{2}.$$

Also, remember you do *not* have to find a common denominator when multiplying or dividing fractions.

TABLE 7.5: RULES FOR OPERATIONS WITH FRACTIONS

OPERATION	RULE	EXAMPLE
Addition	1. To add two fractions that have the same denominator, add the numerators of the fractions to find the numerator of the answer, which is placed over the common denominator, and then reduce to lowest terms, if needed.	$\frac{3}{8}+\frac{1}{8}=\frac{3+1}{8}=\frac{4}{8}=\frac{4 \div 4}{8 \div 4}=\frac{1}{2}$
	2. To add two fractions that have different denominators, first, find a common denominator; next, write each fraction as an equivalent fraction having the common denominator as a denominator; then add the numerators of the fractions to find the numerator of the answer, which is placed over the common denominator; then reduce to lowest terms, if needed.	$\frac{1}{4}+\frac{2}{3}=$ $\frac{1}{4}=\frac{1 \times 3}{4 \times 3}=\frac{3}{12}$ $\frac{2}{3}=\frac{2 \times 4}{3 \times 4}=\frac{8}{12}$ $\frac{1}{4}+\frac{2}{3}=\frac{3}{12}+\frac{8}{12}=\frac{3+8}{12}=\frac{11}{12}$
Subtraction	1. To subtract two fractions that have the same denominator, subtract the numerators of the fractions to find the numerator of the answer, which is placed over the common denominator, and then reduce to lowest terms, if needed.	$\frac{3}{8}-\frac{1}{8}=\frac{3-1}{8}=\frac{2}{8}=\frac{2 \div 2}{8 \div 2}=\frac{1}{4}$
	2. To subtract two fractions that have different denominators, first, find a common denominator; next, write each fraction as an equivalent fraction having the common denominator as a denominator; then subtract the numerators of the fractions to find the numerator of the answer, which is placed over the common denominator, and then reduce to lowest terms, if needed.	$\frac{2}{3}-\frac{1}{4}=$ $\frac{2}{3}=\frac{2 \times 4}{3 \times 4}=\frac{8}{12}$ $\frac{1}{4}=\frac{1 \times 3}{4 \times 3}=\frac{3}{12}$ $\frac{2}{3}-\frac{1}{4}=\frac{8}{12}-\frac{3}{12}=\frac{8-3}{12}=\frac{5}{12}$

continued

TABLE 7.5: RULES FOR OPERATIONS WITH FRACTIONS (CONTINUED)

OPERATION	RULE	EXAMPLE
Multiplication	1. To multiply two proper fractions, two improper fractions, or a proper fraction and an improper fraction: multiply the numerators to obtain the numerator of the product and multiply the denominators to find the denominator of the product; then reduce to lowest terms, if needed.	$\dfrac{1}{4} \times \dfrac{2}{3} = \dfrac{1 \times 2}{4 \times 3} = \dfrac{2}{12} = \dfrac{2 \div 2}{12 \div 2} = \dfrac{1}{6}$
	2. To multiply a fraction times a whole number, write the whole number as an equivalent fraction with denominator 1, then follow multiplication rule 1.	$\dfrac{2}{3} \times 15 =$ $\dfrac{2}{3} \times \dfrac{15}{1} =$ $\dfrac{2 \times 15}{3 \times 1} = \dfrac{30}{3} = 10$
	3. To multiply fractions when mixed numbers are involved, change the mixed numbers to improper fractions, then follow multiplication rule 1.	$1\dfrac{1}{2} \times 2\dfrac{1}{3} =$ $\dfrac{3}{2} \times \dfrac{7}{3} = \dfrac{3 \times 7}{2 \times 3} = \dfrac{21}{6} = \dfrac{21 \div 3}{6 \div 3}$ $\dfrac{7}{2} \text{ or } 3\dfrac{1}{2}$
Division	1. To divide two proper fractions, two improper fractions, or a proper fraction and an improper fraction: multiply the first fraction by the reciprocal of the second fraction using multiplication rule 1.	$\dfrac{3}{2} \div \dfrac{1}{4} = \dfrac{3}{2} \times \dfrac{4}{1} = \dfrac{3 \times 4}{2 \times 1} = \dfrac{12}{2} = 6$
	2. To divide a fraction by a whole number, write the whole number as an equivalent fraction with denominator 1, then follow division rule 1.	$\dfrac{3}{2} \div 5 = \dfrac{3}{2} \div \dfrac{5}{1} = \dfrac{3}{2} \times \dfrac{1}{5} = \dfrac{3 \times 1}{2 \times 5}$ $\dfrac{3 \times 1}{2 \times 5} = \dfrac{3}{10}$
	3. To divide fractions when mixed numbers are involved, change the mixed numbers to improper fractions, then follow division rule 1.	$3\dfrac{1}{2} \times 1\dfrac{1}{4} =$ $\dfrac{7}{2} \div \dfrac{5}{4} =$ $\dfrac{7}{2} \times \dfrac{4}{5} =$ $\dfrac{7 \times 4}{2 \times 5} = \dfrac{28}{10} = \dfrac{14}{5} \text{ or } 2\dfrac{4}{5}$

Operations with Decimals

As with fractions, when doing operations with signed numbers that are decimals, you will need to follow the same rules as given in Tables 7.3 and 7.4. Table 7.6 summarizes additional rules for operations with nonsigned decimals that will be helpful as you perform calculations.

Do not be alarmed about having to do paper and pencil computations on the PPST. Since you are not allowed to use a calculator, you will not be expected to perform long, tedious calculations. Most of the required computations will be simple calculations, some of which you will probably be able to do mentally.

TABLE 7.6: RULES FOR OPERATIONS WITH DECIMALS

OPERATION	RULE	EXAMPLE
Addition	1. To add decimals, line up the decimal points vertically. Then add as you would with whole numbers and place the decimal point in the answer directly under the decimal points in the problem. Hint: Fill in empty decimal places with zeros to avoid adding incorrectly.	$15.3 + .54 + 1.002 =$ 15.300 0.540 + 1.002 ——— 16.842
Subtraction	1. To subtract decimals, line up the decimal points vertically, then subtract as you would with whole numbers, filling in empty decimal places with zeros when needed. Place the decimal point in the answer directly under the decimal points in the problem.	$5.8 - 1.75 =$ 5.80 − 1.75 ——— 4.05
Multiplication	1. To multiply decimals, multiply the numbers as whole numbers, then place the decimal point in the proper place in the product. The number of decimal places in the product is the sum of the number of decimal places in the numbers being multiplied. If there are not enough places, insert one or more zeros at the *left* end of the number.	$55.3 \times 0.05 =$ 55.3 (1 place) × 0.05 (2 places) ——— 2.765 (3 places)
Division	1. To divide two decimals, rewrite the division as an equivalent problem with a whole-number divisor by moving the decimal point the same number of places to the right in both the divisor and dividend (each time you move the decimal to the right, you multiply by 10). After moving the decimal points, divide as with whole numbers. Place the decimal point in the quotient directly above the decimal point in the dividend.	$51.375 \div 0.05 =$ $0.05 \overline{)5137.5} =$ $\dfrac{1027.5}{5\overline{)5137.5}}$

Division Involving Zero

When zero is involved in division, you need to be *extra* careful. Zero can be a dividend; that is, you can divide a nonzero number into zero. However, zero **cannot** be a divisor, which means that you cannot divide by zero. The quotient of any number divided by zero has no meaning; that is, **division by zero is undefined—you can't do it!** Table 7.7 summarizes division involving zero.

TABLE 7.7: SUMMARY OF DIVISION INVOLVING ZERO

RULE	EXPLANATION
1. Division by zero is undefined.	Which means: any number $\div$ 0 can't be done! $\dfrac{\text{any number}}{0}$ can't be done! $0\overline{)\text{any number}}$ can't be done! $0 \div 0,\ \dfrac{0}{0},\ 0\overline{)0} =$ can't be done!
2. The quotient of 0 divided by any number, except 0, is 0.	Which means: $0 \div$ any nonzero number $= 0$ $\dfrac{0}{\text{any nonzero number}} = 0$ any nonzero number $\overline{)0}$

Order of Operations

When a computation has more than one operation involved, you must follow the **order of operations**:

1. Perform computations inside parentheses.
2. Multiply as indicated by exponents.
3. Multiply and divide in the order these operations occur, from left to right.
4. Add and subtract in the order these operations occur, from left to right.

A good way to remember the order of operations is to memorize the sentence: "Please Excuse My Dear Aunt Sally"—abbreviated as **PE(MD)(AS)**. The first letter of each word stands for the various operations described in the previous list.

Note that multiplication does not have to be done before division, or addition before subtraction. That's why we put **MD** and **AS** in parentheses in **PE(MD)(AS)**. You multiply and divide in the order they occur in the problem. Similarly, you add and subtract in the order they occur in the problem.

Look at these examples:

$80 - 5 \times 3^2 + 30 \div (4 + 1)$

1. Perform computations inside parentheses: $80 - 5 \times 3^2 + 30 \div (5)$
2. Multiply as indicated by exponents: $80 - 5 \times 9 + 30 \div (5)$
3. Multiply and divide, from left to right: $80 - 45 + 6$
4. Add and subtract, from left to right: $80 - 45 + 6 = 41$

$60 + 32 \div 2^3 - 5(4 + 6)$

1. Perform computations inside parentheses: $60 + 3^2 \div 2^3 - 5(10)$
2. Multiply as indicated by exponents: $60 + 32 \div 8 - 5(10)$
3. Multiply and divide, from left to right: $60 + 4 - 50$
4. Add and subtract, from left to right: $60 + 4 - 50 = 14$

$5(43 + 7) - 2 \times 100$

1. Perform computations inside parentheses: $5(50) - 2 \times 100$
2. Multiply as indicated by exponents—none, so skip this step.
3. Multiply and divide, from left to right: $250 - 200$
4. Add and subtract, from left to right: $250 - 200 = 50$

$12 \div 6 - 2 \times 10 + 48$

1. Perform computations inside parentheses—none, so skip this step.
2. Multiply as indicated by exponents—none, so skip this step.
3. Multiply and divide, from left to right: $2 - 20 + 48$
4. Add and subtract, from left to right: $2 - 20 + 48 = 30$

Ratios and Proportions

A ratio is the quotient of two numbers. In a paint mixture that uses three parts yellow paint to five parts blue paint, the ratio of yellow paint to blue paint is 3 to 5, 3:5, or $\frac{3}{5}$. The numbers 3 and 5 are called the **terms** of the ratio. A ratio is a pure number; it does not have any units. When you find the ratio of two quantities, you must make sure they have the same units so that when you write the ratio, the units will "cancel out." For example, you cannot write the ratio of two pints to three quarts as $\frac{2}{3}$ because these quantities are not expressed in the same units. Since 2 pints = 1 quart, the ratio is 1 quart to 3 quarts $= \frac{1 \text{ qt}}{3 \text{ qt}} = \frac{1}{3}$. If you cannot convert the two quantities into the same unit, then you must keep the units and write the quotient as a **rate**. For instance, $\frac{100 \text{ mi}}{2 \text{ hr}} = 50$ mph is a rate of speed.

A **proportion** is a mathematical statement that two ratios are equal. The **terms** of the proportion are the four numbers that make up the two ratios. For example, take the proportion $\frac{2}{3} = \frac{8}{12}$. This proportion has terms 2, 3, 8, and 12. In a proportion, cross products are equal; that is, the numerator of the first ratio multiplied by the denominator of the second ratio equals the denominator of the first ratio multiplied by the numerator of the second ratio.

Here's an example.

For the proportion $\frac{2}{3} = \frac{8}{12}$, you get $2 \times 12 = 3 \times 8 = 24$

When you are solving proportion problems on the PPST, you will have to solve a proportion in which one of the terms is missing. You can put an x or other letter in for the missing term or simply use a question mark. To solve the proportion, find a cross product that you can calculate, and then divide by the number in the proportion that you didn't use.

Look at these examples:

Solve $\frac{x}{12} = \frac{2}{3}$

Since you don't know what x is, the only cross product you can calculate is 2×12, so multiply 2×12, then divide by 3, the number you didn't use:

$$x = \frac{2 \times 12}{3} = \frac{24}{3} = 8$$

Solve $\frac{25}{100} = \frac{P}{300}$

Since you don't know what P is, the only cross product you can calculate is 25×300, so multiply 25×300, then divide by 100, the number you didn't use:

$$P = \frac{25 \times 300}{100} = \frac{7500}{100} = 75$$

Solve $\frac{24}{t} = \frac{12}{3}$

Since you don't know what t is, the only cross product you can calculate is 24×3, so multiply 24×3, then divide by 12, the number you didn't use:

$$t = \frac{24 \times 3}{12} = 6$$

Now try a word problem. In a paint mixture that uses 3 parts yellow paint to 5 parts blue paint, how many quarts of yellow paint are needed to mix with 15 quarts of blue paint?

Set up a proportion. The first sentence gives you the first ratio:

$$\frac{3 \text{ parts yellow paint}}{5 \text{ parts blue paint}}$$

The second sentence gives you the second ratio:

$$\frac{x \text{ quarts yellow paint}}{15 \text{ quarts blue paint}}$$

Set the two ratios equal to each other:

$$\frac{3 \text{ quarts yellow paint}}{5 \text{ quarts blue paint}} = \frac{x \text{ quarts yellow paint}}{15 \text{ quarts blue paint}}$$

Omit the units, and solve:

$$\frac{3}{5} = \frac{x}{15}$$

$$x = \frac{3 \times 15}{5} = \frac{45}{5} = 9 \text{ quarts of yellow paint are needed.}$$

Percent Problems

Most percent problems on the PPST can be solved using a proportion that has the following form: $\frac{R}{100} = \frac{\text{"is"}}{\text{"of"}}$. R is the number in front of the % sign; "is" is the percentage in the problem, which is usually near the word *is*; and "of" is the number that comes *immediately after* the word *of* in the problem. With practice, you can learn to identify these three parts.

Here's a hint. Start with R and "of" because they are usually easier to find, and "is" will be what remains. If you can, it's a really good idea to state the percent problem in words because it makes identifying the three parts easier. Unfortunately, for some test takers, that's hard to do. If you are one of these individuals, you may want to just scan the problem for the information needed. The value of two of the parts will be given in the problem, and you will be solving for the third part. After you identify the three parts, plug the two you know into the proportion, and solve for the one that you don't know.

Consider the following problem:

Out of 180 workers at a company, 20% take public transportation to work. How many workers at the company take public transportation to work?

To solve the problem, you need to identify the three parts for $\frac{R}{100} = \frac{\text{"is"}}{\text{"of"}}$. You can see from the problem that $R = 20$, "of" = 180, and "is" is not given. Let x = "is," plug into the proportion, and solve:

$$\frac{20}{100} = \frac{x}{180}$$

$$x = \frac{20 \times 180}{100} = \frac{3600}{100} = 36 \text{ workers take public transportation to work.}$$

In words, the same problem can be stated as follows: "What is 20% of 180?" You may be saying to yourself, "Why not just find 20% of 180 by multiplying 0.20 by 180?" That is another correct way to work the problem: 20% of 180 = 0.20 × 180 = 36 workers. However, many non–math-types struggle with percent problems.

The $\frac{\text{"is"}}{\text{"of"}}$ -method is a way for those individuals to have successful experiences when solving percent problems. If you are comfortable with a different method and it works for you, then you can skip this discussion and go on to the next topic.

Following are some additional examples of percent problems worked using the $\frac{\text{"is"}}{\text{"of"}}$ -method:

If 40% of P = 232, then P = ?

Identify the three parts for $\frac{R}{100} = \frac{\text{"is"}}{\text{"of"}}$: R = 40, "of" = P, and "is" = 232. Now, plug into the proportion, and solve:

$$\frac{40}{100} = \frac{232}{P}$$

$$P = \frac{100 \times 232}{40} = 580.$$

Hint: The problem asks, "If 40% of P is 232, what is P?"

There are 1200 students at a high school. If 300 student are seniors, what percent of the students are seniors?

For this problem, identifying the three parts for $\frac{\text{"is"}}{\text{"of"}}$ is a little tricky. The question question asks, "what percent," so you know the value of R is unknown. There is no number following the word "of." Instead, the question asks, "what percent of the students are seniors?" If you look back at the first sentence, you see there are 1200 students, so "of" = 1200, which means "is" = 300.

Now, plug those values into the proportion, and solve:

$$\frac{R}{100} = \frac{300}{1200}$$

$$R = \frac{100 \times 300}{1200} = \frac{3000}{1200} = 25, \text{ so } 25\% \text{ of the students are seniors.}$$

Hint: The problem asks, "What percent of 1200 is 300?"

There are 96 girls and 64 boys competing in a contest. What percent of the contestants are boys?

For this problem identifying the three parts for $\frac{\text{"is"}}{\text{"of"}}$ takes some thought. The question asks, "what percent"; so you know the value of R is unknown. There is no number following the word "of"; instead the question asks, "what percent of the contestants are boys?" If you look back at the first sentence, you see there are 96 girls and 64 boys who are contestants, giving a total of 96 + 64 = 160 contestants. Thus, "of" = 160, which means "is" equals either 96 or 64. The question is asking about the percent of boys, so "is" = 64.

Now, plug those values into the proportion, and solve:

$$\frac{R}{100} = \frac{64}{160}$$

$$R = \frac{100 \times 64}{160} = \frac{6400}{160} = 40, \text{ so 40\% of the contestants are boys.}$$

Hint: The problem asks, "What percent of 160 is 64?"

Probability

On the PPST, you be will be asked to find simple probabilities. If all outcomes are equally likely, the **probability** that a possible event will occur is determined this way:

$$\frac{\text{number of outcomes favorable to the event}}{\text{number of total outcomes possible}}$$

For instance, if a bag contains 3 red marbles, 5 green marbles, and 2 yellow marbles. The probability of randomly drawing a red marble from the box =

$$\frac{\text{number of red marbles in the bag}}{\text{number of marbles in the bag}} = \frac{3}{3 + 5 + 2} = \frac{3}{10}$$

Probabilities can be expressed as fractions, decimals, or percents. In the previous problem, the probability of drawing a red marble can be expressed as $\frac{3}{10}$, 0.3, or 30%. The probability that an event is certain to happen is 1, 1.00, or 100%. For instance, if a jar contains 10 green marbles, the probability of drawing a green marble from the jar is $\frac{10}{10} = 1$. If an event *cannot* occur, then it has probability 0. For instance, if a jar contains only 10 red marbles, the probability of drawing a blue marble from the jar is $\frac{0}{10} = 0$.

Thus, 0 is the lowest probability and 1 is the highest probability you can have—all other probabilities fall between 0 and 1. If we use the variable P to represent a probability, then we can write: $0 \leq P \leq 1$. Consequently, if you work a probability problem and your answer is greater than 1 or your answer is negative, you've made a mistake! Go back and check your work. In a probability problem, the number of total outcomes will always be greater than or equal to the number of outcomes favorable to the event, so check to make sure your denominator is *larger* than your numerator when you set up the probability.

If you know the probability of an event, you can compute the probability that the event does *not* occur, called its **complement**, like this:

Probability of complement = 1 − (probability of event)

For example, if the probability that you will win a drawing is $\dfrac{2}{100} = 0.02$, then the probability that you will *not* win the drawing is $1 - 0.02 = 0.98$.

Look at these examples:

A box contains tiles numbered 1 to 30. If one tile is randomly drawn from the box, what is the probability that the number on the tile is divisible by 5? Work the problem in two steps:

1. Figure out what numbers between 1 and 30 are divisible by 5 (5, 10, 15, 20, 25, 30).
2. Determine the probability of drawing a tile with one of these 6 numbers on it.

Probability of drawing 5, 10, 15, 20, 25, or 30 $= \dfrac{6 \text{ tiles}}{30 \text{ (the total number of tiles)}} = \dfrac{1}{5}$

Statistics

Four measures that are used to describe a set of numbers are the **mean, median, mode,** and **range.** The **mean** of a set of numbers is another name for the arithmetic average of the numbers. You calculate the mean by adding up the numbers and dividing by how many numbers you have. In other words,

$$\text{mean} = \frac{\text{the sum of the numbers}}{\text{how many numbers in the set}}$$

For example, to find the mean for the numbers 80, 72, 45, 98, 65, you would proceed as follows:

$$\text{mean} = \frac{80 + 72 + 45 + 98 + 65}{5} = \frac{360}{5} = 72$$

On the PPST, you may be given a set of numbers and asked to find the number that gives the set a certain average (mean). For example, suppose you are given four exam scores, of 75, 62, 91, and 82, and the goal of achieving an average of at least 80 on five exams. What score do you need on the fifth exam to have an average of at least 80? There are two ways to work this problem on the PPST. You can take advantage of the fact that the PPST is a multiple-choice test, which means you are given the answers to the questions—you just have to figure out which one of the five answer choices you are given is the correct one. In this case, you would plug each answer into the formula for the mean until you found the one that gives you an average of at least 80—like a "guess and check" approach. Another way to work the problem is to use an equation. If you let $x =$ the score on the fifth exam, you would set up the problem as follows:

$$80 = \frac{75 + 62 + 91 + 82 + x}{5}$$

You can simplify the numerator on the right and, also, write this equation as a proportion:

$$\frac{80}{1} = \frac{310 + x}{5}$$

Cross-multiplying gives you:
$80 \times 5 = 1 \times (310 + x)$
$400 = 310 + x$
$400 - 310 = 310 + x - 310$ (See the discussion on p. 91 under "Equations" to clarify this step.)
$90 = x$, so 90 is the lowest score that will give an average of 80 for the five exams.

The **median** is the middle number or the average of the two middle numbers in a set of numbers that have been placed in ascending or descending order. Finding the median of a set of numbers is a two-step process:

1. Put the numbers in order from smallest to largest.
2. Find the middle number. If there is no single middle number, average the two middle numbers.

Look at these examples:

Find the median for the numbers 70, 80, 65, 80, 45.
1. Put the numbers in order from smallest to largest: 45, 65, 70, 80, 80.
2. Find the middle number, which is the median. In this example, which contains an odd number of values, there is a middle number. The median = 70.

Note: When you are asked to find a median, don't make the common mistake of forgetting to put the numbers in order first (step 1). In this problem, the middle number is 65 (wrong answer) if you do not order the numbers first.

Find the median for the numbers 52, 30, 30, 30, 60, 75.
1. Put the numbers in order from smallest to largest: 30, 30, 30, 52, 60, 75.
2. Find the middle number. This example contains an even number of values, and there is no single middle number. In this case, the median is the average of the two middle numbers, 30 and 52. Median = the average of 30 and 52 = $\frac{30 + 52}{2} = 41$

The **mode** is the number or numbers that occur most frequently in a set of numbers; there can be one mode, more than one mode, or no mode. If two or more numbers occur most frequently, then each will be a mode. If no number occurs most frequently, there is no mode.

For example:

In the set that includes the numbers 52, 30, 30, 30, 60, 75, the mode = 30.

In the set that includes the numbers 20, 20, 4, 5, 5, 80, 90, the modes = 5 and 20.

In the set that includes the numbers 80, 72, 45, 98, 65, there is no mode.

The **range** for a set of numbers is the largest number minus the smallest number.

For example, to find the range for the numbers 80, 72, 45, 98, 65, you would subtract the smallest number (45) from the largest number (98): $98 - 45 = 53$.

Equations

An **equation** is a statement that two mathematical expressions are equal. An equation may be true or false. For instance, the equation $-8 + 5 = -3$ is true, but the equation $10 = 2$ is false. An equation has two sides. Whatever is on the left side of the equal sign is the *left side,* and whatever is on the right side of the equal sign is the *right side.*

A **variable** is a symbol used in an equation to represent some unknown quantity that can take the value of a specific number. On the PPST, letters are used as variables. If there is a number in front of the letter, that number is called the **coefficient** of the variable. For instance, in the expression $2x$, 2 is the coefficient of the variable x. If no number is written in front of the variable, it is understood that the coefficient is 1. Writing a variable with a coefficient is a way to show multiplication. In other words, $2x$ means 2 times x.

Variable expressions that are the same except for their coefficients are called **like terms**. To add or subtract like terms, you add or subtract their coefficients and use the answer as the coefficient for the common variable. For example, $2x + 3x = 5x$. The addition or subtraction of terms that are *not* like terms can only be indicated. You cannot put them together into a single term. For instance, you would have to leave $2a + 3b$ as it is—you can't make it into a single term.

To **solve an equation** means to find a value for the variable that makes the equation true. Sometimes you can do this by "guessing and checking," which is a good test-taking strategy for multiple-choice math tests. Check the answer choices by substituting the values into the equation, being careful to enclose the substituted value in parentheses and to follow the order of operations PE(MD)(AS) when you do your calculations.

Look at these example test questions:

Solve $7s - 8 = 2s + 12$

A. 2

B. 4

C. 5

D. 6

E. 8

Choice A. On the left side of the equation, using $s = 2$ gives us $7(2) - 8 = 14 - 8 = 6$. On the right side of the equation, you get $2(2) + 12 = 4 + 12 = 16$. Therefore, choice A is not the correct response because $6 \neq 16$.

Choice B. On the left side of the equation, $s = 4$ gives us $7(4) - 8 = 28 - 8 = 20$. On the right side of the equation, you get $2(4) + 12 = 8 + 12 = 20$. Bingo! Choice B is the correct response because $s = 4$ makes the equation true—both sides equal 20.

You would not have to keep going because the correct answer is B.

Another way to work the problem is to solve the equation until you find the value for the variable. In this case, you would end up with an expression like this: variable = number. An equation is like a balanced scale. To keep the equation in balance, whatever you do to one side of the equation you must do to the other side of the equation. The main tools you use in solving equations are the following:

1. Adding the same number to both sides.
2. Subtracting the same number from both sides.
3. Multiplying both sides by the same nonzero number.
4. Dividing both sides by the same nonzero number.

What has been done to the variable determines the operation you choose to do. You perform the same operation on both sides to keep the balance. You "undo" an operation by using the inverse of the operation. To undo addition, subtract, and vice versa. To undo multiplication, divide, and vice versa. An important note: If the variable appears on both sides of the equation, start off by adding or subtracting a variable expression so that the variable appears on only one side of the equation.

Let's solve the following equation: $7s - 8 = 2s + 12$.

In this example, the variable appears on both sides of the equation, so subtract $2s$ from the right side to take it off of that side. To keep the equation balanced, subtract $2s$ from the left side, too:

$$7s - 8 - 2s = 2s + 12 - 2s$$
$$5s - 8 = 12$$

You want to get the variable by itself so that you end up with $s =$ a number, so add 8 to both sides to get rid of the -8 on the left side:

$$5s - 8 + 8 = 12 + 8$$
$$5s = 20$$

You want the coefficient of s to be 1, so divide both sides by 5:

$$\frac{5s}{5} = \frac{20}{5}$$

$$1s = 4$$
$$s = 4$$

You may also be given equations that contain more than one variable in which you solve for a given expression. Let's take an example. If $5x = 45 - 5y$, what is the value of $x + y$?

You want to find $x + y$, so get x and y on the same side. You can do this easily by adding $5y$ to both sides:

$$5x + 5y = 45 - 5y + 5y$$
$$5x + 5y = 45$$

You want $x + y$, so factor out your coefficient:

$$5(x + y) = 45$$

Now get rid of your coefficient by dividing both sides by 5:

$$\frac{5(x + y)}{5} = \frac{45}{5}$$

$$5(x + y) = 45$$
$$x + y = 9$$

7.3

Representations of Quantitative Information

Quantitative information can be presented in various ways. On the PPST, you will be expected to read and interpret information from charts and tables, pictographs, bar graphs, pie charts, and line graphs.

Charts and tables are used to put related information into an organized form. Pictographs, bar graphs, and pie charts show information that is organized into categories. Line graphs show trends, usually over time.

In the case of **charts** and **tables**, information is organized in columns and rows. Each column or row is labeled to explain the entries. Here's an example.

According to the chart shown, in which month was attendance at Little League baseball games in Summerville the highest?

Summer Attendance at Little League Baseball Games in Summerville

MONTH	NUMBER OF FANS ATTENDING
June	200
July	500
August	300

Examination of the chart shows that the highest monthly attendance was 500 fans, which occurred in July.

In a **pictograph**, pictures or symbols are used to represent numbers. Each symbol represents a given number of a particular item. The symbol, its meaning, and the quantity it represents (that is, its scale) should be stated on the figure. To read a pictograph, count the number of symbols in a row and multiply this number by the scale indicated on the graph. Sometimes, a fraction of a symbol is shown. In that case, approximate the fraction and use the value accordingly.

Here's an example of a pictograph.

According to the graph shown below, what was the attendance at Little League baseball games in Summerville during the month of June?

Summer Attendance at Little League Baseball Games in Summerville

According to the graph, each glove-and-baseball symbol stands for 100 fans. The pictograph shows two symbols for June, so June attendance at Little League baseball games was $2 \times 100 = 200$.

A **bar graph** consists of a set of rectangular bars corresponding to different categories. The category for each bar is labeled at the base of the bar. The bars in a bar graph may be arranged vertically or horizontally. The widths of the bars are equal. The length or height of the bar shows the number or amount for the category for that particular bar. A scale (usually beginning at zero) marked with equally spaced values will be shown on the graph. To read a bar graph, examine the scale to determine the units and the amount between the marked values. Then determine where the endpoints of the bars fall in relation to the scale.

Here's an example of how to read a bar graph.

According to the graph shown below, what was the attendance at Little League baseball games in Summerville during the month of August?

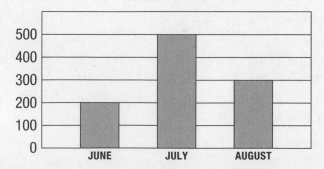

Summer Attendance at Little League Baseball Games in Summerville

Looking at the graph, you can see that the scale is marked in intervals of 100. The endpoint of the bar labeled "August" is at 300. Thus, the attendance at Little League baseball games in August was 300 fans.

Bar graphs can show two or more sets of data on the same graph. This allows you to compare how the data sets compare to each other. For example, the following bar graph shows the quarterly number of new car sales for three salesmen at a car dealership. According to the graph, which salesman appears to have had the poorest performance for the year?

The bar corresponding to Salesman 3 is the shortest of the three bars for all four quarters. Therefore, Salesman 3 had the poorest performance for the year.

A **pie chart,** or **circle graph**, is a graph in the shape of a circle. It is called a pie chart because it looks like a pie cut into wedge-shaped slices. The wedges are labeled to show the categories that make up the graph and, usually, to show the percent amount that corresponds to each category. The total amount in percentage shown on the graph is 100. Reading a pie chart is a simple matter of reading the percents displayed on the graph for the different categories.

Here's an example of how to read a pie chart.

The following pie chart shows how the recreation budget of $1200 was spent in the summer months for Little League baseball activities. According to the graph, how much money was spent in the month of June?

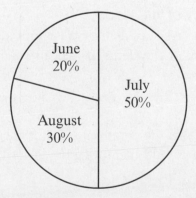

Recreation Budget Expenditures for Summer Total Budget = $1200

The graph shows that 20% of the recreation budget was spent in the month of June. To find how much money was spent, find 20% of $1200 = $240.

A **line graph** uses lines or broken lines for representing data. It has both a horizontal and a vertical scale. The data for the graph are plotted as points according to the two scales. Line segments are used to connect consecutive points. Sometimes, two or more sets of data are plotted on the same graph. The slant of the line between the points shows whether the data values are increasing, decreasing, or remaining at a constant value. If the line slants upward, the data values are increasing; if the line slants downward, the data values are decreasing; and a horizontal line (no slant) means that the data values remain constant.

Here's an example of how to read a line graph.

The following line graph shows the temperature as recorded at 9:00 A.M. every morning over an eight-day period. According to the graph, between which two days was the increase in temperature the greatest?

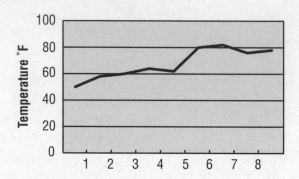

Temperature Readings at 9:00 A.M. for Day 1 Through Day 8

From the graph, you can see that the greatest increase in temperature occurred between Day 5 and Day 6.

7.4

Measurement and Informal Geometry

On the PPST you will be asked to demonstrate your knowledge of measurement, of the U.S. customary and metric systems of measurement, and your understanding of basic geometric concepts.

Units of Measure

The following list contains the common units of measure you will be expected to know for the PPST. You should memorize this information as part of your test preparation.

Conversion Facts for Units of Measure

UNITS OF LENGTH

METRIC	CUSTOMARY
1 kilometer (km) = 1000 meters	1 mile (mi) = 1760 yards
1 meter (m) = 100 centimeters	1 mile (mi) = 5280 feet
1 centimeter (cm) = 10 millimeters	1 yard (yd) = 3 feet
	1 foot (ft) = 12 inches (in.)

UNITS OF CAPACITY AND VOLUME

METRIC	CUSTOMARY
1 liter (L) = 1000 milliliters (mL)	1 gallon (gal) = 4 quarts
	1 gallon (gal) = 128 ounces
	1 quart (qt) = 2 pints
	1 pint (pt) = 2 cups
	1 cup (c) = 8 ounces (oz)

UNITS OF MASS AND WEIGHT

METRIC	CUSTOMARY
1 kilogram (kg) = 1000 grams	1 ton (T) = 2000 pounds
1 gram (g) = 1000 milligrams (mg)	1 pound (lb) = 16 ounces (oz)

MEASURES OF TIME

1 year (yr) = 365 days	1 day (d) = 24 hours
1 year (yr) = 12 months (mo)	1 hour (h) = 60 minutes
1 year (yr) = 52 weeks	1 minute (min) = 60 seconds (sec)
1 week (wk) = 7 days	

On the PPST you may be asked to make an estimate or choose the most appropriate units for a measurement. You probably already are comfortable doing these tasks with units in the U.S. customary system of measurement. You will find the following list of references helpful when estimating or choosing appropriate metric units for a measurement.

Meter: a little longer than a yard
Centimeter: the width of a large paper clip
Millimeter: about the thickness of a dime
Kilometer: about 5 city blocks or a little further than half a mile
Liter: a little more than a quart
Milliliter: five of them to make a teaspoon
Gram: the weight of a small paper clip
Kilogram: the weight of a liter of water or a little more than 2 pounds

For some problems on the PPST, you may need to convert units to different units so that you can solve the problem. You can convert from one unit to another by using an appropriate "conversion fraction." You make conversion fractions by using the conversion facts in the preceding tables. For each conversion fact, you can write *two* conversion fractions. For example, for the conversion fact 1 foot = 12 inches, you have $\dfrac{1 \text{ ft}}{12 \text{ in.}}$ and $\dfrac{12 \text{ in.}}{1 \text{ ft}}$ as your two conversion fractions. Each of these conversion fractions is equivalent to the number 1 because the numerator and denominator are different names for the same length, so they are equal. Therefore, if you multiply something by either of these fractions, you will not change its value.

When you want to change one unit to another unit, multiply by the conversion fraction whose *denominator is the same as the units of the quantity to be converted.* When you do the multiplication, the units you started out with will divide out, and you will be left with the new units. If this doesn't happen, then you used the wrong conversion fraction, so repeat the operation with the other conversion fraction.

Look at these examples:

Convert 5 feet to inches.

The conversion fractions are $\dfrac{1 \text{ ft}}{12 \text{ in.}}$ and $\dfrac{12 \text{ in.}}{1 \text{ ft}}$ You would choose the second because the denominator is in feet, the same unit as in the quantity to be converted.

$$5 \text{ ft} \times \frac{12 \text{ in.}}{1 \text{ ft}} = \frac{5 \ \cancel{\text{ft}}}{1} \times \frac{12 \text{ in.}}{1 \ \cancel{\text{ft}}} = 60 \text{ in.}$$

Notice that the feet (ft) units divide out, and you are left with inches, the unit you were looking for.

Change 3200 centimeters to meters.

The conversion fractions are $\dfrac{1 \text{ m}}{100 \text{ cm}}$ and $\dfrac{100 \text{ cm}}{1 \text{ m}}$. Use the first one because the denominator is centimeters, the same as in the quantity to be converted.

$$3200 \text{ cm} \times \frac{1 \text{ m}}{100 \text{ cm}} = \frac{3200 \ \cancel{\text{cm}}}{1} \times \frac{1 \text{ m}}{100 \ \cancel{\text{cm}}} = 32 \text{ m}$$

Notice that the centimeters (cm) units divide out, and you are left with meters, the unit you were looking for.

When you have a word problem involving units of measurement and conversion, convert the units first, and then work the problem using the converted units. Let's look at an example.

A punch recipe mixes 3 quarts of cranberry juice with 4 quarts of orange juice. How many quarts of cranberry juice will be needed to mix with 5 gallons of orange juice using this recipe?

Solve the problem by using a proportion. The first sentence gives you the first ratio:

$$\frac{3 \text{ quarts cranberry juice}}{4 \text{ quarts of OJ}}$$

The second sentence gives you the second ratio:

$$\frac{x \text{ (quarts) of cranberry}}{5 \text{ gallons of OJ}}$$

Notice that you have a problem. The denominator for the first ratio is in quarts, but the denominator of the second ratio is in gallons. You will need to change

5 gallons to quarts before going on. 5 gallons $= \dfrac{5 \text{ gal}}{1} \times \dfrac{4 \text{ qt}}{\text{gal}} = 20$ quarts.

Set the two ratios equal to each other:

$$\frac{3 \text{ quarts cranberry juice}}{4 \text{ quarts of OJ}} = \frac{x \text{ (quarts) of cranberry}}{20 \text{ quarts of OJ}}$$

Now, for convenience you can omit the units, then solve the proportion:

$$\frac{3}{4} = \frac{x}{20}$$

$$\frac{3 \times 20}{4} = 15 \text{ quarts of cranberry juice}$$

In a computation involving quantities that have units attached, the units must undergo all the operations of the computation. You can always add or subtract quantities that have the same units, and the sum or difference will have those same units. Here are a few examples:

20 ft + 10 ft = 30 ft
$400.00 − $250.75 = $149.25
190 lbs + 86 lbs − 34 lbs = 242 lbs

You can also add or subtract quantities that can be converted to the same unit, provided you convert them before you add or subtract. For example:

5800 g + 2 kg = 5.8 kg + 2 kg = 7.8 kg
1 mile + 176 yards = 1 mile + 0.1 miles = 1.1 miles
2 pints − 1 cup = 2 pints − 0.5 pints = 1.5 pints

You can *never* add or subtract quantities whose units are not the same or that cannot be converted to the same units, such as the following:

5 feet + 40 pounds
$50 + 7 liters
10 centimeters – 400 kilograms
30 inches – 25 (a pure number without any units)
50% + 200 ft

These operations cannot be performed because you cannot convert these pairs to quantities of the same unit.

Multiplication or division of quantities that have units attached is allowed, but you will have to decide whether the product or quotient makes sense in the context of the problem. Look at these examples:

10 ft × 8 ft = 80 ft². Okay because ft² is a legitimate unit of measure (ft² = square feet).

$$\frac{110 \text{ miles}}{2 \text{ hours}} = 55 \frac{\text{mi}}{\text{h}}.$$ Okay because $\frac{\text{mi}}{\text{h}}$ means miles per hour (mph), a legitimate unit of measure.

3 cm × 10 cm × 5 cm = 150 cm³. Okay because cm³ is a legitimate unit of measure (cm³ = cubic centimeters).

(70 cm)(5 g) = 350 cm-g. This unit, "centimeter-gram," might not be okay because cm-g is the unit of the answer.

You can always multiply or divide a quantity of any unit by a pure number (one with no unit associated with it). The product or quotient will have the same units as the original quantity. Here are a few examples:

8 L × 2 = 16 L
75 yds ÷ 3 = 25 yds
25 lbs × 4 = 100 lbs

Informal Geometry

The geometry on the PPST involves terms and formulas that most students learn in elementary or middle school. You will need to know basic terminology and be able to use formulas for area, perimeter, and volume for common geometric figures. You also will need to know how to plot points on a coordinate grid.

Angles are measured in degrees. The degree symbol (90°, 45°, etc.) is used to indicate that unit of measure. The following terminology is used to talk about angles:

Acute angle—an angle with a measure between 0° and 90°
Right angle—an angle with a measure of 90°
Obtuse angle—an angle with a measure between 90° and 180°
Straight angle—an angle with a measure of 180°

Here are some examples of the different kinds of angles.

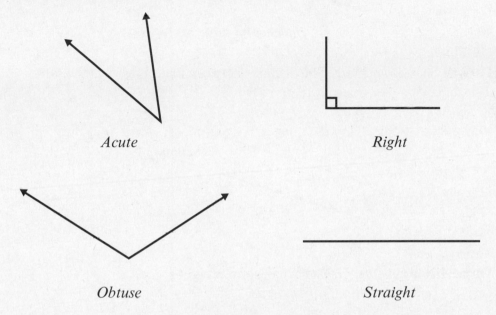

Acute   *Right*

Obtuse   *Straight*

Two angles whose sum is 90° are **complementary angles.**

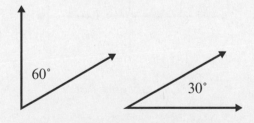

Sample Complementary Angles

Two angles whose sum is 180° are **supplementary angles.**

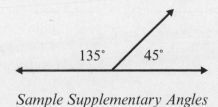

Sample Supplementary Angles

Parallel and Perpendicular

A **plane** is a set of points that forms a flat surface. Lines in a plane can be parallel or intersecting.

Intersecting lines cross at a point on the plane.

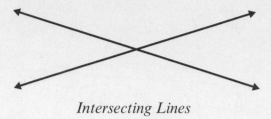

Intersecting Lines

Parallel lines never meet. The distance between them is always the same.

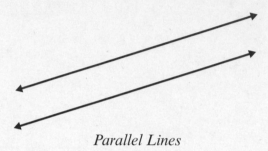

Parallel Lines

Perpendicular lines intersect each other at a right angle.

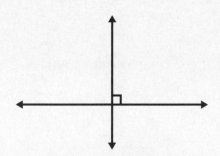

Perpendicular Lines

Congruence, Similarity, and Symmetry

Congruent geometric figures have the same size and shape. If they were superimposed, they would fit exactly on top of each other.

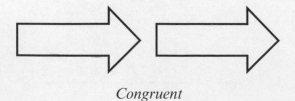

Congruent

Similar geometric figures have the same shape, but they are not necessarily the same size. The sides of similar shapes are proportional to each other.

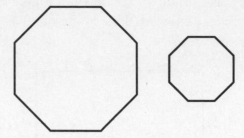

Similar, but not congruent

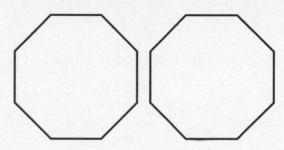

Similar and congruent

Symmetry describes the shape of a figure. Basically, a figure has symmetry if it can be folded along a center line (horizontal or vertical) so that the two resulting parts match exactly.

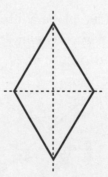

Key Geometric Plane Figures

Two-dimensional (plane) figures are flat shapes (that is, shapes that lie in a plane). The plane figures that are most important for you to know for the PPST are listed below.

A **rectangle** is a closed, four-sided plane figure that has four right angles. It has two dimensions: **length** and **width**.

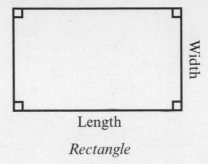

Length

Rectangle

A **square** is a rectangle that has four congruent **sides**. Its two dimensions, length and width, are equal.

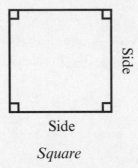

Side

Square

A **triangle** is a closed, three-sided plane figure. It has two dimensions: **base**, the length of one side, and **height**, the perpendicular distance from the base to the opposite point (vertex) where the other two sides meet.

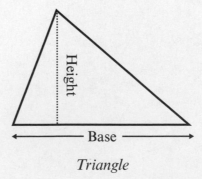

Triangle

A **circle** is a closed plane figure for which all points are the same distance from a point within, called the **center**. A line segment drawn from the center of the circle to a point on the circle is called a **radius** of the circle. A **diameter** is a line segment through the center of the circle with endpoints on the circle. The diameter of a circle is twice the length of a radius.

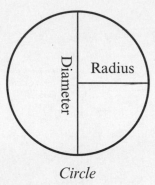

Circle

Perimeter and Circumference

The **perimeter** of a figure is the distance around it. Perimeter is measured in units of length, such as inches, feet, yards, miles, kilometers, meters, centimeters, or millimeters. If no diagram is given in a perimeter problem, be on the safe side and draw your own diagram to figure out your answer.

The following examples show how to solve perimeter problems that deal with different figures:

The formula for the perimeter of a rectangle is $P = 2L + 2W$, where L is the length and W is the width. How many feet of fencing are needed to enclose a rectangular garden that is 20 feet by 30 feet?

1. Draw a diagram and label it.

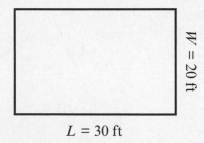

$L = 30$ ft

2. Plug the given values into the formula:
    $P = 2L + 2W$
    $2(30 \text{ ft}) + 2(20 \text{ ft})$
    $60 \text{ ft} + 40 \text{ ft} = 100 \text{ ft}.$

3. Thus, 100 feet of fencing is needed.

The formula for the perimeter of a square is $P = 4s$, where s is the length of a side. The perimeter of a square is 64.8 centimeters; what is the length of one side of the square?

1. Draw a diagram and label it:

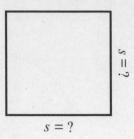

$s = ?$

2. Plug the given values into the formula:

    $P = 4s$

    $68.4 \text{ cm} = 4s$

3. For convenience you can rewrite the equation like this:

    $4s = 68.4 \text{ cm}$

4. Solve for s by dividing both sides by 4 (omitting the units until the final calculation):

    $$\frac{4s}{4} = \frac{68.4}{4}$$

    $s = 17.1 \text{ cm}$

5. 17.1 cm = length of one side of the square.

The formula for the perimeter of a triangle is $P = a + b + c$, where a, b, and c are the lengths of the sides of the triangle. Given that the perimeter of the triangle in the diagram is 38 ft, what is the length of side a?

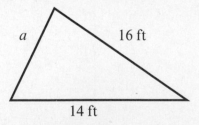

1. From the diagram, you can see that two sides of the triangle have lengths 14 ft and 16 ft. Plug the given values into the formula and simplify:

    $$P = a + b + c$$
    $$38 \text{ ft} = a + 14 \text{ ft} + 16 \text{ ft}$$
    $$38 \text{ ft} = a + 30 \text{ ft}$$

2. For convenience you can rewrite the equation like this:

    $$a + 30 \text{ ft} = 38 \text{ ft}$$

3. Solve for *a* by subtracting 30 from both sides (omitting the units until the final calculation):

$$a + 30 = 38$$
$$a + 30 - 30 = 38 - 30$$
$$a = 8$$

4. The length of side *a* = 8 ft.

The perimeter (or distance around) a circle is known as the **circumference**. The formula for the circumference of a circle is $C = \pi D$, where *D* is the diameter of the circle. The value π is a special number in mathematics that is approximately equal to 3.14.

The diameter of a circle is equal to two times the radius (represented by the variable *r*). Therefore, you can substitute the value *2r* for *D* in the circumference formula: $C = \pi(2r)$, which is usually written as $C = 2\pi r$.

Look at this example.

Find the circumference of the circle in the diagram. (Use π = 3.14.)

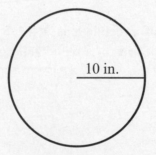

10 in.

1. From the diagram, you can see that *r*, the radius of the circle, is 10 in.
2. Plug that value into the formula:

$$C = 2\pi r$$
$$C = 2\pi(10 \text{ in.})$$
$$C = 2 \times 3.14 \times 10 \text{ in.}$$
$$C = 62.8 \text{ in.}$$

3. The circumference *C* = 62.8 in.

Area

The **area** of a plane figure is the amount of surface inside the figure. Area is measured in square units. Square units are obtained when a unit is multiplied by itself, as follows:

- Square inches (in) = in × in = in²
- Square feet (ft) = ft × ft = ft²
- Square miles (mi) = mi × mi = mi²
- Square millimeters (mm) = mm × mm = mm²
- Square centimeters (cm) = cm × cm = cm²
- Square meters (m) = m × m = m²
- Square kilometers (km) = km × km = km²

If no diagram is given in an area problem, be on the safe side and draw your own diagram to figure out your answer.

The following examples cover problems asking you to find the area of different figures:

The formula for the area of a rectangle is $A = L \times W$, where L is the length and W is the width. What is the area of a rectangular garden that is 30 feet by 20 feet?

1. Draw a diagram and label it.

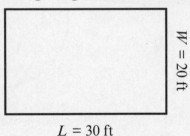

$$W = 20 \text{ ft}$$

$$L = 30 \text{ ft}$$

2. Plug the given values into the formula:

$$A = L \times W$$
$$A = (20 \text{ ft})(30 \text{ ft})$$

3. The answer is $A = 600$ ft.²

The formula for the area of a square is $A = s^2$, where s is the length of a side. Find the area of the square in the diagram.

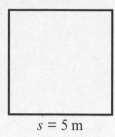

$s = 5$ m

1. From the diagram, you can see that s, the length of a side of the square, is 5 m.
2. Plug the given value into the formula:

$$A = s^2$$
$$A = (5 \text{ m})^2$$

3. The answer is $A = 25$ m^2.

The formula for the area of a triangle is $A = \dfrac{1}{2} bh$, where b is the length of a base of the triangle, and h is the height for that base. Find the area of the triangle in the diagram.

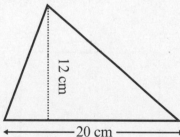

12 cm

20 cm

1. From the diagram, you can see that $b = 20$ cm and $h = 12$ cm.
2. Plug the given values into the formula:

$$A = \frac{1}{2} bh$$

$$A = \frac{1}{2} (20 \text{ cm})(12 \text{ cm})$$

3. Follow the order of operations:

$$A = \frac{(20\text{cm})(12\text{cm})}{2}$$

$$A = \frac{240 \text{ cm}^2}{2}$$

4. The answer is $A = 120$ cm^2.

The formula for the area of a circle is $A = \pi r^2$, where r is the radius of the circle. Find the area of the circle in the diagram. (Use $\pi = 3.14$.)

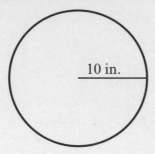

10 in.

1. From the diagram, you can see that the radius is 10 in.
2. Plug that value into the formula:

$$A = \pi r^2$$
$$A = \pi(10 \text{ in.})^2$$
$$A = 3.14 \times 100 \text{ in}^2$$

3. The answer is $A = 314 \text{ in}^2$.

Polygons

A **polygon** is a closed figure whose **sides** are line segments. The point at which any two sides of a polygon intersect is called a **vertex**. A **regular polygon** is one in which all sides are congruent. Some regular polygons are shown here.

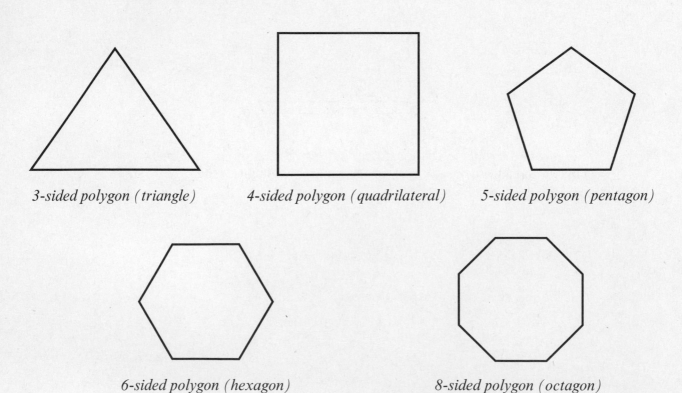

3-sided polygon (triangle)   *4-sided polygon (quadrilateral)*   *5-sided polygon (pentagon)*

6-sided polygon (hexagon)   *8-sided polygon (octagon)*

Right Triangles and the Pythagorean Theorem

A **right triangle** is a triangle that has two sides intersecting at a right angle. These two intersecting sides are called the **legs** of the triangle. The side opposite the right angle is called the **hypotenuse** of the triangle. In a right triangle, the hypotenuse is *always* the longest side. The variable c is traditionally used to represent the hypotenuse of a right triangle, and the variables a and b are used to represent the legs.

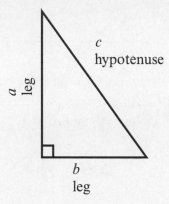

A special relationship, named after the famous Greek mathematician Pythagoras, exists among the sides of a right triangle. The special relationship is the **Pythagorean theorem**, which states that $c^2 = a^2 + b^2$.

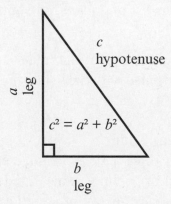

Thus, if you know the value of any two sides of a right triangle, you can find the third side by using the formula $c^2 = a^2 + b^2$.

Look at this example.

Find the diagonal of a rectangular garden that measures 20 feet by 15 feet.

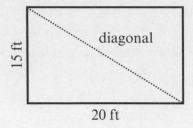

1. From the diagram, you can see that the diagonal of the described rectangle is also the hypotenuse of a right triangle with legs measuring 20 ft and 15 ft.
2. Plug the given values into the formula:

$$c^2 = a^2 + b^2$$
$$c^2 = (20 \text{ ft})^2 + (15 \text{ ft})^2$$
$$c^2 = 400 \text{ ft}^2 + 225 \text{ ft}^2$$
$$c^2 = 625 \text{ ft}^2$$

3. Now you know the value of c^2, but the question asks for the value of c. To solve this equation, you must think of a number that multiplies by itself to give 625 ft^2. From the list of square roots given in Section 7.1, you know that $\sqrt{625} = 25$.

4. When you find the square root of the value 625, you apply the same operation to the units associated with the value (ft^2). The answer is therefore $c = 25$ ft.

Volume of a Rectangular Solid

Volume is the measure of three-dimensional figures. Just as area is measured in square units (such as square feet), volume is measured in cubic units (such as cubic feet). For instance, if the measures of a box were taken in feet, the box's volume would be calculated by multiplying width (in feet) by length (in feet) by height (in feet) = ft × ft × ft = ft^3.

A **rectangular solid (box)** is a three-dimensional figure composed of six **faces**, all of which are rectangles. The dimensions are **length, width,** and **height**. The formula for the volume of a rectangular solid is $V = L \times W \times H$, where L = length, W = width, and H = height.

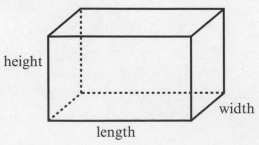

Rectangular Solid

Here's an example of a question concerning the volume of a rectangular solid.

Find the volume (V) of a box-shaped container that measures 5 feet by 8 feet by 2 feet.

  1. Plug the given values into the formula:

$$V = L \times W \times H$$
$$V = (5 \text{ ft})(8 \text{ ft})(2 \text{ ft})$$

  2. The answer is $V = 80 \text{ ft}^3$.

A **cube** is a rectangular solid that has six congruent faces, all of which are squares. Its three dimensions—length, width, and height—are equal. The formula for the volume of a cube is therefore $V = s^3$, where s is the length of a side of one of its square faces.

Look at this example.

Find the volume of the cube in the diagram.

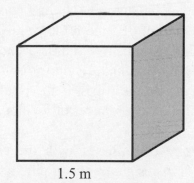

1.5 m

  1. From the diagram you can see $s = 1.5$ m.
  2. Plug the given value into the formula:

$$V = s^3$$
$$V = (1.5 \text{ m})^3$$

  3. The answer is $V = 3.375 \text{ m}^3$.

Coordinate Grid

In Section 7.1, we discussed how rational numbers can be represented on a number line. If you take two number lines, one horizontal and one vertical, and position them at right angles so that they intersect at the 0 point on each line, you have **a coordinate grid**. The horizontal number line with positive direction to the right is usually called the *x* **axis**, and the vertical number line with positive direction upward is called the *y* **axis**. The intersection of the two lines is called the **origin.** The two intersecting *x* and *y* axes divide the coordinate grid into four sections, called *quadrants*. The quadrants are numbered counterclockwise using Roman numerals, as shown in the figure on page 114.

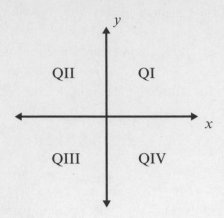

Quadrants of the Coordinate Grid

With this coordinate system we can match points with an **ordered pair** of numbers, called **coordinates**. An ordered pair of numbers is written in a definite order so that one number is first, and the other is second. The first number is called the **x coordinate** and the second number is called the **y coordinate**. In Quadrant 1, both the *x* and *y* coordinates are positive. In Quadrant II, the *x* coordinate is negative and the *y* coordinate is positive. In Quadrant III, both the *x* and *y* coordinates are negative. In Quadrant IV, the *x* coordinate is positive and the *y* coordinate is negative.

Points for which one or both coordinates is zero lie on the axes. If the *x*-coordinate of a point is zero, the point lies on the *y*-axis. If the *y*-coordinate of a point is zero, the point lies on the *x*-axis. If both coordinates of a point are zero, the point is at the origin.

We write ordered pairs in parentheses, with the two numbers separated by commas. The ordered pair (0, 0) designates the origin.

Look at these examples:

(2, 3) is the ordered pair with *x* coordinate = 2 and *y* coordinate = 3.
(−1, 4) is the ordered pair with *x* coordinate = −1 and *y* coordinate = 4.

Think of an ordered pair as giving you directions on how to get to a point on the coordinate grid, starting from the origin (0, 0). The *x* coordinate tells you how far to go right (for positive numbers) or left (for negative numbers) on the *x* axis, and the *y* coordinate tells you how far to go up (for positive numbers) or down (for negative numbers) on the *y* axis.

Use this idea to graph the ordered pairs (2, 3), (–1,4), (–4, –5), and (5, –2) on the coordinate grid, as follows:

To graph the point (2, 3): Start at (0, 0), then go 2 units right and 3 units up.
To graph the point (–1, 4): Start at (0,0), then go 1 unit left and 4 units up.
To graph the point (–4, –5): Start at (0,0), then go 4 units left and 5 units down.
To graph the point (5, –2): Start at (0,0), then go 5 units right and 2 units down.

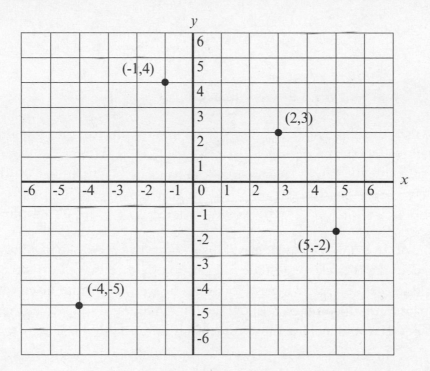

7.5

Formal Mathematical Reasoning

On the PPST, you will need to know the mathematical meaning of certain everyday words, such as *and, or, not, some, all,* and *none.* Do not rely on your intuitive understanding of these words because you might go wrong if you do.

Conjunctions: "And" and "Or"

In logic, the conjunction *and* means "both at the same time." The statement "It is raining and cold outside" means it is both raining *and* cold outside. Similarly, a check written to "Mr. X and Mrs. X," would have to be endorsed by *both* parties to be cashed.

On the other hand, the conjunction *or* means "one or the other, or possibly both at the same time."

"In the winter, it is often raining or cold outside" can mean any one of *three* things. It may mean that on any given day it is raining outside, it is cold outside, or it is both raining and cold outside. A check written to "Mr. X or Mrs. X," may be endorsed by either party, or by both parties. Either way, the check may be cashed.

Notice that the word *or* includes the idea of "both." It is equivalent to what lawyers mean when they use **and/or**.

You can illustrate the use of *and* and *or* with Venn diagrams. **Venn diagrams** are circles that represent the intersection or union of sets. Here's an example.

If the S circle represents the students who play sports, and the B circle represents the students who play in the band, then the oval-shaped section where the two circles overlap, called the **intersection**, contains the students who both play sports *and* are in the band.

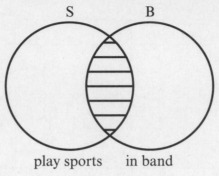

Venn Diagram: "And"

On the other hand, the students who play sports or play in the band would be in the S circle, in the B circle, or in their intersection. Notice that these two circles are drawn so that they intersect. Unless you are told *specifically* that given sets do not overlap, your Venn diagram must show them intersecting. In this case, the intersection of A and B would include those students, if any, who do both activities.

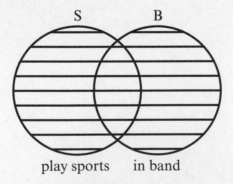

Venn Diagram: "Or"

Negation: "Not"

The word ***not*** is used to negate a statement. For example, "It is *not* raining" is the negation of "It is raining." If you are using a Venn diagram to illustrate a set, the items outside the circle do *not* belong to the set represented by the circle.

If the B circle represents the students at School X who ride the bus to school, the shaded area represents the students at School X who do *not* ride the bus to school. (Notice a rectangle is used to represent the whole group under discussion.)

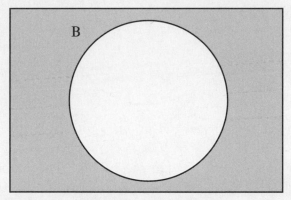

Venn Diagram: "Not"

Quantity: "Some," "All," and "None"

In logic, the word *some* means "at least one," which can also be stated as "one or more." The statement "Some students like opera" means one or more students like opera. In the context of mathematical reasoning, even if just one student likes opera, that situation is consistent with the given statement. That is, "some" means "at least one." In a Venn diagram, "some" is illustrated as follows. A variable *x* is placed in the intersection of the S circle (representing students) and the O circle (representing opera-likers).

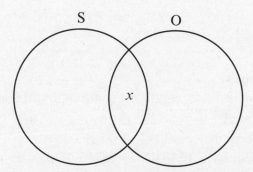

Venn Diagram: "Some"

You do not know how many students the variable *x* represents. You just know for sure that it represents at least one.

The word *all* means "every single one, no exceptions." The statement "All rectangles are parallelograms" means every single rectangle is a parallelogram, and there are no rectangles that are not parallelograms.

In a Venn diagram, "all" is illustrated as follows. The R circle, representing rectangles, is entirely inside the P circle, which represents parallelograms. This is the way to illustrate that all of one thing can be characterized as another thing.

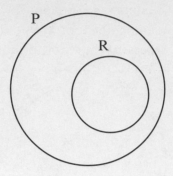

Venn Diagram: "All"

The word **none** means "not one, no exceptions." The statement "None of the contestants wears glasses" means "not one of the contestants wears glasses."

In a Venn diagram, "none" is illustrated as follows. The C circle (representing contestants) is drawn beside the G circle (representing those who wear glasses). The circles do *not* overlap.

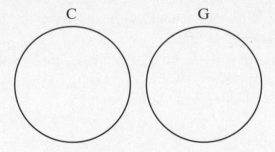

Venn Diagram: "None"

If-Then Statements

The **if-then statement,** also called a **conditional statement,** is used frequently in reasoning. These statements take the form "*if p, then q.*" In the statement "If I receive my check, I'll buy new clothes," you can see that p = "I receive my check" and q = "I'll buy new clothes." In logic terms, the equivalent of an if-then statement (with form *if p, then q*) is its **contrapositive,** which is stated like so: *If not q, then not p.* Notice that in the contrapositive, the q clause (the "then" part of the statement) comes first, and both the q and the p are negated.

The following table includes examples of if-then statements and their contra-positives.

IF-THEN AND CONTRAPOSITIVE

STATEMENT	CONTRAPOSITIVE
"If it rains, I will carry an umbrella."	"If I did not carry an umbrella, it did not rain."
"If my average is 90 or above, then I will make an A."	"If I did not make an A, then my average was not 90 or above."

Chapter 8

Review for the PPST Writing

The writing tests in this preparation guide and in the PPST Writing test are given in two sections. Section I is divided into Part A, Usage Questions (twenty-five questions), and Part B, Sentence Correction Questions (twenty questions). Section II is the essay examination. The purpose of the PPST Writing test is to measure your ability to recognize and use standard written English correctly and effectively. The test is designed to measure writing skills that you will be expected to demonstrate during your academic and professional career. To be successful on the test you should have a working knowledge of the following:

- Parts of speech: prepositions, nouns, verbs, pronouns, adverbs, conjunctions, interjections, appositives
- Punctuation: colon, semicolon, comma, apostrophe
- Sentence structure: verb and noun phrases, parallelism
- Sentence fragments; dependent and independent clauses
- Agreement: pronouns/antecedent, subject/verb
- Idiomatic expressions, figurative language, figures of speech
- Appropriate level of diction; awkwardness and wordiness
- Synonyms and antonyms

Section 1

Usage

Part A

This section presents twenty-five sentences, each of which is marked and underlined in parts. Each underlined part is labeled with a letter (A through D). The directions are to read each sentence and decide whether any of the underlined parts contains an error. If so, on your answer sheet, mark the answer choice that is the same as the letter printed beneath the error in the sentence. If the sentence does not contain an error, mark choice E on your answer sheet. No sentence has more than one error.

These guidelines may be helpful in attacking this part of the writing test:

- It is important to read the entire sentence and look at all parts critically.
- One word may be underlined or several words. In any case, the entire part that is underlined does not have to be incorrect. Instead, the error may depend upon one word only.
- Do not take the parts in isolation. If you read each one in isolation, it may make sense and sound correct. But when read in context with the rest of the sentence, you may see that it is wrong because of other elements in the sentence.
- Choice E (no error) should be used if the sentence looks and sounds correct. Do not be shy about using this choice.
- Try to correct the error in your mind by replacing, changing, or deleting an element.
- A line under a blank space indicates that a punctuation mark may be needed. You must decide what, if any, punctuation to add.
- On the other hand, if a punctuation mark is underlined, you must decide if it is correct, whether another piece of punctuation would be correct, or whether any punctuation is needed at all.

Section 1

Sentence Correction

Part B

The twenty sentences in this part are also underlined in part or in whole. The five answer choices present five ways of writing the underlined part, with choice A being the same as the original. The underlined portion of the sentence correction question may be as short as one or two words or as long as the entire sentence. You must select the answer choice that is best in terms of correctness and effectiveness.

The guidelines may be helpful in attacking this part of the writing test:

- Choice A repeats the portion of the question that is underlined. After reading every answer, choose A if you think the original is the best answer.
- There may be several ways to correct the sentence, but you will need to choose the one that appears in the answer selection.
- Do not choose an answer that changes the meaning of the sentence.
- Read the entire sentence before making your answer selection.
- All parts of the sentence must fit together correctly.
- Do not choose an answer simply because it's lengthy or concise.
- Read all the choices before choosing an answer.

Section 2

Essay

An essay examination plays a significant role in testing, as it provides the best demonstration that you are thinking critically and analytically about a subject. The examiner wants to make sure you can sort through information, identify what is important, and explain your decision. You are tested to see if you understand the concepts necessary to make connections, see relationships, draw conclusions, and find contrasts.

We write for a variety of purposes. Some writing is meant to be persuasive, to convey information, express feelings, or to give pleasure. The process of planning your essay begins before you actually put your thoughts on paper in an organized way. Think about what you want to say and how you want to say it. This planning and organizing is an important part of writing.

The thesis is the central point of your essay, which your argument and details support. An effective thesis clearly communicates your essay's main idea and uses ideas and information to support the central point. When the essay is arranged logically, the paragraphs appear in an appropriate order so that ideas are unified as the essay progresses. There should be enough detail to support the ideas.

The use of correct sentence structure and language is the foundation for the essay. The sentence structure signals the relative importance of clauses in a sentence and their logical relationship to one another. Interesting essays are written with sentences of varying length and follow different grammatical patterns.

How well you do on the essay depends upon the way you attend to the following:

- Organization and development of ideas (unity, coherence, and progression of argument)
- Use of detail to support a thesis or illustrate ideas
- Quality of writing, including syntactic variety and facility in the use of language

After the essay is planned out, think about how each part (sentence or paragraph) prepares the readers for the parts that follow. Look at each section of the essay in turn. The paragraphs should proceed in logical order, with appropriate transitions to help readers connect the points you are making. Generalizations should be strongly supported by detail, examples, or evidence. Adjust sentences that do not say what you intend.

Remember that the purpose of this examination is to test your writing ability within an allotted amount of time. The evaluators are looking for the total overall impression that your essay makes.

Chapter 9

Study Tips for the PPST

The best way to prepare for the PPST is to study the review material in Chapters 6 through 8. Here are some tips for developing an effective study plan:

1. On a calendar, mark the days and times you plan to study. Make your plan realistic, so that you will be more likely to stick to it. Try to set aside at least two hours per session. If possible, spread your study schedule over a period of at least three weeks. You don't have to study every day, but don't let long gaps of more than two or three days separate your study sessions.

2. Find a comfortable place to study, away from distractions and undue noise, with ample room to work. You should have adequate lighting and a room temperature that is not too warm or too cold. Once you've found it, study at the same place every time.

3. Figure out what time of day you are at your best mentally and what times you can work into your schedule. Set that time aside for studying, and decide that, during that study time, preparing for the PPST has priority over all other activities.

4. Try to eliminate distractions from your studying. Other people's conversations should be out of your hearing range, and phone calls should be taken after you've finished studying. Don't try to watch television or listen to loud, distracting music while you study. On the other hand, if too much quiet makes you uncomfortable, and you feel listening to music helps you concentrate, then select music that doesn't interfere with your thought processes. Have your study aids (paper, pen/pencil, calculator) nearby, so that you don't have to interrupt your studying to go get something you need.

5. Concentrate when you study because your mind is more likely to be able to retrieve information you paid attention to when studying. Of course, there will be

times when your attention wanders and you find yourself thinking of something else. When that happens, just calmly call your attention back and concentrate again on your work. It will help if you return to a place one or two sentences before where you were—to refresh your memory on the topic at hand.

6. Stop often to take notes and reflect on the study material. Look away and translate ideas into your own words, your own mental images, and your own specific examples. Learning with pauses and intervals for reflection will help you store the learned information in long-term memory.

7. Make flashcards for concepts you had difficulty understanding. Review your cards periodically, and always carry a few with you to look over when you have spare minutes of idle time.

8. Each time you begin a new study session, briefly review what you have studied last. Of course, don't try to read everything, but do look over your notes and the study material to warm up your mind about the subject. Read slowly enough to see key words and phrases. When you successfully remind yourself and arouse memories, your brain will be ready to link the new information you learn that day with the past learning—and those links improve retention!

9. Spend time practicing skill areas that you think you have learned. This is particularly important in mathematics. Continue to practice the skill until you feel you can apply that skill in a variety of problem contexts.

10. Plan to study or review previously studied material. Reading the same chapters two or three times will improve both your memory and your understanding and will allow you to identify skill areas in which you may need additional practice.

11. Plan to memorize important information and to check yourself to make sure you have got it. The following memory techniques (modified for the purposes of this book) were developed for students at the University of Alabama at Birmingham (see the university Web site at *http://students.uab.edu*). Review each technique, and use those that fit your learning style.

MEMORY TECHNIQUES

Organize It
✓ **Learn from the general to the specific.** For new material, skim for the general idea and then read to get the specifics.
✓ **Make it meaningful.** What do you want from the information? How will it help you? The answers to these questions will make it relevant to you.
✓ **Create associations.** Store the new information with similar or related information that you already know. You will have the ability to recall the new information more effectively.

Use Your Body

✓ **Learn it once, actively.** Enhance your learning with action. Stand up, sit up straight, pace back and forth, and/or gesture with your hands to get your body involved when you study. Learning requires energy.

✓ **Relax.** Your ability for recall is greater when the anxiety level is minimal.

✓ **Create pictures.** You can draw pictures, charts, or cartoons to connect facts. Visualization promotes recall.

✓ **Recite and repeat.** Repetition uses your physical and auditory senses, which you can use to accelerate your concentration. The combination of concentration and hearing the information as you recite in your own words increases your ability to remember.

✓ **Write it down.** Writing, which uses your hand and arms, is active learning. Writing requires you to be logical and reveals missing information.

Use Your Brain

✓ **Reduce interference.** Find a space free of distractions. Sticking to one activity at a time increases your ability to remember.

✓ **Overlearn.** Dissect the information, add to it, and go over it until it becomes second nature.

✓ **Escape the short-term memory trap.** Short-term memory doesn't last long—just a few minutes or hours. For exams, move information to your long-term memory by reviewing until you have overlearned.

✓ **Use daylight.** You should study difficult subjects during the daylight hours when your concentration is more effective.

✓ **Distribute learning.** Schedule time to study into manageable increments, one- to two-hour sessions. You should reward yourself with regular breaks. There is an exception to this technique. When you are engrossed in an idea and cannot think of anything else, keep going.

✓ **Be aware of attitudes.** Your attitude about a subject or topic may be negative. That's all right, as long as you acknowledge that's the case. Your awareness can deflate an attitude that is blocking your memory.

✓ **Choose what not to store in your memory.** Be selective. Decide what is essential to remember, and apply memory techniques to those ideas.

✓ **Combine memory techniques.** Memory techniques work better in combination. Consolidate two or three of the techniques and experiment with them.

Recall It

✓ **Remember something else.** Brainstorming is a technique used to promote recall. Recall similar information, and the answer you need will probably appear.

✓ **Notice when you do remember.** Everyone remembers differently. Pay attention to the styles that work for you.

✓ **Use it before you lose it.** Practice using information regularly—read it, write it, speak it, listen to it, or apply it. The more you use information, the greater the recall.

✓ **Remember that you never forget.** Properly stored information is never lost. You might have problems recalling it. As an aid, use positive statements like "Let me find where I stored it."

12. Use the free ETS resources available at *www.ets.org/praxis.* You will find detailed information about the PRAXIS tests and sample questions and answer explanations in the Tests at a Glance section.

13. Learn from the diagnostic and practice tests in this book. The answer explanations contain review material and test-taking strategies.

14. Be committed to your study plan. Don't make excuses or procrastinate.

15. Pick a realistic test date. Give yourself ample time to get prepared before you attempt the PPST.

Not everyone learns in the same way. Some of the suggestions in this chapter may not work for you. Try them all, then tailor your approach to use those that fit your learning style. After you complete your study plan, you will be confident and prepared to take the PPST. Congratulations on a job well done!

Part 4

PPST and Answers

Chapter 10

Practice PPST

READING

40 Questions
Time—60 minutes

Directions: Each statement or passage in this test is followed by a question or questions based on its content. After reading each statement or passage, read each question that follows, and then choose the one best answer from the five choices given. Answer the questions based on what is stated or implied in the passage.

Mark your answer on the answer sheet. Fill in the space that has the same letter as the answer you have selected.

Questions 1–5

From the firsthand accounts by European observers of the time, Native American life in the Southwest and Great Plains region, Native American life in the Northeast and Great Lakes region, and life in the European countries of France, England, and Spain were greatly different in numerous respects. The major differences described by these eyewitness scribes of history were in lodging, food, clothing, and customs.

The countryside of the Southwest and Great Plains was better in certain respects than in Europe. It consisted of hills and plains and rivers and streams. There were plenty of buffalo and wild plants like prunes, grapes, and flax. The Native Americans of the Southwest who lived near the Rio Grande River had flat-roofed houses, some with two stories, made of mud or stone. The houses had hot rooms underground for shelter from the cold weather in winter. Their agricultural crops included corn, beans, and melons. For clothing they had long robes of braided feathers, cloaks of cotton, and skins of buffalo and deer.

In contrast, the Native Americans in the Great Plains region did not live in houses; instead, their housing consisted of portable huts which were erected from poles stuck into the ground at the bottom, tied together at the top, and covered with buffalo skin. These Native Americans roamed with the buffalo herds, obtaining their food and clothing from these vital animals.

The Native Americans of the Northeast and Great Lakes region were very strange in the eyes of the European observer who recorded their habits and customs. They wore the seams of their stockings between their legs and fastened fringe or spangles to the seam, while the women had fringe or spangles on the outer side of the leg. Their shoes, which they stuffed for warmth in the winter, were flat and wide. They wore their shirts over their clothing to shield them from rain and snow. They did not like to wear breeches and thought that using handkerchiefs was an unclean practice.

They did not wash their meat before cooking it, to keep in the blood and fat. When eating, they sat on the ground and did not eat bread or drink liquids with their meals; rather, they ate the food first, then would drink afterwards and not touch food after that. They did not have soup before meals, but drank the broth of the pot at the end of the meal. Visitors were offered food if they dropped in. The Native Americans preferred to sit or recline on the ground rather than to stand, which they found uncomfortable.

When dancing, they moved their arms and legs energetically and stomped the ground with their feet. Mothers carried their infants bound up to a board on the mother's back. Other customs noted were that the Native Americans wanted to be paid for work before they did it, and they did not like to tell people their names. When couples married, the wife's family received a dowry, and the husband went to live in the wife's house. Also, when people died, they were dressed up, buried with their favorite possessions, and their bodies placed in a fetal position facing west. A man's heirs were his sister's sons, and his small belongings were distributed to his friends. When a man was angry or upset, he was given gifts to get him back in good humor. In interpersonal relationships, the Native Americans were open and honest, being very sincere people.

In comparison, the customs and habits of Europeans were quite different. In Europe, men wore the seams of stockings behind the legs, their shoes had heels, and they wore their shirts next to their skin. They wore breeches and usually carried handkerchiefs. When eating, Europeans sat on chairs at tables, and food and drink were consumed together, not separately. They washed their meat before cooking it, to cleanse it of blood and impurities. They began dinner with soup and ate bread with their meals. When visitors dropped in, they were invited to have a drink, not offered food. Europeans preferred to sit on chairs, benches, or stools, rather than to sit on the ground. When they danced, for example, as in France, they moved their upper body very little and their feet lightly touched the ground. Mothers carried their infants on the arm, clasped to the breast, not strapped to their backs, and used cradles, which stayed at home.

European workers did not expect to be paid until the work was completed, and did not mind giving their names when asked. Dowries were given to a husband's family, and the wife went to live in the husband's house. When people died, they were buried almost naked, their bodies were stretched out lengthwise and, in some parts of France, placed facing east. In Europe, the children inherited the belongings of their parents. Also, in France, when a man was angry or upset, he was not given presents, but was reproached and *castigated*. In interpersonal relationships, in a large part of Europe, the Europeans, unlike Native Americans, were prone to be artificial and insincere.

The contrasts in the cultures of the Native Americans and Europeans are revealed in the firsthand accounts given by European observers. The various differences, which, in many instances, are very stark, are intriguing and interesting.

1. The best title for this selection is:
   A. "Native American Life in the New World"
   B. "A Contrast of Cultures"
   C. "European Scribes of History"
   D. "The Customs and Habits of Early Europeans"
   E. "Early Life in the European Countries of France, England, and Spain"

2. The author's primary purpose in this passage is to:
   A. persuade
   B. entertain
   C. frighten
   D. ridicule
   E. compare

3. The tone of the passage is:
   A. sarcastic
   B. inquiring
   C. humorous
   D. factual
   E. disapproving

4. According to the selection, Native Americans in the Great Plains region:
   A. did not expect to be paid until the work was completed.
   B. had flat-roofed houses, some with two stories, made of mud or stone.
   C. were prone to be artificial and insincere.
   D. did not live in houses.
   E. wore the seams of stockings behind the legs.

5. Which of the following words, if substituted for the word "castigated" in paragraph 4, would introduce the LEAST change in the meaning of the sentence?
   A. profaned
   B. glorified
   C. punished
   D. rewarded
   E. flogged

Questions 6–10

The general situation in high school differs fundamentally from the situation in the grammar school in that the children represent a selected group. Only the brightest children survive long enough in their school careers to reach high school, and the pupils taking a given subject are still further a selected group. Moreover, the children themselves have changed. They are no longer children, but adolescents, and the immediate aims of the high school are not identical with those of the grammar school, however similar the ultimate aims may be. It is, then, to be expected that tests for high school should differ somewhat from those applicable to the grades. The subject matter is certainly different, and the form is very likely to be somewhat changed. The reader will doubtless notice, for instance, that most of these tests require writing—a condition that was severely criticized in the earlier chapters. The tests would probably be easier for the teacher to score if the writing was eliminated, but the demand for writing does not invalidate the results to any dangerous extent, since all the pupils in high school write with a fair rapidity. Also, the examiner may take for granted a certain amount of intelligent understanding of directions and the general problem of the tests, for only the more intelligent children get into high school. It will be seen that the tests are very much less special in form and much more like an ordinary class exercise than is possible in work with younger children.

6. What does the passage state about the immediate aims of high schools?
   A. They are different from those of grammar schools.
   B. They may be similar to those of grammar schools.
   C. It does not matter because the ultimate aims are similar.
   D. Most subject tests require writing.
   E. There should be no differentiation from the variance of grade levels.

7. What is the purpose of the passage?
   A. To discuss whether high school students should be examined based on their writing.
   B. To discuss the use of tests in high school subjects.
   C. To discuss the major differences between high school and grammar school tests.
   D. To advocate the use of informal evaluation rather than testing to evaluate student progress.
   E. To advocate the use of standardized tests for entrance into high school programs.

8. The author believes which of the following?
   A. Students should be tested in high school the same as they were in grammar school because they are used to this format.
   - B. Students in high school are tested over different subjects and, therefore, should be tested somewhat differently.
   C. Evaluating high school students' writing serves no purpose in assessing knowledge.
   - D. Evaluating high school students' writing is important when assessing knowledge.
   E. Prospective high school students should be tested before being admitted to high school.

9. The author assumes which of the following?
   A. All high school students write at a slow pace.
   B. Adolescents (or high school students) have the same interests as grammar school students.
   C. Only the brightest students advance in their educational career to the high school level.
   D. Subject matter is the same for all high school students.
   E. There is no demand for writing.

10. Testing in high school should be _____ according to the author.
    A. written essays
    B. more like ordinary class exercises
    C. specific to the subject
    D. fill in the blank
    E. multiple choice

Questions 11–16

When we are looking at a landscape we think ourselves pleased; but it is only when it comes back upon us by the fire o' nights that we can disentangle the main charm from the thick of particulars. It is just so with what is lately past. It is too much loaded with detail to be distinct; and the canvas is too large for the eye to encompass. But this is no more the case when our recollections have been strained long enough through the hour-glass of time; when they have been burthen of so much thought, the charm and comfort of so many a vigil. All that is worthless has been sieved and sifted out of them. Nothing remains but the brightest lights and the darkest shadows. When we see a mountain country near at hand, the spurs and haunches crowd up in eager rivalry, and the whole range seems to have shrugged its shoulders to its ears, till we cannot tell the higher from the lower: but when we are far off, these lesser prominences are melted back into the bosom of the rest, or have set behind the round horizon of the plain, and the highest peaks stand forth in lone and sovereign dignity against the sky. It is just the same with our recollections. We require to draw back and shade our eyes before the picture dawns upon us in full breadth and outline. Late years are still in limbo to us; but the more distant past is all that we possess in life, the corn already harvested and stored for ever in the grange of memory. The doings of today at some future time will regain the required offing; I shall learn to love the things of my adolescence, as Hazlitt loved them, and as I love already the recollections of my childhood. They will gather interest with every year. They will ripen in forgotten corners of my memory; and some day I shall waken and find them vested with new glory and new pleasantness.

—Robert Louis Stevenson, *A Retrospect*

11. In the first sentence, the "fire o' nights" refers to which of the following?
    A. fireflies
    B. sunset
    C. moon
    D. a fire at night
    E. sunrise

12. The author does not compare a person's recollections to which of the following?
    A. a mountain range
    B. a sunset
    C. a landscape
    D. harvested corn
    E. a picture

13. The value of recollections is found in _____ according to the author.
    A. time that has passed
    B. interest
    C. forgotten corners of memory
    D. detail
    E. charm and comfort

14. The author's description of the mountain range is used to visually depict what point?
    A. We see the details when we are up close.
    B. Being up close is comparable to recollections of the recent past, and being far off is comparable to those of the distant past.
    C. You cannot see the landscape of the mountains against the sky when you are in the midst of a mountain range.
    D. The sovereign dignity of a mountain range against the sky can only be observed from far away.
    E. We cannot tell the higher from the lower when we are in the mountains.

15. According to the author, our recollections are _____ in the recent past and _____ in the distant past.
    A. muddled by detail; clearer
    B. clearer; muddled by detail
    C. distinct with detail; unclear
    D. unclear; distinct with detail
    E. clearer; distinct with detail

16. In the passage, the harvested corn symbolizes what?
   A. distant past
   B. memory
   C. experiences
   D. recollections
   E. agricultural landscape

Questions 17–22

It is commonly supposed that when a man seeks literary power he goes to his room and plans an article for the press. But this is to begin literary culture at the wrong end. We speak a hundred times for every once we write. The busiest writer produces little more than a volume a year, not so much as his talk would amount to in a week. Consequently, through speech it is usually decided whether a man is to have command of his language or not. If he is slovenly in his ninety-nine cases of talking, he can seldom pull himself up the strength and exactitude in the hundredth case of writing. A person is made in one piece, and the same being runs through a multitude of performances. Whether words are uttered on paper or to the air, the effect on the utterer is the same. Vigor or feebleness results according as energy or slackness has been in command. I know that certain adaptations to a new field are often necessary. A good speaker may find awkwardness in himself, when he comes to write; a good writer, when he speaks. And certainly cases occur where a man exhibits distinct strength in one of the two, speaking or writing, and not in the other. But such cases are rare. As a rule, language once within our control can be employed for oral or written purposes. And since the opportunities for oral practice enormously outbalance those for written, it is the oral which is chiefly significant in the development of literacy power. We rightly say of the accomplished writer that he shows a mastery of his own tongue.

—G. H. Palmer, *Self-Cultivation in English*

17. The passage emphasizes the importance of _____ in communication.
   A. oral skills
   B. written skills
   C. command of his language
   D. the development of literacy power
   E. mastery of the writer's own tongue

18. According to the passage, the rule between oral and written communication is which of the following?
   A. The two are directly related; strength in one indicates strength in the other.
   B. The two are inversely related; strength in one indicates weakness in the other.
   C. The two are related by cause and effect.
   D. The two are not related.
   E. The relationship between the two cannot be determined from the passage.

19. The term "slovenly" in the sixth sentence means which of the following?
    A. careful
    B. exact
    C. sloppy
    D. purposeful
    E. weak

20. According to the passage, why is oral communication regarded as more important than written communication?
    A. The accomplished writer shows a mastery of his own tongue.
    B. The busiest writer produces little more than a volume a year, not so much as his talk would amount to in a week.
    C. Through speech it is usually decided whether a man is to have command of his language or not.
    D. As a rule, language once within our control can be employed for oral or written purposes.
    E. We speak a hundred times for every once we write.

21. Why does the author state, "We rightly say of the accomplished writer that he shows a mastery of his own tongue"?
    A. It is another way of saying that oral communication is more important than written.
    B. He is sarcastically making fun of those that say that good speakers have mastered their own tongue.
    C. He is saying that a good writer must also be a good speaker, and must therefore have mastery over his literal tongue.
    D. He is saying that being an accomplished writer means nothing if the writer does not have a mastery of his own tongue.
    E. Oral communication is chiefly significant in the development of literacy power.

22. Which of the following is said about seeking literary power?
    A. Literary power is determined by written communication skills.
    B. The opportunities for oral practice are inferior to the opportunities for written practice.
    C. Good oral communication skills result in good written communication skills.
    D. Written practice outbalances oral practice.
    E. Language is out of our control.

Questions 23–27

Mr. Henry James once suggested as a test of the rank of a novel that we ask ourselves whether it aroused in us the emotions of surprise or the emotions of recognition. If it amuses us only by the ingenuity of its story and by the startling effect of its unsuspected incidents, it stands on a lower plane than if it pleases us by revealing unexpected recesses of the human soul, which we accept as veracious although we have never before perceived them. The same test is as valid in the theater as in the library; and in a serious drama, as well as in high-comedy, mere surprise must always be subordinate to the subtler recognition. We expect the dramatist to explain us to ourselves and to turn his lantern on the hidden corners of character, whether tragic or comic. When we see a personage in a play do this, or when we hear him say that, we ought to feel instantly that, however unforeseen the deed or the saying may be, it was precisely what the personage would have done or said at that particular moment of his life.

—Brander Matthews, *A Study of the Drama*

23. The main idea of the passage is which of the following?
    A. Dramatic works are ranked on the same basis as novels.
    B. The types of emotions that are evoked determine the rank of a novel.
    C. The types of emotions that are evoked determine the rank of a dramatic work.
    D. The element of surprise is secondary to that of recognition in a dramatic work.
    E. If a character says or does something, it should be exactly what that character would have said or done at that particular moment of his life.

24. The term "veracious" in the second sentence means which of the following?
    A. inaccurate
    B. disputed
    C. truthful
    D. dishonest
    E. unread

25. According to the passage, which of the following results in the story being on a higher level?
    A. It amuses us only by the ingenuity of its story and by the startling effect of its unsuspected incidents.
    B. It evokes surprise in the reader/audience.
    C. It shows accepted truth about the human soul, however unforeseen.
    D. It evokes the subtler recognition.
    E. The author turns his lantern on the hidden corners of character, whether tragic or comic.

26. "In a serious drama, as well as in high-comedy, mere surprise must always be subordinate to the subtler recognition." By this statement, the author means _____?
    A. Serious dramas and high-comedies are alike.
    B. The emotion of surprise is very important to the story line.
    C. Recognition in the drama is more important than surprise.
    D. Surprise is unimportant to the drama.
    E. Serious dramas are higher in rank than comedies.

27. "We expect the dramatist to explain us to ourselves and to turn his lantern on the hidden corners of character, whether tragic or comic." Through this strategy, the author/dramatist evokes which of the following emotions?
    A. recognition
    B. interest
    C. surprise
    D. creativity
    E. sadness

Questions 28–30

On his way out of the town he had to pass the prison, and as he looked in at the windows, whom should he see but William himself peeping out of the bars, and looking very sad indeed. "Good morning, brother," said Tom, "have you any message for the King of the Golden River?" William ground his teeth with rage, and shook the bars with all his strength; but Tom only laughed at him, and advising him to make himself comfortable till he came back again, shouldered his basket, shook the bottle of holy water in William's face till it frothed again, and marched off in the highest spirits in the world. It was, indeed, a morning that might have made anyone happy, even with no Golden River to seek for. Level lines of dewy mist lay stretched along the valley, out of which rose the massy mountains—their lower cliffs in pale grey shadow, hardly distinguishable from the floating vapour, but gradually ascending till they caught the sunlight, which ran in bright touches of ruddy colour along the sharp crags, and pierced, in long, level rays, through their fringes of spear-like pine.

—John Ruskin, *King of the Golden River*

28. "Level lines" and "massy mountains" are examples of what literary device?
    A. onomatopoeia
    B. palindrome
    C. alliteration
    D. description
    E. simile

29. What does this passage best describe?
    A. The relationship between Tom and William because they are brothers.
    B. The sunlight and mountain view that Tom sees as he sets out to travel.
    C. The Golden River that Tom is going to find.
    D. Tom's high spirits because it is a beautiful morning.
    E. The sunlight cascading through the pine trees in long, level rays.

30. In the last sentence, the term "ruddy" is used to describe the sunlight. It means:
    A. reddish
    B. bright
    C. patchy
    D. shining
    E. dim

Questions 31–35

There is a widespread opinion among educators that the fourth grade is the crucial grade in our public schools. In it the differentiation among pupils becomes probably more definite than in any other grade. It is there, they believe, that the child experiences a marked transference of attention from the symbols of thought to the ideas themselves; from the laborious to the more nearly automatic use of numbers; and from the slow, studied, large handwriting to the smaller, more natural form that becomes his daily tool. Pupils of normal or unusual intelligence advance more rapidly in their studies; those with various handicaps, including the feeble-minded, move more slowly, or even show that they have about reached the limits of their possible progress in formal studies. New subject matters and mental readjustments difficult to make are often encountered. Moreover, as Professor Judd points out, the fourth grade is a crucial one because the good or the poor quality of the primary instruction will show there most strikingly. Previous good work will lead to a greater interest in meanings; poor preparation will reveal an inability to use the forms or symbols of language well enough to proceed satisfactorily with meanings.

—Author unknown, circa 1920

31. According to the passage, why is the fourth grade regarded as crucial?
    A. Children replace using symbols in their thinking with ideas themselves.
    B. Differentiation among students is greatest in the third grade.
    C. Quality of primary instruction decreases in the fourth grade.
    D. Students have a greater interest in reading.
    E. Poor preparation will reveal the child's ability.

32. What is said about students regarding intelligence abilities in the fourth grade?
    A. Those with stronger abilities seem to advance more quickly than other students.
    B. Those that are learning-disabled struggle more in the fourth grade.
    C. Handicapped students have reached their limit of possible progress by the time they reach the fourth grade.
    D. Students that received poor preparation will find a greater interest in meanings.
    E. It is difficult to readjust mental structures after they have already been set.

33. What challenge does a fourth-grade student face, according to the passage?
    A. using a smaller handwriting
    B. encountering new subject matters
    C. using numbers automatically
    D. using symbols of thought
    E. advancing more rapidly

34. The passage refers to a "differentiation among pupils." What did the author(s) mean by this phrase?
    A. A diverse grouping of students with regard to race, religion, and culture.
    B. Children are being compared to each other.
    C. Students are grouped according to their abilities.
    D. There is a wide range of student cognitive processes.
    E. Some students have stronger social abilities, while others have little social skills.

35. Automatic use of numbers and handwriting changing from large to small are examples of what?
    A. symbols of representational thought
    B. ideas themselves
    C. functions of new ways of thinking
    D. unusual intelligence
    E. poor preparation

Questions 36–40

In Burma, many years ago, the finding of a big round footmark in the soft sand at the bottom of a dry river bed was the beginning of one of the most delightful hunting experiences of my whole life. In a moment all other game was forgotten, and my little brown friend and I gave ourselves up, body and soul to the fascination of following the elephant's trail.

Leaving the watercourse we followed the tracks over a level valley through which the elephant had made a passage, covered above on both sides by tall, thick grass.

The afternoon was drawing to a close, when suddenly the silence was broken by a series of rendering crashes that grew fainter and fainter, until at length all was silent again. Something had startled the great beast, and he was gone.

—Author unknown, circa 1920

36. Where did the event in the passage take place?
    A. in Buerna
    B. near a lake
    C. in a level valley
    D. in the desert
    E. deep in the wilderness

37. What is the best title for the story?
    A. "Leaving the Watercourse"
    B. "The Elephant's Trail"
    C. "Life in Burma"
    D. "The Startled Beast"
    E. "My Little Brown Friend"

38. What are the author and "little brown friend" doing in the passage?
    A. Running away from an elephant.
    B. Hunting an elephant.
    C. Discovering fossils.
    D. Startling an elephant.
    E. All of the above.

39. To what does the term "passage" refer in the second paragraph?
    A. a small selection of text, taken from a larger text source
    B. change from one stage of life to the next
    C. a journey
    D. a trail
    E. a habitation

40. Which of the following best describes the tone of this passage?
    A. depressing
    B. exciting
    C. inquiring
    D. amusing
    E. gloomy

STOP

Go back and check your work if you have not used up all your time.

MATHEMATICS

40 Questions
Time—60 minutes

Directions: Read each question that follows, and then choose the one best answer from the five choices given.

Mark your answer on the answer sheet. Fill in the space that has the same letter as the answer you have selected.

1. Which of the following sets of numbers matches the values of P, Q, and R on the number line below?

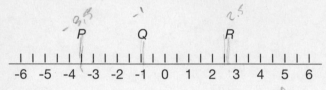

A. $-4.5, -1, 2.75$
B. $-3.5, -1, 2.25$
C. $-3.0, -1, 2.75$
D. $-3.5, -1, 2.75$
E. $-3.5, 1, 2.75$

Be careful

2. Which of the following numbers is greater than $\frac{3}{4}$?

A. 0.60
B. 0.75
C. $\frac{5}{8}$
D. 0.35
E. $\frac{5}{6}$

3. The graph shows a budget for a monthly salary.

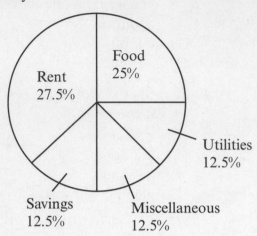

Monthly Budget

   If the monthly salary is $1400, how much money is budgeted for food?

A. $3500
B. $1050
C. $350
D. $56
E. $35

4. Perform the indicated operations:
   $-9(4) - 18 \div 3^2$

A. -6
B. -7
C. -38
D. 7
E. 38

5. Which of the following is the best estimate of $23\frac{7}{8} \div 3\frac{1}{9}$?

A. 5
B. 6
C. 7
D. 8
E. 9

6. In 1960, the tuition at a certain university was $5 per semester credit hour. In 2004, the tuition had increased to $75 per semester credit hour. What is the increase in tuition cost for a 15 semester-credit-hour course load?
   A. $70
   B. $75
   C. $1050
   D. $1125
   E. $1200

7. Which of the following expressions is NOT equivalent to the others?
   A. $4^3 \times 9^2$
   B. $2^4 \times 4 \times 3^4$
   C. 12×18
   D. $36^2 \times 4$
   E. $4 \times 4 \times 4 \times 9 \times 9$

8. Perform the indicated operations:
   $$\frac{56 \times 10^7}{7 \times 10^4}$$
   A. 8×10^{-3}
   B. 8×10^3
   C. 9×10^3
   D. 8×10^{11}
   E. 9×10^{11}

9. If 15 of the 120 customers who purchased items in a department store on a particular Saturday applied for a store credit card, what percent of the customers applied for a store credit card on that Saturday?
   A. 0.125%
   B. 8%
   C. 12.5%
   D. 15%
   E. 80%

10. If $3100 is 20% of P, the original price of a used car, then P = what?
    A. $620
    B. $2480
    C. $3720
    D. $3875
    E. $15,500

11. A student needs an average of at least 90 on four tests to earn a grade of A in a college course. The student has grades of 88, 91, and 82 on the first three tests. What is the lowest grade the student can make on the fourth test and still receive an A in the course?
    A. 90
    B. 95
    C. 96
    D. 99
    E. 100

12. Which of the following represents the number 2.374 rounded to the nearest hundredth?
    A. 2.36
    B. 2.37
    C. 2.38
    D. 2.40
    E. 2.00

13. The liquid ingredients for a recipe consist of milk and water. If the recipe calls for $1\frac{3}{4}$ cups of milk and $2\frac{1}{2}$ cups of water, how much liquid is called for in the recipe?
    A. $3\frac{1}{4}$ cups
    B. $3\frac{4}{6}$ cups
    C. $3\frac{2}{3}$ cups
    D. $3\frac{3}{4}$ cups
    E. $4\frac{1}{4}$ cups

14. Convert 5708 to scientific notation.
    A. 0.5708×10^4
    B. 5.708×10^3
    C. 57.08×10^2
    D. 5708×10^0
    E. 5.708×10^{-3}

15. If $x = -3$ and $y = -5$, then $x - y = $ what?
    A. -8
    B. -2
    C. 2
    D. 8
    E. 15

16. Which of the following statements is true?

    A. $0.5 < \dfrac{4}{9}$

    B. $1\dfrac{2}{3} > 1\dfrac{5}{8}$

    C. 5% of 60 < 10% of 20

    D. $\dfrac{3}{4} = 34\%$

    E. $-14 > -2$

17. After working four nights as a part-time waiter, a student earned $9.50, $14, $9.50, and $11.50 in tips. What was the median amount of money the student earned in tips for those four nights?
    A. $9.50
    B. $10.50
    C. $11.125
    D. $11.75
    E. $44.50

18. Of the following units, the one that would most likely be used to measure the height of a telephone pole is the:
    A. millimeter
    B. centimeter
    C. meter
    D. kilometer
    E. liter

19. The pictograph below shows the number of fans attending baseball games in the summer.

MONTH

June

July

August

Summer Attendance at Baseball Games

According to the pictograph, if 15,000 more fans attended in August than in July, how many fans does each  represent?
    A. 2,000
    B. 3,000
    C. 5,000
    D. 10,000
    E. It cannot be determined from the information given in the graph.

20. If $-2x - 5 = 3x + 15$, which of the following statements is true?
    A. $x = -20$
    B. $x = -4$
    C. $x = -2$
    D. $x = 2$
    E. $x = 4$

21. In which quadrant on a coordinate grid does the point $(-4, 3)$ lie?
    A. Quadrant I
    B. Quadrant II
    C. Quadrant III
    D. Quadrant IV
    E. It cannot be determined from the information given.

22. Which of the following rational numbers is least?
    A. 0.875
    B. $\frac{11}{12}$
    C. −4.33
    D. −0.25
    E. 0

23. Use the drawing below to answer the question that follows.

    1.   2.   3.   4.   5.

    Which two figures are *similar* but not *congruent*?
    A. 1 and 3
    B. 1 and 5
    C. 2 and 4
    D. 2 and 5
    E. 3 and 5

24. Use the following table to answer the question that follows.

x	y
1	0
4	9
5	16
7	36
9	64

    Which of the following formulas expresses the relationship between x and y in the table?
    A. $y = x - 1$
    B. $y = x^2$
    C. $y = \sqrt{x-1}$
    D. $y = 2x + 1$
    E. $y = (x - 1)^2$

25. A small jar contains a number of nickels and dimes. There are three times as many nickels as dimes in the jar. Which of the following is the best expression of the amount of money in cents if D equals the number of dimes in the jar?

    A. $D + 3D$
    B. $10D + 5D$
    C. $10D + 5(3D)$
    D. $15(4D)$
    E. $D + 5(3D)$

26. If temperatures measured in Celsius (°C) and Fahrenheit (°F) are related by the formula $F = \frac{9}{5}C + 32$, what temperature in Celsius converts to 194°F?
    A. 80°C
    B. 90°C
    C. 100°C
    D. 120°C
    E. 200°C

27. What is the greatest common factor of 20 and 30?
    A. 10
    B. 20
    C. 30
    D. 60

28. A box contains tiles numbered 1 through 50. If one tile is drawn from the box, what is the probability that the number on the tile is a prime number?
    A. $\frac{1}{15}$
    B. $\frac{3}{10}$
    C. $\frac{8}{25}$
    D. $\frac{1}{16}$
    D. $\frac{1}{3}$
    E. $3\frac{1}{3}$

29. What is the value of $5x^3 - x^2 + 20$ when $x = -2$?
    A. −984
    B. −24
    C. −16
    D. −14
    E. 56

$5(-2^3) - (-2)^2 + 20 =$

$5(-8) - (4) + 20$

$-40 - 4 + 20$

$-44 + 20 = -24$

30. On a midterm exam, a student correctly answered 87.5 percent of the 160 questions. Which computation shows the number of questions the student answered correctly?
    A. 0.0875×160
    B. 0.875×160
    C. 8.75×160
    D. 87.5×160
    E. 875×160

31. Use the diagram below to answer the question that follows.

10 m

If the perimeter of the rectangle is 64 meters, what is its length?
    A. 54 units
    B. 44 units
    C. 32 units
    D. 22 units
    E. 16 units

64
$- 20$
$\overline{44} \div 2 = 22$

32. Use the figure below to answer the question that follows.

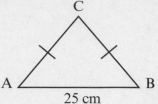

25 cm

$\triangle ABC$ is an isosceles triangle. If the perimeter of the triangle is 55 centimeters, what is the length of side AC?
    A. 5 cm
    B. 10 cm
    C. 15 cm
    D. 20 cm
    E. 30 cm

55
-25
$\overline{30}$

33. The wingspan of a particular airplane is 50 feet. A scale model of the airplane is one-tenth of the plane's actual size. Which proportion should be used to find the measure, w, of the model's wingspan?

    A. $\dfrac{w}{50} = \dfrac{10}{1}$

    B. $\dfrac{50}{w} = \dfrac{1}{10}$

    C. $\dfrac{w}{50} = \dfrac{1}{10}$

    D. $\dfrac{50}{10} = \dfrac{1}{w}$

    E. $\dfrac{50}{1} = \dfrac{w}{10}$

$\dfrac{1}{10} = \dfrac{w}{50}$

34. Determine the value of the eighth term in the sequence that begins 1, 3, 6, 10, 15:
    A. 21
    B. 28
    C. 30
    D. 36
    E. 45

21 28 36

+2 3 4 5 6 7 8

Beautiful

35. Use the diagram below to answer the question that follows.

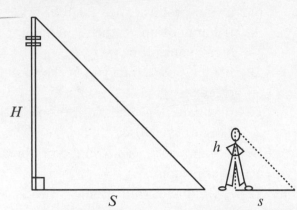

The diagram shows a method that is used to indirectly measure the height, H, of a telephone pole. A person measures his or her own height, h; the length of his or her shadow, s; and the length of the telephone pole's shadow, S. The measured values are inserted into a proportion, which is solved for H.

Calculate H, the height of the telephone pole, when $h = 5.4$ ft, $S = 20$ ft, $s = 3.6$ ft. If necessary, round your answer to the nearest whole number.

A. 13 ft
B. 20 ft
C. 30 ft
D. 97 ft
E. The height of the telephone pole cannot be determined from the information given.

$$\frac{H}{S} = \frac{h}{s} \qquad \frac{H}{20} = \frac{5.4}{3.6}$$

$$108 = 3.6$$

36. The rectangular pool shown below is surrounded by a brick walkway.

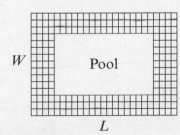

Which method could be used to find the area of the walkway?

A. Multiply the length of the pool by the width of the pool.
B. Multiply W times L, then subtract the area of the pool.
C. Find $2L$ plus $2W$.
D. Find $2L$ plus $2W$, then subtract the perimeter of the pool.
E. Find $2L$ times $2W$, then subtract the area of the pool.

37. A delivery person used the elevator to make deliveries to different floors of an office building. The list of deliveries was in alphabetical order, which the delivery person was instructed to follow as the deliveries were made. The delivery person entered the elevator, rode up 4 floors, rode down 2 floors, rode up 6 floors, and rode down 1 floor, where the last delivery was made. Which expression can be used to find the floor on which the delivery person made the last delivery?

A. $4 - 2 + 6 - 1$
B. $4 + 2 - 6 + 1$
C. $1 + 4 - 2 + 6 - 1$
D. $4 + 2 + 6 + 1$
E. $-4 + 2 - 6 - 1$

$+4 - 2 + 6 - 1$

38. In a survey of 1,000 people regarding television programs, the following information was collected:

600 people said they liked sitcoms.
250 people said they liked dramas.
150 people said they liked both sitcoms and dramas.

How many people liked neither sitcoms nor dramas?

A. 0
B. 150
C. 300
D. 700
E. 850

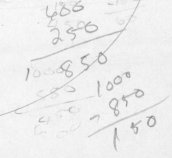

39. What conclusion logically can be drawn from the following statements?

All squares are rectangles.
All rectangles are parallelograms.
All parallelograms are quadrilaterals.

   A.   All parallelograms are rectangles.
   B.   All quadrilaterals are squares.
   C.   All quadrilaterals are rectangles.
   D.   All squares are parallelograms.
   E.   All rectangles are squares.

40. Which of the following statements is logically equivalent to the statement, "If you break your promise, then I will be upset."
   A.   If I am not upset, then you did not break your promise.
   B.   If I am upset, then you broke your promise.
   C.   If you do not break your promise, then I will not be upset.
   D.   If I am upset, then you did not break your promise.
   E.   If you break your promise, I will not be upset.

STOP
Go back and check your work if you have not used up all your time.

SECTION 1

WRITING

45 Questions
Time—30 minutes

PART A

_-3_

25 Questions
Suggested Time—10 minutes

Directions: In the sentences below, four parts are underlined and lettered. Read each sentence and decide whether any of the underlined parts contains an error. If so, on your answer sheet, mark the answer choice that is the same as the letter printed beneath the error in the sentence. If the sentence does not contain an error, mark choice E on your answer sheet. No sentence has more than one error.

1. When our family <u>goes</u> on vacation we <u>always</u> leave our two dogs with our <u>next-door</u> neighbor.
           A   B C   D

    <u>No error</u>
    E

2. <u>Each</u> of the participants had <u>their</u> own personal reasons <u>for wanting</u> to be a contestant <u>on a</u>
     A   B   C   D

    television game show. <u>No error</u>
                          E

3. A group of enthusiastic students, cheering loudly, <u>were</u> heard as the band marched <u>onto</u> the field.
                        A   B   C   D

    <u>No error</u>
    E

4. <u>Giving</u> Logan more responsibility has <u>had</u> a positive <u>affect</u> on his attitude <u>in</u> school. <u>No error</u>
     A   B   C   D   E

5. <u>From</u> a survey of parents and teachers the administration obtained data <u>that</u> <u>show</u> strong
     A   B C

    support <u>for</u> school uniforms. <u>No error</u>
          D   E

6. The camp director sent a letter <u>informing</u> parents that <u>their</u> children must bring sheets, pillows,
                                  A   B

    towels, and bathroom supplies when <u>they</u> come to camp. <u>No error</u>
        C   D   E

7. The <u>reason</u> you <u>were</u> not invited to the meeting is <u>because</u> the supervisor plans to meet later with
       A   B   C

   you <u>individually</u>. <u>No error</u>
        D   E

8. The <u>couple</u> invited <u>whoever</u> was related to the bride or groom to <u>their</u> wedding <u>reception</u>. <u>No error</u>
       A   B   C   D   E

9. <u>Unfortunately</u>, <u>every one</u> of the ten <u>student's</u> pictures <u>was</u> out of focus. <u>No error</u>
      A   B   C   D   E

10. My father's favorite poem is Alfred Lord <u>Tennyson's</u> "The Charge of the Light Brigade"<u>,</u> <u>which</u>
                                       A   B C

    he can recite <u>from</u> memory. <u>No error</u>
                  D   E

11. The <u>principle</u> justification for <u>increasing</u> the tuition rates at state institutions of <u>higher</u> education
         A   B   C

    is the large state budget <u>deficit</u>. <u>No error</u>
                               D   E

12. The policeman felt <u>badly</u> <u>about</u> having <u>to issue</u> a speeding ticket to the <u>mayor's</u> wife. <u>No error</u>
                       A   B   C   D   E

13. I <u>want</u> you to know <u>that</u> I <u>treasure</u> the warm friendship between you and I. <u>No error</u>
       A   B   C   D   E

14. <u>Them</u> talking <u>while</u> class <u>is</u> going on <u>disrupts</u> my thought processes. <u>No error</u>
       A   B   C   D   E

15. Sabrina <u>was</u> in high spirits<u>,</u> because her older brother <u>would</u> be coming home after <u>being</u> away in
           A   B   C   D

    Europe for a year. <u>No error</u>
                         E

16. Kevin's dad, who is a war veteran, has a <u>most unique</u> tattoo of <u>an</u> eagle on <u>his</u> upper arm. <u>No error</u>
        A   B   C   D   E

17. My aunt, <u>who</u> owns a bookstore<u>,</u> has <u>given</u> me hundreds of books <u>over</u> the years. <u>No error</u>
             A   B   C   D   E

18. If a person <u>wants</u> to be considered for the position, <u>you</u> must submit an application no later than
                 A   B C

    <u>5:00</u> p.m. today. <u>No error</u>
     D   E

19. My <u>children</u> had <u>too</u> many books, <u>so</u> I gave <u>them</u> as a donation to our local library. <u>No error</u>
         A   B   C   D   E

20. The test <u>it</u> was <u>really</u> hard, <u>but</u> I think I did <u>all right</u> on it. <u>No error</u>
             A   B   C   D   E

21. <u>As</u> director of the new facility, <u>you</u> will be responsible for keeping records, organizing events,
     A   B

    <u>meet</u> <u>with</u> the board members, and preparing financial statements. <u>No error</u>
     C   D   E

22. The runner <u>found</u> it <u>real</u> hard to keep on going <u>when</u> the course became muddy and <u>slick</u>. <u>No error</u>
           A   B   C   D   E

23. <u>You</u> <u>should</u> carry an umbrella today, the forecast <u>said</u> it was supposed to rain. <u>No error</u>
      A   B   C   D   E

24. <u>After</u> the city purchased the old department store building, a fundraising project was <u>begun</u> to try
      A   B   C

    <u>and</u> raise money for renovations. <u>No error</u>
     D   E

25. <u>Some</u> residents of other states are surprised when they learn <u>that</u> the state <u>capitol</u> of California is
      A   B   C

    Sacramento, <u>rather than</u> San Francisco or Los Angeles. <u>No error</u>
                   D   E

GO ON TO THE NEXT PAGE

PART B

20 Questions
Suggested Time—20 minutes

Directions: In the sentences below, part or all of the language is underlined. The five answer choices present five ways of writing the underlined part—with choice A being the same as the original. Select the answer choice that is best in terms of correctness and effectiveness.

1. The New York Comedy Club has the <u>most funniest comedians</u> I ever heard.

   A. The New York Comedy Club has the most funniest comedians I ever heard.
   B. The New York Comedy Club has the funnest comedians I ever heard.
   C. The New York Comedy Club has funnier comedians I ever heard.
   D. The New York Comedy Club has the funniest comedians I ever heard.
   E. The New York Comedy Club, has the funniest comedians I ever heard.

2. It is important to know the <u>evacuation procedures for your building in case of a fire because you cannot take the time to learn them when there is a fire.</u>

   A. It is important to know the evacuation procedures for your building in case of a fire because you cannot take the time to learn them when there is a fire.
   B. Because you cannot take time to learn them when there is a fire, it is important to know the evacuation procedures for your building.
   C. Evacuation procedures are important to know for your building because you cannot take time to learn them when there is a fire.
   D. You must know evacuation procedures for your building in case of a fire because you cannot take time to learn them when there is one.
   E. You must know evacuation procedures for your building because you cannot take time to learn them when there is a fire.

3. <u>Chocolate, which is made from the cocoa bean,</u> has been used as medicine in many civilizations.

   A. Chocolate, which is made from the cocoa bean, has been used as medicine in many civilizations.
   B. Chocolate that is made from the cocoa bean has been used as medicine in many civilizations.
   C. Chocolate is made from the cocoa bean, it has been used as medicine in many civilizations.
   D. Chocolate, made from the cocoa bean, has been used as medicine in many civilizations.
   E. Chocolate made from the cocoa bean has been used as medicine in many civilizations.

4. The Mexicans defeat the Texans at the Battle of the Alamo, but the fallen Texans were able to provide Sam Houston with two additional weeks to prepare his army.

    A. Mexicans defeat the Texans
    B. Mexicans' defeat of the Texans
    C. Mexicans' victory over the Texans
    D. Mexicans defeated the Texans
    E. Mexicans were victorious over the Texans

5. John slammed the door forcefully, which resulted in the cake falling.

    A. which resulted in the cake falling.
    B. causing the cake to fall.
    C. and the cake falling was the effect.
    D. which caused the falling of the cake.
    E. which resulted in the falling of the cake.

6. By means of organizing a financial campaign, the candidate sought to win the election with donated funds.

    A. By means of organizing a financial campaign,
    B. Through organizing a financial campaign,
    C. Through the organizing of a financial campaign,
    D. By organizing a financial campaign
    E. Through the means of organizing a financial campaign,

7. Research tells us that spatial reasoning problems occur when someone is not able to walk, but no one knows if as a cause or effect of a more significant problem with the brain.

    A. if as a cause or effect of
    B. whether this is a cause or an effect of
    C. if they are a cause or an effect of
    D. if they cause, or are they effect
    E. if they cause it, or as an effect of

8. The ancient Egyptians wrote hieroglyphics on cave walls and the tombs of pharaohs.

    A. Egyptians wrote hieroglyphics on
    B. Egyptians' wrote in hieroglyphics in
    C. Egyptians' writings were hieroglyphics on
    D. Egyptians wrote hieroglyphics in
    E. Egyptians wrote hieroglyphics, on

9. The symptom of having dried lips and headaches is probably due to the condition of dehydration.

    A. The symptom of having dried lips and headaches is probably due to the condition of dehydration.

    B. Having dried lips and headaches is probably due to the condition of dehydration.

    C. Dried lips and headaches are probably due to the condition of dehydration.

    D. Due to the condition of dehydration, one may have the symptoms of dried lips and headaches.

    E. The symptoms of having dried lips and headaches are probably due to the condition of dehydration.

10. The Florida ballots lost Al Gore the presidential election in 2000.

    A. ballots lost Al Gore the presidential election

    B. ballots caused the loss of Al Gore in the presidential election

    C. ballots caused Al Gore's loss of the presidential election

    D. ballots made Al Gore loose the presidential election

    E. ballots lost Al Gore's presidential election

11. Due to the Soviet launch of *Sputnik,* American schools began focusing on teaching their students more math and science.

    A. Due to the Soviet launch of *Sputnik,* American schools began focusing on teaching their students more math and science.

    B. As a result of the Soviet's launch of *Sputnik,* American schools began focusing on teaching their students more math and science.

    C. The Soviet's launch of *Sputnik* caused American schools to begin focusing on teaching their students more math and science.

    D. The Soviets launched *Sputnik,* and as an effect, American schools began focusing on teaching their students more math and science.

    E. When Soviets launched *Sputnik,* American schools began focusing on teaching their students more math and science as a result.

12. Because it is punishable by heavy fines and even jail time, drivers are wearing their seat belts more.

    A. Because it is punishable by heavy fines and even jail time, drivers are wearing their seat belts more.

    B. Because not wearing seat belts is punishable by heavy fines and even jail time, drivers are wearing their seat belts more.

    C. Not wearing seat belts is punishable by heavy fines and even jail time, and drivers are wearing them more.

    D. The cause is that it is punishable by heavy fines and even jail time, and the effect is that drivers are wearing their seat belts more.

    E. If it is punishable by heavy fines and even jail time, drivers will wear their seat belts more.

13. The man known <u>as being Honest Abe earned him the respect of many Americans</u> because he never lied.

   A. as being Honest Abe earned him the respect of many Americans
   B. as being Honest Abe earned the respect of many Americans
   C. as being Honest Abe earned himself the respect of many Americans
   D. as Honest Abe earned him the respect of many Americans
   E. as Honest Abe earned himself the respect of many Americans

14. <u>Irrespective of</u> the highly flammable chemicals in the back of his truck, the driver drove recklessly on the highway.

   A. Irrespective of
   B. Disregarding
   C. Not considerate of
   D. Despite
   E. Ignorant of

15. The planet Mars <u>is believed to have once had</u> life because it shows signs of prehistoric rivers.

   A. is believed to have once had
   B. is believed to once have had
   C. is believed to have
   D. it was believed to have once had
   E. that was believed to have once had

16. <u>More capable using music than words to describe how he felt, Beethoven wrote his Ninth Symphony as a deaf man.</u>

   A. More capable using music than words to describe how he felt, Beethoven wrote his Ninth Symphony as a deaf man.
   B. More capable of using music than words to describe how he felt, Beethoven wrote his Ninth Symphony as a deaf man.
   C. Beethoven wrote his Ninth Symphony as a deaf man due to his being more capable at using music instead of words to describe how he felt.
   D. As a deaf man, Beethoven wrote his Ninth Symphony as a result of his being more capable using music than words to describe how he felt.
   E. More capable of using music and not words to describe how he felt, Beethoven wrote his Ninth Symphony as a deaf man.

17. To get bluebonnets to grow, it is best to <u>soak the seeds in water overnight and then plant them in good soil and water them frequently.</u>

   A. soak the seeds in water overnight and then plant them in good soil and water them frequently.
   B. soak the seeds in water overnight, and then plant them in good soil, and water them frequently.
   C. soak the seeds in water overnight, plant them in good soil, and water them frequently.
   D. soak the seeds in water, overnight, and then plant them in good soil and water them frequently.
   E. soak the seeds in water overnight and water them frequently after planting them in good soil.

18. The edge of the mountain is a <u>hazard</u> area, so do not exceed the posted speed limit.

   A. hazard
   B. danger
   C. dangerous
   D. harmful
   E. secure

19. The climate of Cypress is somewhat <u>like Florida</u>.

   A. like Florida
   B. like Florida's
   C. as Florida
   D. as Florida's
   E. similar to Florida

20. Women never <u>have and never will be</u> respected in Afghanistan.

   A. have and never will be
   B. have and never will have been
   C. have been and never will be
   D. have been nor will be
   E. have been and will be

STOP
Go back and check your work if you have not used up all your time.

SECTION 2

ESSAY

Time—30 minutes

1 Topic

Directions: Write an essay on the topic presented on the next page. You will have thirty minutes for this portion of the test. BE SURE TO WRITE ON THE ASSIGNED TOPIC. No credit will be given for essays that are off-topic.

Write your entire essay below, keeping in mind that you'll write your essay at the actual test on the answer sheet provided.

GO ON TO THE NEXT PAGE

Recently, the controversy about whether women should be subjected to the draft has been a topic of discussion. Write an essay in which you describe your position on this issue.

You may use the space below to write notes for your essay. However, only what you write on the answer sheet will be scored.

Practice PPST Answer Sheet

READING

1. Ⓐ Ⓑ Ⓒ Ⓓ Ⓔ
2. Ⓐ Ⓑ Ⓒ Ⓓ Ⓔ
3. Ⓐ Ⓑ Ⓒ Ⓓ Ⓔ
4. Ⓐ Ⓑ Ⓒ Ⓓ Ⓔ
5. Ⓐ Ⓑ Ⓒ Ⓓ Ⓔ
6. Ⓐ Ⓑ Ⓒ Ⓓ Ⓔ
7. Ⓐ Ⓑ Ⓒ Ⓓ Ⓔ
8. Ⓐ Ⓑ Ⓒ Ⓓ Ⓔ
9. Ⓐ Ⓑ Ⓒ Ⓓ Ⓔ
10. Ⓐ Ⓑ Ⓒ Ⓓ Ⓔ
11. Ⓐ Ⓑ Ⓒ Ⓓ Ⓔ
12. Ⓐ Ⓑ Ⓒ Ⓓ Ⓔ
13. Ⓐ Ⓑ Ⓒ Ⓓ Ⓔ
14. Ⓐ Ⓑ Ⓒ Ⓓ Ⓔ
15. Ⓐ Ⓑ Ⓒ Ⓓ Ⓔ
16. Ⓐ Ⓑ Ⓒ Ⓓ Ⓔ
17. Ⓐ Ⓑ Ⓒ Ⓓ Ⓔ

18. Ⓐ Ⓑ Ⓒ Ⓓ Ⓔ
19. Ⓐ Ⓑ Ⓒ Ⓓ Ⓔ
20. Ⓐ Ⓑ Ⓒ Ⓓ Ⓔ
21. Ⓐ Ⓑ Ⓒ Ⓓ Ⓔ
22. Ⓐ Ⓑ Ⓒ Ⓓ Ⓔ
23. Ⓐ Ⓑ Ⓒ Ⓓ Ⓔ
24. Ⓐ Ⓑ Ⓒ Ⓓ Ⓔ
25. Ⓐ Ⓑ Ⓒ Ⓓ Ⓔ
26. Ⓐ Ⓑ Ⓒ Ⓓ Ⓔ
27. Ⓐ Ⓑ Ⓒ Ⓓ Ⓔ
28. Ⓐ Ⓑ Ⓒ Ⓓ Ⓔ
29. Ⓐ Ⓑ Ⓒ Ⓓ Ⓔ
30. Ⓐ Ⓑ Ⓒ Ⓓ Ⓔ
31. Ⓐ Ⓑ Ⓒ Ⓓ Ⓔ
32. Ⓐ Ⓑ Ⓒ Ⓓ Ⓔ
33. Ⓐ Ⓑ Ⓒ Ⓓ Ⓔ
34. Ⓐ Ⓑ Ⓒ Ⓓ Ⓔ
35. Ⓐ Ⓑ Ⓒ Ⓓ Ⓔ

36. Ⓐ Ⓑ Ⓒ Ⓓ Ⓔ
37. Ⓐ Ⓑ Ⓒ Ⓓ Ⓔ
38. Ⓐ Ⓑ Ⓒ Ⓓ Ⓔ
39. Ⓐ Ⓑ Ⓒ Ⓓ Ⓔ
40. Ⓐ Ⓑ Ⓒ Ⓓ Ⓔ

MATHEMATICS

1. Ⓐ Ⓑ Ⓒ Ⓓ Ⓔ
2. Ⓐ Ⓑ Ⓒ Ⓓ Ⓔ
3. Ⓐ Ⓑ Ⓒ Ⓓ Ⓔ
4. Ⓐ Ⓑ Ⓒ Ⓓ Ⓔ
5. Ⓐ Ⓑ Ⓒ Ⓓ Ⓔ
6. Ⓐ Ⓑ Ⓒ Ⓓ Ⓔ
7. Ⓐ Ⓑ Ⓒ Ⓓ Ⓔ
8. Ⓐ Ⓑ Ⓒ Ⓓ Ⓔ
9. Ⓐ Ⓑ Ⓒ Ⓓ Ⓔ
10. Ⓐ Ⓑ Ⓒ Ⓓ Ⓔ
11. Ⓐ Ⓑ Ⓒ Ⓓ Ⓔ

12. Ⓐ Ⓑ Ⓒ Ⓓ Ⓔ
13. Ⓐ Ⓑ Ⓒ Ⓓ Ⓔ
14. Ⓐ Ⓑ Ⓒ Ⓓ Ⓔ
15. Ⓐ Ⓑ Ⓒ Ⓓ Ⓔ
16. Ⓐ Ⓑ Ⓒ Ⓓ Ⓔ
17. Ⓐ Ⓑ Ⓒ Ⓓ Ⓔ
18. Ⓐ Ⓑ Ⓒ Ⓓ Ⓔ
19. Ⓐ Ⓑ Ⓒ Ⓓ Ⓔ
20. Ⓐ Ⓑ Ⓒ Ⓓ Ⓔ
21. Ⓐ Ⓑ Ⓒ Ⓓ Ⓔ
22. Ⓐ Ⓑ Ⓒ Ⓓ Ⓔ
23. Ⓐ Ⓑ Ⓒ Ⓓ Ⓔ
24. Ⓐ Ⓑ Ⓒ Ⓓ Ⓔ
25. Ⓐ Ⓑ Ⓒ Ⓓ Ⓔ
26. Ⓐ Ⓑ Ⓒ Ⓓ Ⓔ
27. Ⓐ Ⓑ Ⓒ Ⓓ Ⓔ
28. Ⓐ Ⓑ Ⓒ Ⓓ Ⓔ
29. Ⓐ Ⓑ Ⓒ Ⓓ Ⓔ
30. Ⓐ Ⓑ Ⓒ Ⓓ Ⓔ
31. Ⓐ Ⓑ Ⓒ Ⓓ Ⓔ
32. Ⓐ Ⓑ Ⓒ Ⓓ Ⓔ
33. Ⓐ Ⓑ Ⓒ Ⓓ Ⓔ
34. Ⓐ Ⓑ Ⓒ Ⓓ Ⓔ
35. Ⓐ Ⓑ Ⓒ Ⓓ Ⓔ
36. Ⓐ Ⓑ Ⓒ Ⓓ Ⓔ
37. Ⓐ Ⓑ Ⓒ Ⓓ Ⓔ
38. Ⓐ Ⓑ Ⓒ Ⓓ Ⓔ

39. Ⓐ Ⓑ Ⓒ Ⓓ Ⓔ
40. Ⓐ Ⓑ Ⓒ Ⓓ Ⓔ

WRITING

SECTION 1: PART A

1. Ⓐ Ⓑ Ⓒ Ⓓ Ⓔ
2. Ⓐ Ⓑ Ⓒ Ⓓ Ⓔ
3. Ⓐ Ⓑ Ⓒ Ⓓ Ⓔ
4. Ⓐ Ⓑ Ⓒ Ⓓ Ⓔ
5. Ⓐ Ⓑ Ⓒ Ⓓ Ⓔ
6. Ⓐ Ⓑ Ⓒ Ⓓ Ⓔ
7. Ⓐ Ⓑ Ⓒ Ⓓ Ⓔ
8. Ⓐ Ⓑ Ⓒ Ⓓ Ⓔ
9. Ⓐ Ⓑ Ⓒ Ⓓ Ⓔ
10. Ⓐ Ⓑ Ⓒ Ⓓ Ⓔ
11. Ⓐ Ⓑ Ⓒ Ⓓ Ⓔ
12. Ⓐ Ⓑ Ⓒ Ⓓ Ⓔ
13. Ⓐ Ⓑ Ⓒ Ⓓ Ⓔ
14. Ⓐ Ⓑ Ⓒ Ⓓ Ⓔ
15. Ⓐ Ⓑ Ⓒ Ⓓ Ⓔ
16. Ⓐ Ⓑ Ⓒ Ⓓ Ⓔ
17. Ⓐ Ⓑ Ⓒ Ⓓ Ⓔ
18. Ⓐ Ⓑ Ⓒ Ⓓ Ⓔ
19. Ⓐ Ⓑ Ⓒ Ⓓ Ⓔ
20. Ⓐ Ⓑ Ⓒ Ⓓ Ⓔ
21. Ⓐ Ⓑ Ⓒ Ⓓ Ⓔ
22. Ⓐ Ⓑ Ⓒ Ⓓ Ⓔ

23. Ⓐ Ⓑ Ⓒ Ⓓ Ⓔ
24. Ⓐ Ⓑ Ⓒ Ⓓ Ⓔ
25. Ⓐ Ⓑ Ⓒ Ⓓ Ⓔ

SECTION 1: PART B

1. Ⓐ Ⓑ Ⓒ Ⓓ Ⓔ
2. Ⓐ Ⓑ Ⓒ Ⓓ Ⓔ
3. Ⓐ Ⓑ Ⓒ Ⓓ Ⓔ
4. Ⓐ Ⓑ Ⓒ Ⓓ Ⓔ
5. Ⓐ Ⓑ Ⓒ Ⓓ Ⓔ
6. Ⓐ Ⓑ Ⓒ Ⓓ Ⓔ
7. Ⓐ Ⓑ Ⓒ Ⓓ Ⓔ
8. Ⓐ Ⓑ Ⓒ Ⓓ Ⓔ
9. Ⓐ Ⓑ Ⓒ Ⓓ Ⓔ
10. Ⓐ Ⓑ Ⓒ Ⓓ Ⓔ
11. Ⓐ Ⓑ Ⓒ Ⓓ Ⓔ
12. Ⓐ Ⓑ Ⓒ Ⓓ Ⓔ
13. Ⓐ Ⓑ Ⓒ Ⓓ Ⓔ
14. Ⓐ Ⓑ Ⓒ Ⓓ Ⓔ
15. Ⓐ Ⓑ Ⓒ Ⓓ Ⓔ
16. Ⓐ Ⓑ Ⓒ Ⓓ Ⓔ
17. Ⓐ Ⓑ Ⓒ Ⓓ Ⓔ
18. Ⓐ Ⓑ Ⓒ Ⓓ Ⓔ
19. Ⓐ Ⓑ Ⓒ Ⓓ Ⓔ
20. Ⓐ Ⓑ Ⓒ Ⓓ Ⓔ

SECTION 2

ESSAY

Begin your essay on this page, and continue on the next page if you need more space.

_____

_____

_____

_____

_____

_____

_____

_____

_____

_____

_____

_____

_____

_____

_____

_____

_____

_____

_____

_____

_____

_____

_____

_____

_____

Chapter 11

Answer Explanations for Practice PPST

READING

1. Choice B is the best response because it summarizes the points the selection makes about the major differences between Native American life in the New World and life in the European countries of France, England, and Spain. The other answer choices are too narrow in scope.

2. Choice E is the best response. The author's purpose is to compare the cultures of Native Americans in the New World with that of Europeans in the countries of France, England, and Spain. No argument is presented to persuade (choice A) the reader. Although the reader may find entertainment in reading about the differences in the cultures, to entertain (choice B) is clearly not the primary purpose of the selection. Also, no attempt is made to frighten (choice C) the reader or to ridicule (choice D) the cultures described.

3. Choice D is the best response. The author reports the situation in a factual manner. The author does not show a mocking, sarcastic tone (choice A); a questioning, inquiring tone (choice B); an amusing, humorous tone (choice C); or a critical, disapproving tone (choice E).

4. Choice D is the best response. In the second paragraph, the author states, " . . . the Native Americans in the Great Plains region did not live in houses; instead, their housing consisted of portable huts which were erected from poles stuck into the ground at the bottom, tied together at the top, and covered with buffalo skin." According to the selection, choices A, C, and E are customs and habits of Europeans, and choice B describes the dwellings of the Native Americans of the Southwest who lived near the Rio Grande River.

5. Choice C is the best response. Castigated and punished both mean "disciplined." Profaned carries the meaning of "treating a sacred object with irreverence." Glorified means "praised." Rewarded means "compensated" in some manner. Without having additional information, flogged, which means "beaten severely

with a rod or whip," is too strong a replacement for castigate. Punished best retains the original meaning of the sentence.

6. Choice A is the best response. The second sentence discusses how the immediate aims of high schools are not identical with those of the grammar school.

7. Choice C is the best response. Choice A is incorrect because this particular passage uses writing only as an example in a more general comparison of grammar school and high school tests. Choice B is too vague to be the purpose. Choice D is too specific and not supported directly by the passage. Choice E is not supported by the passage.

8. Choice B is the best response. Choice A is incorrect because the author believes the students need to be tested differently because the subjects are different in high school. Choice C is incorrect because the author states that writing is required on subject tests in high school. Choices D and E are not supported by any information from the passage.

9. Choice C is discussed in the passage and is the best response. The other choices are not mentioned as assumptions.

10. Choice B is the best response. Choice A is incorrect because the author never says that the tests need to be written essays. Choice C is also not directly supported by the text.

11. Choice D is the best response. The "fire o' nights" refers to a figurative night, when as old people we can sit around the fire and recollect our days. This is borne out by the remainder of the passage, which talks about the ripening of memory over time.

12. Choice B is the best response. All of the answers were compared to a person's recollections except B.

13. Choice A is correct and stated in the twelfth sentence; it is the best response.

14. Choice B is the best response. Choice A does not convey that we become confused by too many details by seeing them up close. Choices C, D, and E do not address the comparison between the mountains and a person's recollections.

15. Choice A is the best response. The third sentence of the passage discusses how the recent past is too muddled by details to be distinct. The fourth sentence discusses how the distant past becomes clearer when strained through the "hourglass" of time.

16. Choice D is the best response. Choices A and B are not recollections. Choice E is just a visual example of the same symbol as corn. Choice C is incorrect because it does not include the memory aspect of experience.

17. Choice A is the best response. Choice B is incorrect because the passage discusses how oral communication is more important than written communication.

Choices C, D, and E are incorrect because they are too specific for the main topic of the paragraph.

18. Choice A is the best response. The thirteenth sentence discusses how strength in one form of communication usually indicates strength in the other.

19. Choice C is the best response. Choices A, B, and D do not make sense in the context of the sentence. The word *slovenly* means "sloppy" or "unkempt," so *weak* (choice E) is not the best answer.

20. Choice C is the best response. Choices A, B, and E do not address the importance or influence of oral communication being greater than that of written communication. Choice D stresses the importance but not the influence of oral communication. Choice C addresses the influence of oral communication on a man's ability to have command over his language.

21. Choice C is the best response. There is not enough evidence to support either choices B or D as being the correct answer. Choices A and E do not address the cause-and-effect relationship between good oral and written communication skills.

22. Choice C is the only choice stated in the passage and is the best response.

23. Choice D is the best response. Choice A is incorrect because it is too vague to be the main idea of the passage. Choice B is incorrect because the passage is about dramatic works and uses novels as a comparison. Choice C is true; however, it is the incorrect choice because the main idea discusses how the emotion of surprise ranks the work on a lower level than the emotion of recognition. Choice E is incorrect because it is too specific to be the main idea of the passage. It is an example of the main idea (expressed in choice D).

24. Choice C is the best response. This is the best definition of *veracious*.

25. Choice C is the best response. Choices A and B are incorrect because the passage states that this is what puts the story on a lower level. Choice C is stated directly in the second sentence of the passage.

26. Choice C is the best response. Choice A is untrue because they are only alike in that particular way. Choices B and D are incorrect because the passage discusses the importance of both recognition and surprise, but it states that surprise is subordinate to recognition.

27. Choice A is the best response. Choices B, D, and E are incorrect because the passage never discusses these emotions. Choice C is incorrect because the sentence is discussing the importance of the emotion of recognition.

28. Choice C is the best response. Alliteration is defined as "the repetition of the same sounds or of the same kinds of sounds at the beginning of words or in stressed syllables." Choice A is incorrect because onomatopoeia is "the formation or use of words such as buzz or murmur that imitate the sounds associated

with the objects or actions they refer to." Choice B is incorrect because a palindrome is "a word, phrase, verse, or sentence that reads the same backward or forward." Choice D is not a literary device. Choice E is defined as "a figure of speech in which two essentially unlike things are compared."

29. Choice B is the best response. Choice A is incorrect because the passage describes the morning view. Choice C is incorrect because the passage does not describe the Golden River. Choice D is incorrect because the passage does not describe Tom's spirits. Choice E is incorrect because it does not describe the view of the mountain.

30. Choice A is the best response. The term *ruddy* means "reddish."

31. Choice A is mentioned in the third sentence and is the best response.

32. Choice A is the best response. Choice B is not mentioned or implied from the text. Choice C assumes that is the case for all handicapped fourth-graders. Choice D is untrue—those with "previous good work" will show greater interest in meanings. Choice E does not represent intelligence abilities of fourth graders.

33. Choice B is the best response. The fifth sentence states that new subject matters and mental adjustments difficult to make are often encountered. The passage does not indicate that the other answer choices are challenges for the student.

34. Choice C is the best response. Choice A is incorrect because none of these characteristics is mentioned in the passage and because they do not reflect mental structures of individuals. Choice B is untrue because it does not address on what basis the students are compared to each other. Choice D is untrue because students are grouped according to their chronological age and grade, not individual ability. Choice E is incorrect because social skills are not being discussed in the passage.

35. Choice C is the best response. Choices A, D, and E are clearly incorrect from the text. Choice B is incorrect because they are not the actual ideas; they are the new ways that children express or represent those ideas.

36. Choice C is the best response. The level valley is mentioned in the sixth line.

37. Choice B is the best response. The central theme of the passage is the hunting of the elephant. The other choices are supporting ideas.

38. Choice B is the best response. The answer is stated in the first paragraph of the passage.

39. Choice D is the best response. The elephant had made a trail with its tracks, not a journey, text, or change in stages of life.

40. Choice C is the best response. The author recounts a story in which he is seeking information.

MATHEMATICS

1. Choice D is the correct response. Start with R, the positive value, because positive values are usually easier to read on the number line. R is at 2.75. Eliminate any choice that does not include 2.75; thus choice B is eliminated. Clearly, Q is at –1, so eliminate any choice that does not include –1. Eliminate E. Now decide whether P is at –4.5 (choice A), –3 (choice C), or –3.5 (choice D). Obviously, P is not at –3, so eliminate choice C. Now as you look at the number line from left to right, P is halfway between –4 and –3. Remember, however, that you read the negative numbers starting from zero, so P is at –3.5, making choice D the correct response.

2. Choice E is the correct response. Since some of the answer choices are written as decimals, change $\frac{3}{4}$ to a decimal value:

$$3 \div 4 = 4\overline{)3.00}^{\;.75}$$

   Eliminate choices A and D since neither 0.60 nor 0.35 is greater than 0.75. Eliminate choice B because 0.75 equals $\frac{3}{4}$, equal to but not *greater than* $\frac{3}{4}$. Now compare $\frac{3}{4}$ and $\frac{5}{8}$ by writing $\frac{3}{4}$ as an equivalent fraction with denominator 8:

   $\frac{3}{4} = \frac{3 \times 2}{4 \times 2} = \frac{6}{8}$, which is greater than $\frac{5}{8}$. Eliminate choice C. Choice E must be the correct response. You can verify this by writing each fraction as an equivalent fraction having the common denominator 12:

$$\frac{3}{4} = \frac{3 \times 3}{4 \times 3} = \frac{9}{12} \text{ and } \frac{5}{6} = \frac{5 \times 2}{6 \times 2} = \frac{10}{12}. \text{ Thus, } \frac{5}{6} > \frac{3}{4} \text{ because } \frac{10}{12} > \frac{9}{12}$$

3. Choice C is the correct response. From the pie chart, you can see that 25% of the monthly salary is budgeted for food. To answer the question, you must find 25% of $1400.
   Method 1: Change 25% to a decimal fraction and multiply:
   25% of $1400 = 0.25 × $1400 = $350, choice C.
   Method 2: Set up a percent proportion and solve it:

$$\frac{25}{100} = \frac{x \text{ (``is'')}}{1400 \text{ (``of'')}}$$

   Multiply 1400 by 100 and then divide by 100:

$$\frac{1400 \times 25}{100} = \$350, \text{ choice C.}$$

   Choice B results if you solve the problem incorrectly by finding 75% of $1400. Choice D results if you solve the problem incorrectly by dividing $1400 by 25. Choice E results if you calculate incorrectly.

4. Choice C is the correct response. Follow "Please Excuse My Dear Aunt Sally."

   $-9(4) - 18 \div 3^2 =$

   $-9(4) - 18 \div 9$ There are no parentheses, so do exponentiation first;

   $-36 - 2$ Multiply and divide from left to right, next.

   $-36 - 2 = -36 + -2 = -38$ Then subtract, yielding the answer in choice C.

   Choice A results if you work the problem from left to right without following the order of operations. The other choices result if you fail to follow the order of operations and make sign mistakes as you do the computations.

5. Choice D is the correct response. $23\frac{7}{8} \div 3\frac{1}{9}$ is approximately $24 \div 3 = 8$, choice D. The other choices result if you round the mixed fractions incorrectly.

6. Choice C is the correct response. Three steps are needed to solve the problem:
   Step 1. Find the cost for a 15 semester-credit-hour (s.c.h.) course load in 1960:

   $$\frac{\$5}{\text{s.c.h.}} \times 15 \text{ s.c.h.} = \$75 \text{ in } 1960$$
   (Hint: Quantities following the word *per* should be written in the denominator of a fraction.)

   Step 2. Find the cost for a 15 semester-credit-hour (s.c.h.) course load in 2004:

   $$\frac{\$75}{\text{s.c.h.}} \times 15 \text{ s.c.h.} = \$1125 \text{ in } 2004$$

   Step 3. Find the difference in cost between the two years:
   $\$1125 - \$75 = \$1050$, choice C.

   Choice A is the difference in tuition for one semester credit hour, not 15 semester credit hours. Choice B is the tuition for 15 semester credit hours in 1960, not the difference between the two years. Choice D is the tuition for 15 semester credit hours in 2004, not the difference between the two years. Choice E is the sum of the two tuitions, not the difference.

7. Choice C is the correct response. To compare the expressions, perform all the indicated operations:
   Choice A: $4^3 \times 9^2 = 4 \times 4 \times 4 \times 9 \times 9 = 5184$
   Choice B: $2^4 \times 4 \times 3^4 = 2 \times 2 \times 2 \times 2 \times 4 \times 3 \times 3 \times 3 \times 3 = 5184$
   Choice C: $12 \times 18 = 216$
   Choice D: $36^2 \times 4 = 36 \times 36 \times 4 = 5184$
   Choice E: $4 \times 4 \times 4 \times 9 \times 9 = 5184$
   Choice C is NOT equivalent to the other choices, so it is the correct response.

8. Choice B is the correct response. Work the problem in two parts as follows:

   $$\frac{56 \times 10^7}{7 \times 10^4} = \frac{56}{7} \times \frac{10^7}{10^4} = 8 \times 10^{7-4} = 8 \times 10^3, \text{ choice B.}$$

    Choices A and D occur if you deal with the exponents incorrectly. Choice C occurs if you divide 56 by 7 incorrectly, and choice E occurs if you divide incorrectly and deal with the exponents incorrectly.

9. Choice C is the correct response. To solve the problem, you must answer the question: 15 is x % of 120?

Set up a percent proportion and solve it:

$$\frac{x}{100} = \frac{15 \text{ ("is")}}{120 \text{ ("of")}}$$

Multiply 15 by 100 and then divide by 120:

$$\frac{15 \times 100}{120} = 12.5, \text{ choice C.}$$

Choice A results if you make a decimal point mistake. The other choices occur if you fail to set up a correct proportion.

10. Choice E is the correct response. Set up a percent proportion and solve it:

$$\frac{20}{100} = \frac{1300 \text{ ("is")}}{P \text{ ("of")}}$$

Multiply 3100 by 100 and then divide by 20:

$$\frac{3100 \times 100}{20} = 15,500, \text{ choice E.}$$

The other choices occur if you fail to set up a correct proportion.

11. Choice D is the correct response. A quick way to work this problem is to check the answer choices—a good test-taking strategy for multiple-choice math tests.

Checking A: $\dfrac{\text{sum of 4 test grades}}{4} = \dfrac{88 + 91 + 82 + 90}{4} = \dfrac{351}{4} = 87.75 < 90$

Checking B: $\dfrac{\text{sum of 4 test grades}}{4} = \dfrac{88 + 91 + 82 + 95}{4} = \dfrac{356}{4} = 89 < 90$

Checking C: $\dfrac{\text{sum of 4 test grades}}{4} = \dfrac{88 + 91 + 82 + 96}{4} = \dfrac{357}{4} = 89.25 < 90$

Checking D: $\dfrac{\text{sum of 4 test grades}}{4} = \dfrac{88 + 91 + 82 + 99}{4} = \dfrac{360}{4} = 90, \text{ correct.}$

A grade of 100 (choice E) on the fourth test would also yield an A in the course (with an average of 90.25), but 100 is not the *lowest* grade that will yield an average of 90.

12. Choice B is the correct response. To round to the nearest hundredth, you look at the digit in the thousandths place. Since the digit 4 in the thousandths place is less than 5, you drop it and do not change any of the other digits. Therefore, 2.374 rounded to the nearest hundredth is 2.37, choice B. Choice A results if you make the mistake of dropping the 4 and reducing the 7 to 6. Choice C results if you mistakenly round the 7 up to 8. Choice D results if you mistakenly round to the nearest tenth, and choice E results if you mistakenly round to the nearest whole number.

13. Choice E is the correct response. You are asked to find a total, so add the two numbers in the problem. Since they are fractions, find a common denominator, write the fractions as equivalent fractions with that denominator, and then add (omitting the units until the end):

    $1\frac{3}{4}$ cups $+ 2\frac{1}{2}$ cups $= 1\frac{3}{4} + 2\frac{2}{4} = 3 + \frac{5}{4} = 3 + 1\frac{1}{4} = 4\frac{1}{4}$ cups, choice E.

    Choice A results if you fail to add the whole numbers correctly. Choice B results if you add the fractions by adding the numerators, then adding the denominators together. Choice C is equivalent to choice B because $\frac{4}{6}$ reduces to $\frac{2}{3}$, which means neither of these answer choices could be correct. Choice D results if you fail to add in the $\frac{1}{2}$ in the second fraction.

14. Choice B is the correct response. A number written in scientific notation is written as a product of two numbers: a number that is greater than or equal to 1, but less than 10, and a power of 10. Eliminate A because the first number is less than 1. Eliminate C and D because the first number is greater than 10. Now look at B and E. They are the same except B has a positive exponent on the 10 and E has a negative exponent on the 10. Multiply each out to see which one equals 5708.
    Choice B: $5.708 \times 10^3 = 5.708 \times 1000 = 5708$, correct.

    Choice E: $5.708 \times 10^{-3} = 5.708 \times \frac{1}{1000} = \frac{5.708}{1000} = 0.005708$, wrong.

15. Choice C is the correct response. Substitute into the expression, being sure to enclose the substituted value in parentheses:
    $x - y = (-3) - (-5) = -3 + 5 = 2$, choice C.

    Choices A, B, and D result if you make a sign mistake. Choice E results if you multiply instead of subtract.

16. Choice B is the correct response. Check each choice to determine the correct response:

    Choice A is false, because $0.5 = \frac{1}{2} > \frac{4}{9}$. This is clear when you find a common denominator of 18 and rewrite the fractions as equivalent fractions with denominators of 18:

    $\frac{1}{2} = \frac{9}{18}$ and $\frac{4}{9} = \frac{8}{18}$, so $\frac{1}{2}$ is not less than $\frac{4}{9}$ because $\frac{9}{18}$ is not less than $\frac{8}{18}$

Choice B is true. You can show this by finding a common denominator of 24 for the two fractions:

$$1\frac{2}{3} = 1\frac{16}{24}, \text{ and } 1\frac{5}{8} = 1\frac{15}{24}, \text{ so } 1\frac{2}{3} > 1\frac{5}{8} \text{ because } 1\frac{16}{24} > 1\frac{15}{24}$$

Checking the remaining choices, you would find:

Choice C is false because 5% of 60 = 0.05 × 60 = 3, which is not less than 10% of 20 = 2.

Choice D is false because $\frac{3}{4} = 3 \div 4 = 4\overline{)3.00}^{.75}, = 0.75 = 75\%$, not 34%.

Choice E is false, because –14 lies to the left of –2 on the number line, which means –14 < –2.

17. Choice B is the correct response. The median of an ordered set of numbers is the middle number if there is a middle number; if there is no single middle number, the median is the average of the two middle numbers. Finding the median of a set of numbers is a two-step process.

Step 1: Put the numbers in order from smallest to largest:

$9.50, $9.50, $11.50, $14.00

Step 2: Find the middle number; if there is no single middle number, average the two middle numbers:

There is no middle number. The two middle numbers are $9.50 and $11.50. Their average is $\dfrac{\$9.50 + \$11.50}{2} = \dfrac{\$21.00}{2} = \$10.50$, choice B.

Choice A is the mode, not the median. Choice C is the mean (average), not the median. Choice D is the result if you forgot to order the set of numbers before averaging the two middle numbers. Choice E is the sum of the numbers, not the median.

18. Choice C is the correct response. A telephone pole would most likely be measured in meters. A meter is about 3 inches longer than a yard. A telephone pole would measure a little over 9 meters tall. Millimeters (choice A) and centimeters (choice B) are too small. Kilometers (choice D) would be too large. Choice E is incorrect because liters are used to measure volume, not length or height.

19. Choice C is the correct response. In a pictograph, each symbol represents the same quantity. You can see that for August, there are three more baseball symbols than there are for July. Since these three baseball symbols represent a total of 15,000 fans, you must divide 15,000 by 3 to determine how many fans one baseball symbol represents:

15,000 ÷ 3 = 5,000 fans, choice C. The other choices result if you interpret the graph incorrectly.

20. Choice B is the correct response. A good strategy for this problem is to check the answer choices by substituting the value into the equation, being careful to enclose the substituted value in parentheses:

   Choice A: When you substitute –20 for x on the left side of the equation, you get $-2(-20) - 5 = 40 - 5 = 35$. When you substitute –20 for x on the right side of the equation, you get $3(-20) + 15 = -60 + 15 = -45$. Therefore, choice A is not the correct response because $35 \neq -45$.

   Choice B: When you substitute –4 for x on the left side of the equation, you get $-2(-4) - 5 = 8 - 5 = 3$. When you substitute –4 for x on the right side of the equation, you get $3(-4) + 15 = -12 + 15 = 3$. Therefore, choice B is the correct response because –4 makes the two sides of the equation equal.

   When –2 (choice C) is substituted for x, you get –1 on the left side of the equation and 9 on the right side; when 2 (choice D) is substituted for x, you get –9 on the left side of the equation and 21 on the right side; and when 4 (choice E) is substituted for x, you get –13 on the left side of the equation and 27 on the right side.

21. Choice B is the correct response. The two intersecting x and y axes divide the coordinate grid into four sections, called quadrants.

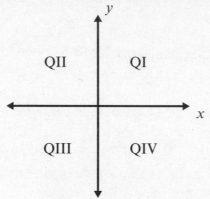

   The quadrants are numbered counterclockwise using Roman numerals, as shown in the figure above. In Quadrant I, both the x coordinate and the y coordinate are positive; in Quadrant II, the x coordinate is negative and the y coordinate is positive; in Quadrant III, both the x coordinate and the y coordinate are negative; and in Quadrant IV, the x coordinate is positive and the y coordinate is negative. The point $(-4, 3)$ has -4 as the x coordinate and 3 as the y coordinate. Since the x coordinate is negative and the y coordinate is positive, the point $(-4, 3)$ lies in Quadrant II.

22. Choice C is the correct response. Since positive numbers and zero are greater than negative numbers, you can immediately eliminate choices A, B, and E. To decide which negative number is least, pick the one that is farthest to the left on a number line:

Since –4.33 is to the left of –0.25, it is the *least* of the numbers given.

23. Choice A is the correct response. Similar geometric figures must have the same shape, but they do not have to be the same size. Congruent geometric figures must have the same shape and the same size; in other words, congruent figures are exactly the same size and shape. For the shapes given, two pairs are similar: 1 and 3 (choice A) are similar because they have the same shape, and 2 and 4 (choice C) are similar because they have the same shape. However, 2 and 4 are also congruent because they are the same size. Therefore, 1 and 3 (choice A) are the only two figures that are similar, but not congruent. Pairs 1 and 5 (choice B), 2 and 5 (choice D), and 3 and 5 (choice E) are neither similar nor congruent.

24. Choice E is the correct response. Look for a pattern from left to right. Notice that every number in the right-hand column is the square of one less than its partner in the left-hand column. Choice E expresses this relationship. None of the other choices expresses the relationship shown in the table. Another and probably easier way to work the problem is to check the answers using the values in the table. The formula must work for every pair in the table or it is not correct. Even if it works for one or more of the pairs, it is not the correct formula unless it works for all the pairs in the table.

    Choice A: The first pair, $x = 1$ and $y = 0$, works because $0 = 1 - 1$; but the next pair, $x = 4$ and $y = 9$, does not work because $9 \neq 4 - 1$. Eliminate A because you found a pair that did not work in the formula.

    Choice B: The first pair, $x = 1$ and $y = 0$, doesn't work because $0 \neq 1^2$. Eliminate B because you found a pair that did not work in the formula.

    Choice C: The first pair, $x = 1$ and $y = 0$, works because $0 = \sqrt{1 - 1} = \sqrt{0} = 0$; but the next pair, $x = 4$ and $y = 9$, does not work because $9 \neq \sqrt{4 - 1}$. Eliminate C because you found a pair that did not work in the formula.

    Choice D: The first pair doesn't work because $0 \neq 2(1) + 1$. Eliminate D because you found a pair that did not work in the formula.

    Choice E: The first pair, $x = 1$ and $y = 0$, works because $0 = (1 - 1)^2$; the second pair, $x = 4$ and $y = 9$, also works because $9 = (4 - 1)^2$; the third pair, $x = 5$ and $y = 16$, also works because $16 = (5 - 1)^2$; $x = 7$ and $y = 36$ works because $36 = (7 - 1)^2$; and $x = 9$ and $y = 64$ work because $64 = (9 - 1)^2$. Choice E is therefore correct because *all* the pairs in the table work in the formula.

25. Choice C is the correct response. You are finding the amount of money in cents, so you will have to multiply the number of dimes by 10 (to get the amount in cents) and the number of nickels by 5 (again, to get the amount in cents):

    Amount of money in cents = 10(no. of dimes) + 5(no. of nickels)

    D is the number of dimes.

    The number of nickels is three times the number of dimes = $3D$.

    Substituting, you get: Amount of money in cents = 10(no. of dimes) + 5(no. of nickels) = $10D + 5(3D)$.

    Choice A is the total number of coins and results if you forget to multiply to get the value of each coin. Choice B results if you use the same number of nickels and dimes. Choice D results if you combine terms incorrectly. Choice E results if you forget to multiply D by 10.

26. Choice B is the correct response. A good strategy for this problem is to check the answer choices.

    Choice A: Substitute 80 for C in the formula: $F = \dfrac{9}{5} \times 80 + 32 = 144 + 32 = 176°F$, wrong.

    Choice B: Substitute 90 for C in the formula: $F = \dfrac{9}{5} \times 90 + 32 = 162 + 32 = 194°F$, correct.

    Choice C gives $F = 212°F$. Choice D gives $F = 248°F$, and choice E gives $F = 382°F$, all of which are incorrect.

27. The greatest common factor is the largest factor that the two numbers have in common. Clearly, the greatest common factor should divide into each of the numbers without a remainder. Looking at the answer choices, only 10 (choice A) will divide into each of the numbers 20 and 30 without a remainder ($20 \div 10 = 2$ and $30 \div 10 = 3$). None of the other answer choices will divide into each of the two numbers without a remainder. You can also work the problem by factoring each of the two numbers into its prime factors, then selecting each factor the most number of times it appears in each number:

    $20 = 2 \times 2 \times 5$ and $30 = 3 \times 2 \times 5$; therefore, $2 \times 5 = 10$ is the greatest common factor.

28. Choice B is the correct response. This is a two-step problem.

    Step 1: Determine the prime numbers between 1 and 50: 2, 3, 5, 7, 11, 13, 17, 19, 23, 29, 31, 37, 41, 43, 47. (Remember, the number 1 is neither prime nor composite.)

    Step 2: Determine the probability of drawing a tile with one of these 15 numbers on it from the 50 tiles:

    $$\text{Probability} = \frac{15 \text{ prime tiles}}{50 \text{ (the total number of tiles)}} = \frac{3}{10}, \text{ choice B.}$$

    You should have eliminated choice E right off because you know a probability cannot be greater than 1. Choice C occurs if you mistakenly count the number 1 as a prime. Choices A and D occur if you make a mistake in step 1 and you use 15 (choice A) or 16 (choice D) as the total number of tiles, instead of 50.

29. Choice B is the correct response. First, rewrite the expression, putting parentheses in place of x: $5(\ )^3 - (\ )^2 + 20$. Put -2 inside the parentheses and evaluate, being sure to follow the order of operations—PE(MD)(AS)—and to follow the rules for multiplying signed (positive and negative) numbers:

    $5(-2)^3 - (-2)^2 + 20 = 5(-8) - 4 + 20 = -40 - 4 + 20 = -24$, choice B.

    Choice A occurs if you multiply 5 times -2 before applying the exponent. Choice C occurs if you square the $-$ sign before $(-2)^2$. Choice D occurs if you evaluate $(-2)^3$ as -6. Choice E occurs if you evaluate $(-2)^3$ as 8.

30. Choice B is the correct response. To find the number of questions the students answered correctly, you must find 87.5% of 160. Looking at the answers, you can see that means you must multiply the decimal equivalent of 87.5% by 160. To

change 87.5% to a decimal, write it as a ratio with denominator 100 (as you would if you were to actually work out the problem using a percent proportion): $87.5\% = \frac{87.5}{100} = 0.875$, choice B. (Hint: To divide by 100, move the decimal point 2 places to the left.) The other answer choices result if you change 87.5% to a decimal fraction incorrectly.

31. Choice D is the correct response. The perimeter of a rectangle is given by the formula: $P = 2L + 2W$, where L is the length of the rectangle and W is its width. You know the perimeter is 64 meters, and you can see from the figure that the width is 10 meters, so substitute these values into the formula (omitting the units as you do the calculations):

    $64 = 2L + 2W$
    $64 = 2L + 2(10)$
    $64 = 2L + 20$. Now check the answers to see which one works in this equation:

    Choice A: For $L = 54$, $64 = 2(54) + 20 = 108 + 20 = 128$, doesn't work.
    Choice B: For $L = 44$, $64 = 2(44) + 20 = 88 + 20 = 108$, doesn't work.
    Choice C: For $L = 32$, $64 = 2(32) + 20 = 64 + 20 = 84$, doesn't work.
    Choice D: For $L = 22$, $64 = 2(22) + 20 = 44 + 20 = 64$, works.
    Choice E: For $L = 16$ gives a perimeter of 52, not 64.

32. Choice C is the correct response. The perimeter of a triangle equals the sum of the lengths of its sides. For convenience, let $x =$ the length of side AC. You are told that this is an isosceles triangle. Notice the single slash marks on sides AC and BC of the triangle. This means line segments AC and BC are congruent, which in turn means these two sides have the same length.

    You know from the figure that the other side (AB) has a length of 25 centimeters. Thus, the perimeter of the triangle (omitting the units) = (length of side AB) + (length of side AC) + (length of side BC) = $25 + x + x = 25 + 2x$. You are told the perimeter is 55 centimeters, so you can write: $55 = 25 + 2x$.

    Now check the answers to see which one works in this equation.
    Choice A: For $x = 5$, $55 = 25 + 2(5) = 25 + 10 = 35$, doesn't work.
    Choice B: For $x = 10$, $55 = 25 + 2(10) = 25 + 20 = 45$, doesn't work.
    Choice C: For $x = 15$, $55 = 25 + 2(15) = 25 + 30 = 55$, works.
    Choice D: For $x = 20$, $55 = 25 + 2(20) = 25 + 40 = 65$, doesn't work.
    Choice E: For $x = 30$, $55 = 25 + 2(30) = 25 + 60 = 85$, doesn't work.

33. Choice C is the correct response. From the information given in the problem, you know that the wingspan of the model is one-tenth the size of the wingspan of the actual airplane. You can set up a proportion (omitting the units) to show the relationship as follows:

    $$\frac{\text{wingspan of model } (w)}{\text{wingspan of plane } (50)} = \frac{1}{10}, \text{ choice C.}$$

    The other answer choices result if you set up the proportion incorrectly.

34. Choice D is the correct response. You are given 5 terms of the sequence and asked to find the 8ᵗʰ term. Note that you must find the 8ᵗʰ term, not the next term in the sequence. Number the terms of the sequence, leaving blanks for the missing terms:

$$1, \ 3, \ 6, \ 10, \ 15, \ \_\_\_, \ \_\_\_, \ \_\_\_, \ \ldots$$
$$1^{st} \ 2^{nd} \ 3^{rd} \ 4^{th} \ 5^{th} \ \ 6^{th} \ \ 7^{th} \ \ \ 8^{th}$$

Look for a pattern from term to term. If you do not see a pattern right away, determine if the sequence is arithmetic by subtracting each term from the term that follows it:

$3 - 1 = 2$, difference between the 1ˢᵗ and 2ⁿᵈ terms
$6 - 3 = 3$, difference between the 2ⁿᵈ and 3ʳᵈ terms
$10 - 6 = 4$, difference between the 3ʳᵈ and 4ᵗʰ terms
$15 - 10 = 5$, difference between the 4ᵗʰ and 5ᵗʰ terms

The sequence is *not* arithmetic because you did not find the *same* difference every time, but you can see a pattern in the differences. Each time, the difference is one more than the previous difference. Therefore, you can predict that the difference between the 5ᵗʰ and 6ᵗʰ terms is 6, the difference between the 6ᵗʰ and 7ᵗʰ term is 7, and the difference between the 7ᵗʰ and 8ᵗʰ terms is 8. The 5ᵗʰ term is 15, so the 6ᵗʰ term is 21 because $21 - 15 = 6$.

$$1, \ 3, \ 6, \ 10, \ 15, \ 21, \ \_\_\_, \ \_\_\_, \ \ldots$$
$$1^{st} \ 2^{nd} \ 3^{rd} \ 4^{th} \ 5^{th} \ 6^{th} \ \ 7^{th} \ \ \ 8^{th}$$

The difference between the 6ᵗʰ term and the 7ᵗʰ term is 7, so the 7ᵗʰ term is 28 because $28 - 7 = 21$.

$$1, \ 3, \ 6, \ 10, \ 15, \ 21, \ 28, \ \_\_\_, \ \ldots$$
$$1^{st} \ 2^{nd} \ 3^{rd} \ 4^{th} \ 5^{th} \ 6^{th} \ 7^{th} \ \ \ 8^{th}$$

The difference between the 7ᵗʰ term and the 8ᵗʰ term is 8, so the 8ᵗʰ term is 36 because $36 - 28 = 8$.

$$1, \ 3, \ 6, \ 10, 15, \ 21, \ 28, \ 36, \ \ldots$$
$$1^{st} \ 2^{nd} \ 3^{rd} \ 4^{th} \ 5^{th} \ 6^{th} \ 7^{th} \ 8^{th}$$

Choice A is the 6ᵗʰ term, not the 8ᵗʰ term. Choice B is the 7ᵗʰ term, not the 8ᵗʰ term. Choice C results if you fail to identify the pattern correctly. Choice E is the 9ᵗʰ term, not the 8ᵗʰ term.

35. Choice C is the correct response. The triangle created at the telephone pole and the triangle with the person standing are two similar triangles. Similar triangles have the same shape. Their corresponding angles are equal, and corresponding sides are proportional. Looking at the triangle, you can see that side H and side h are corresponding sides, and side S and side s are corresponding sides. You can write a proportion that expresses that these corresponding sides are proportional:

$$\frac{H}{h} = \frac{S}{s}$$

Now plug in the values given for h, S, and s and solve the resulting proportion (omitting the units until the final calculation):

$$\frac{H}{5.4 \text{ ft}} = \frac{20 \text{ ft}}{3.6 \text{ ft}}$$

$$H = \frac{20 \times 5.4}{3.6 \text{ ft}} = \frac{108}{3.6} = 30 \text{ feet}$$

The other answer choices result if you set up the proportion incorrectly.

36. Choice B is the correct response. From the figure, you can see that the larger rectangular region consists of the walkway plus the pool; therefore, the area of the walkway is equal to the area of the larger rectangular region minus the area of the pool. The formula for the area of a rectangle is $A = L \times W$. The larger rectangular region has width W and length L, so you can find its area by multiplying L times W. Thus, the area of the walkway = L times W minus the area of the pool, which is the same as choice B. Choice A gives the area of the pool, not the area of the walkway. Choice C gives the perimeter of the larger rectangular region. Choice D gives the difference in the perimeter of the larger rectangular region and the pool perimeter. Choice E uses the wrong formula for the area of the larger rectangular region.

37. Choice A is the correct response. You can use signed numbers to track the delivery person, with positive numbers indicating "up" and negative numbers indicating "down" in the elevator. The path is as follows:

4 up, 2 down, 6 up, 1 down = $4 + (-2) + 6 + (-1) = 4 - 2 + 6 - 1$, choice A. Choices B, D, and E result if you are inconsistent in assigning positive to "up" and negative to "down," and choice C results if you incorrectly add an additional 1.

38. Choice C is the correct response. You can draw a Venn diagram to illustrate the survey results:

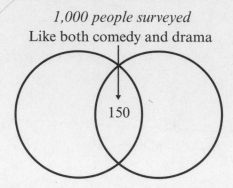

1,000 people surveyed
Like both comedy and drama

150

From the Venn diagram, you can determine that 600 – 150 = 450 people like sitcoms only and 250 – 150 = 100 people like dramas only.

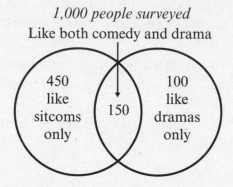

1,000 people surveyed
Like both comedy and drama

450 like sitcoms only

150

100 like dramas only

Now the Venn diagram shows that 450 + 100 + 150 = 700 people who like sitcoms or dramas or both, leaving 1000 – 700 = 300 people who like neither. Choice A results if you incorrectly add 600 + 250 + 150 = 1000 to determine how many people like sitcoms or dramas or both. This is a mistake because you are counting the 150 people that like both sitcoms and dramas three times, instead of once. Choice B results if you count the 150 people that like both sitcoms and dramas two times, instead of once. Choice D results if you fail to subtract 300 from 1,000. Choice E results if you try to find the answer by subtracting 150 from 1,000.

39. Choice D is the correct response. You can draw a Venn diagram to illustrate the problem:

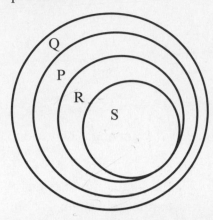

The smallest circle, circle S, is the circle containing all squares. That circle is completely contained in circle R, the circle containing all rectangles, because the first statement says, "All squares are rectangles." Circle R is completely contained in circle P, the circle containing all parallelograms, because the second statement says, "All rectangles are parallelograms." Circle P is completely contained in circle Q, the circle containing all quadrilaterals, because the third statement says, "All parallelograms are quadrilaterals." Now check the answer choices to see which logically can be concluded from the Venn diagram:

Choice A: The statement "All parallelograms are rectangles" is not a logical conclusion because the P circle is not completely contained in the R circle.

Choice B: The statement "All quadrilaterals are squares" is not a logical conclusion because the Q circle is not completely contained in the S circle.

Choice C: The statement "All quadrilaterals are rectangles" is not a logical conclusion because the Q circle is not completely contained in the R circle.

Choice D: The statement "all squares are parallelograms" is a logical conclusion because the S circle is completely contained in the P circle.

Choice E: The statement "All rectangles are squares" is not a logical conclusion because the R circle is not completely contained in the S circle.

40. Choice A is the correct response. The statement "If you break your promise, then I will be upset" has the form *if p, then q*, where *p* = "you break your promise" and *q* = "I will be upset." The form *if p, then q* is called a conditional statement and is used frequently in reasoning. Logically, the statement that is equivalent to *if p, then q* is the statement called its contrapositive: *If not q, then not p.* Look at the answer choices. You want to find one where the part after the word "if" is "I will *not* be upset" and the part after the word "then" is "you did *not* break your promise." Choice A comes closest to this. It makes sense, too. Knowing that I didn't get upset does imply that you did not break your promise. You can check the other choices to convince yourself that they are not logically equivalent to the original statement:

Choice B: Not logically equivalent because I could get upset for other reasons besides that you broke your promise.

Choice C: Not logically equivalent because not breaking your promise is no guarantee that I won't get upset since there may be other things that upset me.

Choice D: Not logically equivalent because this statement contradicts the original statement.

Choice E: Not logically equivalent because this statement contradicts the original statement.

SECTION 1

WRITING

PART A

1. Choice B is the correct response. A comma is needed following the introductory subordinate clause.

2. Choice B is the correct response. The word *Each* is the singular antecedent of the pronoun at B. Do not use the plural pronoun *their* to refer to a singular noun.

3. Choice B is the correct response. A collective noun like *group, committee, family,* or *team* is singular when the members of the collection are acting together. The "group of enthusiastic students" in the sentence is being heard as a group, so the noun *group* is singular. The singular subject group requires a singular verb. Change *were* at B to *was* to make the sentence grammatically correct.

4. Choice C is the correct response. The word *affect* is a verb. Replace *affect* with *effect* to make the sentence grammatically correct.

5. Choice E is the correct response. This sentence is correct as written. (The plural verb *show* at C is correct because the word *data* is a plural noun.)

6. Choice C is the correct response. No comma is necessary after the word *and.* Delete the comma at C to correct the error.

7. Choice C is the correct response. The sentence contains a redundant construction because the word *because* means "for the reason that." Change *because* to *that* to make the sentence grammatically correct.

8. Choice E is the correct response. This sentence is correct as written. (The word *whoever* at B is correct because it is the subject of the verb *was related.*)

9. Choice C is the correct response. To form the possessive of a plural noun ending in *s,* put an apostrophe after the *s.* Change *student's* to *students'* to make the sentence grammatically correct.

10. Choice B is the correct response. The comma should be placed inside the quotation marks, not outside.

11. Choice A is the correct response. The word at A should be an adjective. The word *principle* is a noun. Change *principle* to *principal* to make the sentence grammatically correct.

12. Choice A is the correct response. In this sentence, the word following the verb *felt* modifies the subject (a noun). The word *badly* is an adverb. It should not be used to modify a noun. The adjective *bad* should be used instead. Replace the word *badly* with *bad* to make the sentence grammatically correct.

13. Choice D is the correct response. The word *between* is a preposition. The object of a preposition should be in the objective case. Change *I* to *me* to make the sentence grammatically correct.

14. Choice A is the correct response. Gerunds take pronouns in the possessive case. The word *Them* should be changed to *Their*.

15. Choice B is the correct response. No comma is needed before the subordinate clause.

16. Choice B is the correct response. The adjective *unique* is absolute in its meaning and thus does not have degrees of comparison. Something is either unique or it isn't. Replace *most unique* with *unique* to make the sentence grammatically correct.

17. Choice E is the correct response. This sentence is correct as written.

18. Choice B is the correct response. The pronoun *you* at B does not agree with its antecedent, *person*.

19. Choice D is the correct response. Does *them* refer to *children* or *books*? Change *them* at D to *the books* to avoid ambiguity.

20. Choice A is the correct response. Delete the word *it* to make the sentence grammatically correct.

21. Choice C is the correct response. To make the sentence grammatically correct, change *meet* to *meeting* so that the construction is parallel, with all verbs in the same tense: *keeping, meeting,* and *preparing.*

22. Choice B is the correct response. The word at B should be an adverb. The word *real* is an adjective. Replace *real* with an adverb like *really* or *very.*

23. Choice C is the correct response. This sentence is an example of a comma splice, where two independent clauses are joined by a comma without a coordinating conjunction. It can be made grammatically correct by substituting a semicolon for the comma at C.

24. Choice D is the correct response. Changing *and* to *to* makes the sentence grammatically correct.

25. Choice C is the correct response. The word *capitol* refers to a building, not to a city. Change *capitol* to *capital* to make the sentence grammatically correct.

PART B

1. Choice D is the best response. Use either the suffixes *er* and *est* or the words *more* and *most* to form the comparative and superlative degrees of adverbs and adjectives. This sentence contains a double comparison because it states the comparison twice.

2. Choice B is the best response. A complex sentence consists of one independent clause and one or more subordinate clauses. Because it is long, this sentence is more correctly written when the subordinate clause, introduced by *because,* comes before the independent clause.

3. Choice A is the best response. A comma should be used to set off parenthetical expressions that add information that is not essential to the meaning of the sentence.

4. Choice D is the best response. The past tense of the verb is needed in this sentence.

5. Choice B is the best response. Choice B is less wordy and more precise in this complex sentence.

6. Choice B is the best response. In choice B, *Through* is used to introduce the subordinate clause.

7. Choice B is the best response. The word *whether* should be used when expressing alternatives.

8. Choice A is the best response. Hieroglyphics is a noun in this sentence meaning "a written language composed of pictures and symbols." These symbols were written on, not in, cave walls.

9. Choice E is the best response. Choice E has agreement between the subject and verb.

10. Choice C is the best response. The ballots didn't lose Al Gore the election. It was the cause of the loss. Choice C indicates that it was Al Gore's loss, not the loss of Al Gore as indicated in choice B.

11. Choice B is the best response. Introducing this sentence with a subordinate clause is the correct response.

12. Choice B is the best response. The second clause of the original sentence contains no antecedent for it. B corrects this mistake and most effectively expresses what is presented in the original sentence in comparison to the other choices.

13. Choice E is the best response. Choice E is free from logic, structure, and grammar problems.

14. Choice D is the best response as it is the response with the best word usage.

15. Choice B is the best response. This answer contains two auxiliary verbs plus the main verb. Choice B indicates that at some time earlier, people believed there was life on Mars.

16. Choice B is the best response. Choice C is a run-on sentence. Choices A and D incorrectly exclude a preposition between *capable* and *using.* Choice E would be more properly written using *instead.*

17. Choice C is the best response. Commas should be used to separate three or more phrases in a series.

18. Choice C is the best response. The use of the adjective *dangerous* clearly describes the situation in the sentence.

19. Choice B is the best response. *Like* indicates resemblance. Choice B is correct with its use of the possessive form of the word *Florida*.

20. Choice D is the best response. It completes the past verb tense and contrasts the situation to be expected in the future.

SECTION 2

ESSAY

A Well-Written Sample Response

Living in the twenty-first century, we assume that women and men are treated equally in almost all ways. When it comes to fighting and dying for our country, this is not true. Our young men between the ages of 18 and 25 are required by law to register with selective service. One might say that this is their passage into manhood. They are good sons and loyal Americans.

On the other hand, young women are free to choose whether they go into the military or not. They have a choice to go to war or stay at home. We proudly send our sons to war while we keep our daughters safely tucked away on the home front. Where, then, is the equality that women have asked for over the years? Is it not right that at the age of 18 our daughters should nobly step forward and sign up for selective service, too?

Most women are proud of their American heritage. Many already show their loyalty to our country by serving in the military. They have made great strides against being treated as second-class citizens. By not being eligible for the draft, as are their male counterparts, women are being discriminated against—and so are the men who are forced to register and serve if called to duty. Furthermore, being exempt from the draft does not benefit women's causes. This practice brings to mind the stereotype that women are the "weaker sex" and need preferential treatment.

Clearly, we should all support the registering of all Americans who are of eligible age for selective service, including women. Women have fought injustices for generations. They deserve to be treated as equals.

ESSAY CHECKLIST
My essay:
- ✓ Is well-organized and coherent
- ✓ Has key ideas clearly explained and illustrated
- ✓ Has varied sentence structure
- ✓ Shows command of the language
- ✓ Follows rules of standard English

Part 5

PLT

Chapter 12

Principles of Learning and Teaching Diagnostic Test

Two Case Histories and Constructed Response Questions

Case History 1—Ms. Almira

Directions: The following case history is accompanied by two short answer questions. You should allow yourself approximately twenty minutes to read the case history and create a constructed response for both questions. The sample questions that follow illustrate the kinds of questions on the test. They are not, however, representative of the entire scope of the test in terms of content or difficulty. Answers with explanations and a general scoring guide follow the questions.

Scenario

Ms. Almira is a seventh grade social studies teacher in an urban middle school. As a part of each unit in her U.S. history course, Ms. Almira tries to incorporate one or more lessons on local history. She is currently teaching a unit on the Great Depression and has made arrangements through the local senior center for students in her class to interview some local residents who lived through that period.

Document 1: Interview Project Assignment

Students will work in pairs on the interview project. In preparing for the interviews, Ms. Almira explains,

"The primary purpose of the interviews is to find out how people were *personally* affected by the Great Depression, not to find out specific facts or statistics about the Depression." She asks students to discuss the kinds of questions that are most appropriate to the primary purpose of the interviews and formulate a list of interview questions.

At the conclusion of the discussion, Ms. Almira says to the class, "The list of interview questions we have formulated is a good starting point, and you should try to stick to it because the more similar the questions are from interview to interview, the easier it will be for us to compare and contrast different interviewees' responses when the interviews are over. However, I would encourage everyone to remain flexible because additional questions that are worth pursuing may come up during the course of the interviews."

Document 2: Two Entries from Ms. Almira's Teacher Reflection Journal

March 23rd:

WOW! The interview process went very smoothly. I think the students feel that they have made new friends with the people they interviewed. Many of them expressed an interest in continuing this dialogue with the members of the senior center.

I plan to invite the director of the senior center to the school to give a talk to my students about how the senior center works and what it does for people in the community. I hope we can explore ways we might help each other.

March 27th:

Ms. Murray's talk was excellent. I can't get over how excited the students are about getting involved with the senior citizens. We have agreed to set up a partnership between the class and the senior center. The students are going to make the arrangements for a partnership start-up meeting to be held the next week at the senior center.

Document 3: Minutes from Partnership Meeting

April 2nd:

The partnership start-up meeting of students and senior citizens was called to order at 1:30 P.M. by Director Murray. Ms. Murray asked students to first meet with residents for an informal half-hour "social." After the informal meeting, Ms. Murray provided lists for interested students to sign up to provide a specific volunteer service. Students met enthusiastically with the senior citizens and developed new lists of tasks to share with one another. Some of the services that the students suggested included reading aloud to residents or visiting and talking with a resident for an hour or two. The residents offered the students tutoring in a variety of school subjects and teaching a range of skills (e.g., quilt making, carpentry). The meeting was adjourned promptly at 3:00 P.M.

Document 4: A Phone Conversation with Ms. Almira

School Newspaper Editor: Hi, Ms. Almira. We recently heard about your class partnership with the residents of the senior center, and we would like you to write an article for the school newspaper about how to plan partnership activities.

Ms. Almira: I would be delighted. But I have a question. Is it all right if I ask my students to serve as co-authors? They could develop articles about their individual partnerships.

School Newspaper Editor: Absolutely, I don't see why not. I think we should encourage other members of the school community to become involved in this partnership. In fact, I think this whole effort could grow to include other classes and teachers as well as other individuals in the community.

Ms. Almira: Great! Thank you for calling me. I will get started on the first story right away!

The following two questions address **Case History 1—*Ms. Almira***. Use the information presented in the case history to analyze and answer the following questions. Base your answers on your understanding of basic principles of teaching and learning. Read the question carefully and make sure to answer all parts of the question. Write your constructed response answers on the lined pages indicated on the pages that follow.

QUESTION 1
Review the initial planning and early implementation phase of the interview research project. Describe two activities that Ms. Almira could have planned and introduced at the beginning of the project to ensure the likelihood of student success on the interviews. Base your response on principles of communication, motivation theory, and planning instruction.

QUESTION 2
Review the minutes from the first partnership meeting (Document 3) and the conversation with the local news editor (Document 4). In addition to publicizing the partnership through the local newspaper, describe two ways in which Ms. Almira could strengthen student involvement and extend the activity of the partnership within the school and the community. Base your response on principles of motivation, human development, and behavior.

Principles of Learning and Teaching Test

Write your response to Question 1 here.

Principles of Learning and Teaching Test
Write your response to Question 2 here.

_____

_____

_____

_____

_____

_____

_____

_____

_____

_____

_____

_____

_____

_____

_____

_____

_____

_____

_____

_____

_____

_____

_____

Case History 2—Carl

Directions: The following case history is accompanied by two short answer questions. You should allow yourself approximately twenty minutes to read the case history and create a constructed response for both questions.

Scenario

Carl is a thirteen-year-old boy in Mr. Garrett's eighth grade science class. Carl is an only child who lives with his mother. She works two jobs and is not at home in the evenings. Carl prefers to work alone and is having difficulty working in cooperative groups. Mr. Garrett designs the following activity to provide Carl with the opportunity to work in pairs on the upcoming research project.

Document 1: Research Assignment

To help students get started on their research, Mr. Garrett distributes the following instructions and introduces the activity, called "I Say, You Say." After students have chosen partners and selected topics for their collaborative research projects, students begin to search and select texts for the activity.

"I Say, You Say"

Step 1: Using the science library in the classroom, pairs of students will choose two different texts that include information on the research topic they have selected.

Step 2: For five minutes, partners silently read their own texts.

Step 3: Students take turns commenting briefly to their partners about what they have just read. These comments may be open-ended and take any form (such as paraphrases, observations, questions, comparisons, or predictions).

Step 4: When both partners have commented, they repeat steps 2 and 3 several times.

Document 2: Observation Conversation between Carl and Mr. Garrett

Soon after the activity begins, Mr. Garrett notices that Carl appears restless and anxious during the initial silent reading period and is glancing repeatedly in his direction. Ms. Garrett quietly asks Carl if he has any questions. He nods and opens the following conversation.

Carl: I don't get this. It doesn't make any sense.

Mr. Garrett: What doesn't make any sense?

Carl: This reading for five minutes thing. It's so stupid.

Mr. Garrett: Sounds like you're pretty frustrated about this. Would you like to talk a little about how the activity is set up and why we're doing it this way?

Carl: Well, I get that it's supposed to help us understand the stuff we're reading, and I know I'm supposed to read for five minutes, and then say something. But I can't read much in five minutes, and I'm not going to have anything good to say afterward.

Mr. Garrett: Sounds to me like you know exactly what to do. Don't worry—I'm sure you'll do just fine.

Document 3: Conversation with Colleague, Ms. Washington

Later that afternoon Mr. Garrett reflects on his response to Carl about the "I Say, You Say" activity. He decides to discuss the activity with a colleague, Ms. Washington, to find out other ways he might address Carl's anxiety. Ms. Washington suggests that he explain to Carl that the students can read at their own pace during the silent reading phase and their responses will not be judged as "good" or "bad." Mr. Garrett decides to approach Carl the next day and talk with him further.

Document 4: Entry from Mr. Garrett's Reflection Log, the Following Week

I think Ms. Washington's ideas last week about the "I Say, You Say" activity were right. I talked with Carl about not worrying about his reading pace and he seemed to lighten up. Today he worked with another student who was having difficulty with the chapter in the textbook. I have noticed that he does not seem as restless and fidgety when working in pairs. Perhaps this activity will help Carl become more comfortable when working with other students. I think I will try to vary the activity and use it in other ways since Carl is showing such progress.

QUESTION 3

Explain two strengths in Mr. Garrett's instructional approach in this lesson. Base your response on principles of learning theory, instructional design, and communication.

QUESTION 4

Review Mr. Garrett's conversations with Carl (Document 2) and the colleague, Ms. Washington. Explain two additional ways that Mr. Garrett might modify the assignment further to better meet the needs of Carl and other students. Base your response on principles of learning theory, human development, and instructional design.

Principles of Learning and Teaching Test

Write your response to Question 3 here.

_____

_____

_____

_____

_____

_____

_____

_____

_____

_____

_____

_____

_____

_____

_____

_____

_____

_____

_____

_____

_____

_____

_____

_____

Principles of Learning and Teaching Test

Write your response to Question 4 here.

_____

_____

_____

_____

_____

_____

_____

_____

_____

_____

_____

_____

_____

_____

_____

_____

_____

_____

_____

_____

_____

_____

_____

Principles of Learning and Teaching Diagnostic Test
Practice Multiple-Choice Questions Answer Sheet

1. Ⓐ Ⓑ Ⓒ Ⓓ Ⓔ   9. Ⓐ Ⓑ Ⓒ Ⓓ Ⓔ   17. Ⓐ Ⓑ Ⓒ Ⓓ Ⓔ

2. Ⓐ Ⓑ Ⓒ Ⓓ Ⓔ   10. Ⓐ Ⓑ Ⓒ Ⓓ Ⓔ   18. Ⓐ Ⓑ Ⓒ Ⓓ Ⓔ

3. Ⓐ Ⓑ Ⓒ Ⓓ Ⓔ   11. Ⓐ Ⓑ Ⓒ Ⓓ Ⓔ   19. Ⓐ Ⓑ Ⓒ Ⓓ Ⓔ

4. Ⓐ Ⓑ Ⓒ Ⓓ Ⓔ   12. Ⓐ Ⓑ Ⓒ Ⓓ Ⓔ   20. Ⓐ Ⓑ Ⓒ Ⓓ Ⓔ

5. Ⓐ Ⓑ Ⓒ Ⓓ Ⓔ   13. Ⓐ Ⓑ Ⓒ Ⓓ Ⓔ   21. Ⓐ Ⓑ Ⓒ Ⓓ Ⓔ

6. Ⓐ Ⓑ Ⓒ Ⓓ Ⓔ   14. Ⓐ Ⓑ Ⓒ Ⓓ Ⓔ   22. Ⓐ Ⓑ Ⓒ Ⓓ Ⓔ

7. Ⓐ Ⓑ Ⓒ Ⓓ Ⓔ   15. Ⓐ Ⓑ Ⓒ Ⓓ Ⓔ   23. Ⓐ Ⓑ Ⓒ Ⓓ Ⓔ

8. Ⓐ Ⓑ Ⓒ Ⓓ Ⓔ   16. Ⓐ Ⓑ Ⓒ Ⓓ Ⓔ   24. Ⓐ Ⓑ Ⓒ Ⓓ Ⓔ

Principles of Learning and Teaching Diagnostic Test

Practice Multiple-Choice Questions

24 Multiple-Choice Questions
Time: 25 minutes

Suggested Approach: Read the stimulus first.

Use the following information to answer the question that follows.

Ms. Hadley is a ninth grade science teacher. At the start of the school year, Ms. Hadley administers a pretest to each of her classes. The test consists of questions related to everyday experience.

Now you are prepared with information about the context for the first question. Read the question carefully and critically. Think about the question being asked. Eliminate any wrong answers and select the answer choice that best answers the question. Mark the correct answer choice on your answer sheet.

Question 1 assesses the INTASC Standard Principle 7: *The teacher plans instruction based upon knowledge of subject matter, students, the community, and curriculum goals.*

1. The purpose of the pretest is most likely to help Ms. Hadley design appropriate instruction by:
   A. furnishing her with a basis for grouping students by gender and ethnicity.
   B. providing her with information about what students already know.
   C. helping her identify social biases among students.
   D. helping her rank students based on their achievement levels.

Now you are ready to answer two questions associated with the next stimulus.

Use the following information to answer the two questions that follow.

Ms. Hadley includes the following question in the pretest: "If you simultaneously drop a one-pound weight and a ten-pound weight, which one will hit the floor first?" Students are asked to state reasons for their answers to each question. When sharing responses, the students become very interested and demand to know the correct answer. Ms. Hadley replies, "Well, as a matter of fact, the weights would hit the floor at the same time." She continues the discussion by challenging the students to determine why this is true.

Question 2 assesses the INTASC Standard Principle 5: *The teacher uses an understanding of individual and group motivation and behavior to create a learning environment that encourages positive social interaction, active engagement in learning, and self-motivation.*

2. Ms. Hadley's approach to the inquiry question will most likely promote positive student attitudes by:
   A. enhancing students' confidence in their ability to learn successfully.
   B. reinforcing a sense of the uncertainty of all knowledge.
   C. correcting students' opinions about what they are learning.
   D. teaching students how to apply their knowledge appropriately.

Question 3 assesses the INTASC Standard Principle 6: *The teacher uses knowledge of effective verbal, nonverbal, and media communication techniques to foster active inquiry, collaboration, and supportive interaction in the classroom.*

3. When Ms. Hadley asks the students to explain their reasoning behind their predictions she is using a technique that allows students to:
   A. develop perseverance in critical thinking skills.
   B. encourage them to compromise on disputed issues.
   C. help them take greater responsibility for their learning.
   D. motivate them to record their observations more carefully.

Use the following information to answer the following question.

Ms. Hadley organizes her physics course in terms of content units. She introduces every new unit with a number of hands-on activities that involve a variety of different roles and responsibilities to be distributed among individual team members.

The activities are designed to familiarize students with key concepts and principles that will be explored during the unit. Ms. Hadley groups students in teams of four that will work together on all the hands-on activities throughout the course.

Question 4 assesses the INTASC Standard Principle 3: *The teacher understands how students differ in their approaches to learning and creates instructional opportunities that are adapted to diverse learners.*

4. Which of the following factors does Ms. Hadley need to consider first when making the student assignments on the activity teams?
   A. Include students with a range of academic strengths.
   B. Include students from diverse cultural backgrounds.
   C. Include students who work well with each other outside school.
   D. Include equal or representative numbers of male and female students.

Question 5 assesses the INTASC Standard Principle 5: *The teacher uses an understanding of individual and group motivation and behavior to create a learning environment that encourages positive social interaction, active engagement in learning, and self-motivation.*

5. Mr. Coulter, a sixth grade math teacher, wants to create transitions during instruction by dividing long blocks of time into shorter blocks. Which of the following represents Mr. Coulter's understanding of adolescent growth and how to design instruction that is developmentally appropriate for middle school students?

A. Adolescents need to set aside a part of their daily schedule for self-evaluation of their learning.

B. Adolescents' physical and emotional development may make it difficult for them to sustain attention.

C. Variety in instructional routine will lessen adolescent students' resistance to being guided by adult authority figures.

D. Briefer intervals of instruction foster adolescent learners' class participation.

Question 6 assesses the INTASC Standard Principle 4: *The teacher understands and uses a variety of instructional strategies to encourage students' development of critical thinking, problem-solving, and performance skills.*

6. At times, Mr. Coulter uses the direct instruction lesson cycle for teaching math concepts and skills. Which of the following strategies offers Mr. Coulter the best use of guided practice during this instructional block during the direct-instruction segment?

A. Connect students' prior knowledge with new concepts and skills.

B. Demonstrate new concepts and skills.

C. Provide students opportunity to apply new concepts and skills.

D. Review concepts and skills previously covered.

Question 7 assesses the INTASC Standard Principle 3: *The teacher understands how students differ in their approaches to learning and creates instructional opportunities that are adapted to diverse learners.*

7. Ms. Smith, a third grade teacher, engages her students in class discussions before facilitating learning activities that involve first-hand experience. Which of the following tenets of classroom management theory supports this practice?

A. Model respect for a variety of divergent points of view.

B. Exhibit a skeptical attitude toward most opinions.

C. Monitor the discussion so that it conforms to the lesson plan.

D. Establish authority to control behavior in the classroom.

Question 8 assesses the INTASC Standard Principle 4: *The teacher understands and uses a variety of instructional strategies to encourage students' development of critical thinking, problem-solving, and performance skills.*

8. Having students journal in response to metacognitive prompts is most likely to benefit students by helping them develop:

A. the communicative skills needed to write clearly and effectively.

B. the self-monitoring skills needed for independent learning.

C. the organizational skills needed to finish their work on schedule.

D. the interpersonal skills needed for cooperative learning.

Use the following information to answer the question that follows.

Susan Donahue is a ninth grade English teacher. Membership in PTA and parent volunteers have dwindled this year, and some teachers have reported difficulty in getting parents and guardians to come in for parent/teacher conferences.

Raising her concern at a faculty meeting, Ms. Donahue suggests that a school-wide effort is needed to motivate parents and guardians to become more involved in the school. The faculty approves of her suggestion and appoints a special faculty task force on family outreach that Ms. Donahue will coordinate.

The task force sets three goals to accomplish during the next school year:

Increase the outreach and involvement of parents and guardians in class and school activities.

Conduct a survey among the faculty and students to determine how teachers are currently communicating with parents and guardians and ask for suggestions.

Collect and summarize faculty recommendations for increasing family involvement now to discover how teachers communicate with parents and guardians at the beginning and throughout the school year.

Question 9 assesses the INTASC Standard Principle 5: *The teacher uses an understanding of individual and group motivation and behavior to create a learning environment that encourages positive social interaction, active engagement in learning, and self-motivation.*

9. The task force considers ways to involve students in encouraging parents and guardians to take a more active role in the school. Which of the following strategies has the best potential to involve students in this role?
   A. Teachers help students draft a list of classroom/school tasks and invite parents and guardians to volunteer.
   B. Students work together to design a contract for parents and guardians to sign to show their commitment and intent to participate in school activities.
   C. Teachers meet individually with students to suggest ways they can encourage their parents/guardians to be more involved in the school.
   D. Students participate in preparing a monthly calendar of class and school activities to which parents and guardians are invited.

Use the following information to answer the question that follows.

During a task force meeting, Ms. Donahue points out that although the ethnic and cultural diversity of the student body has broadened substantially over the past few years, this diversity is rarely represented in school activities involving students' families.

Question 10 assesses the INTASC Standard Principle 10: *The teacher fosters relationships with school colleagues, parents, and agencies in the larger community to support students' learning and well-being.*

10. Which of the following actions should the faculty consider first in order to encourage all families to become more involved in the school?
    A. Host a schoolwide, multicultural festival organized by the teaching staff.
    B. Recruit interested students to serve as outreach representatives who contact families.
    C. Enrich the curriculum through multicultural activities.
    D. Conduct a needs assessment among parents and guardians to determine their interest and need for school involvement.

Question 11 assesses the INTASC Standard Principle 3: *The teacher understands how students differ in their approaches to learning and creates instructional opportunities that are adapted to diverse learners.*

11. Ms. Donahue and the task force consider various professional development options to help teachers interact effectively with the parents or guardians of students whose home language is other than English. Which of the following options would likely be most helpful to teachers in this regard?
    A. a workshop on cultural factors that can affect communication between teachers and parents/guardians
    B. a minicourse focusing on commonly used phrases in the home languages of students enrolled in the school
    C. a seminar on efficient techniques for directing teacher conferences with parents/guardians
    D. a presentation on the history of discrimination in the United States and the negative consequences of cultural stereotyping

Question 12 assesses the INTASC Standard Principle 3: *The teacher understands how students differ in their approaches to learning and creates instructional opportunities that are adapted to diverse learners.*

12. When sending school notices to the parents or guardians of students whose home language is other than English, teachers should make every effort to ensure that:
    A. students translate the school notices for their parents or guardians.
    B. the notices include the school's Internet address for an interpretation in the home language.
    C. the notices are written in the home language of the students' parents or guardians.
    D. an interpreter makes home visits to translate the notices for parents or guardians.

Use the following information to answer the question that follows.

Ms. Shelley, a fourth grade teacher, receives her students' score reports from a standardized achievement test taken earlier in the year. The score report includes both a grade-equivalent score and a national percentile rank. Lisandra, one of Ms. Shelley's students, scored in the national percentile rank of 97% with a grade equivalent score of 5.5.

Question 13 assesses the INTASC Standard Principle 8: *The teacher understands and uses formal and informal assessment strategies to evaluate and ensure the continuous intellectual, social, and physical development of the learner.*

13. Lisandra's national percentile rank indicates which of the following statements is true?
    A. Lisandra answered 97% of the test items correctly.
    B. Lisandra scored at the same level or higher than 97% of the rest of the students in the test population.
    C. Lisandra scored higher than 3% of the students in the test population.
    D. Lisandra scored in the top three percent of her class.

Question 14 assesses the INTASC Standard Principle 8: *The teacher understands and uses formal and informal assessment strategies to evaluate and ensure the continuous intellectual, social, and physical development of the learner.*

14. Lisandra's grade equivalent score suggests that which of the following statements is true?
    A. Lisandra performed at the level that an average fifth grade student in the fifth month of school would perform on the same test.
    B. Lisandra may encounter some difficulty next year with the fifth grade curriculum.
    C. Lisandra performed at the level that an average fifth grade student in the fifth month of school would perform on a fifth grade test.
    D. Lisandra should be promoted to fifth grade during the second semester of the school year.

Question 15 assesses the INTASC Standard Principle 8: *The teacher understands and uses formal and informal assessment strategies to evaluate and ensure the continuous intellectual, social, and physical development of the learner.*

15. Which of the following statements best describes information that can be determined from a standardized criterion-referenced test?
    A. A comparison of an individual student's knowledge to other students across the school district.
    B. A comparison of an individual student's knowledge to other students at the same age level in a national sample.
    C. An assessment of how much of the student's prior knowledge is reflected in a student's score.
    D. An assessment of the student's knowledge of particular elements of the standard curriculum.

Question 16 assesses the INTASC Standard Principle 8: *The teacher understands and uses formal and informal assessment strategies to evaluate and ensure the continuous intellectual, social, and physical development of the learner.*

16. Mr. Stamos, a ninth grade language arts teacher, wishes to informally monitor students' understanding of a particular lesson. Which of the following techniques offers Mr. Stamos the best potential to check the students' understanding?

    A. Ask the students to work in reflective inquiry teams.
    B. Ask the students to signal their understanding in a game format.
    C. Ask each student to respond to a journal writing prompt at the beginning of the lesson.
    D. Ask the students to complete a pop quiz.

Use the following information to answer the question that follows.

Ms. Ross, a fifth grade social studies teacher, provides students with a list of general focus questions to help students get started with their research projects exploring a specific culture they have chosen to study. As the students begin their projects, Mr. Ross encourages students to add their own questions to the list.

Question 17 assesses the INTASC Standard Principle 7: *The teacher plans instruction based upon knowledge of subject matter, students, the community, and curriculum goals.*

17. By providing the focus questions, Mr. Ross demonstrates his understanding of the importance of designing instruction that:

    A. Helps students determine their own areas of strength.
    B. Allows students to be self-regulating and guide their understanding of an activity.
    C. Adapts instruction to meet individual students' learning styles.
    D. Assesses students' achievement of predefined learning goals in relation to the activity.

Use the following information to answer the question that follows.

Mr. DeLeon's eighth grade career exploration class expresses interest in serving as interns in different kinds of media internships. Mr. DeLeon offers to speak with managers at local newspapers, radio stations, and television stations about the possibility of arranging internships for interested students.

Question 18 assesses the INTASC Standard Principle 10: *The teacher fosters relationships with school colleagues, parents, and agencies in the larger community to support students' learning and well-being.*

18. By seeking to arrange a variety of media internships for students, Mr. DeLeon clearly shows his appreciation for the importance of:
    A. addressing the community about problems concerning teens.
    B. helping his students to stay informed about local community issues.
    C. taking the opportunity to use community resources to foster student growth.
    D. remaining sensitive to the community's needs for a well-educated work force.

Question 19 assesses the INTASC Standard Principle 8: *The teacher understands and uses formal and informal assessment strategies to evaluate and ensure the continuous intellectual, social, and physical development of the learner.*

19. Mr. Sutton, a fourth grade self-contained classroom teacher, is planning to use a combination of assessment strategies for evaluating student performance during an interdisciplinary unit. In evaluating the group projects, which strategies would be most appropriate for Mr. Sutton to include?
    A. teacher observation, peer and student self-assessment
    B. standardized test on interactive CD Rom
    C. teacher observation only
    D. unit review with concept mapping

Use the following information to answer the question that follows.
Ms. Hanson, a fifth grade reading teacher, effectively engages students of varying reading levels during a ninety minute language arts/reading block of instruction. Typically, she divides direct instruction into short, meaningful chunks and offers students choices during individualized learning experiences.

Question 20 assesses the INTASC Standard Principle 5: *The teacher uses an understanding of individual and group motivation and behavior to create a learning environment that encourages positive social interaction, active engagement in learning, and self-motivation.*

20. Which of the following principles of effective classroom management is best demonstrated by Ms. Hanson's lesson design?
    A. Offer students consistent routines to minimize student confusion.
    B. Establish high standards of behavior to minimize disruptions.
    C. Adapt the physical setting according to different instructional goals.
    D. Vary the pace of instruction to accommodate all students.

The following passages are taken from an extended essay on the assessment process and the need for implementing developmentally appropriate assessment. Read the passage below to interpret and address questions 21–24, which follow the passage.

Understanding Assessment

The assessment process consists of three stages during the instructional cycle. These stages are preassessment, formative assessment, and summative assessment. In the preassessment phase, information about a student is gathered prior to instruction, such as a screening or diagnostic test. The information collected during preassessment is used to place the students in special programs or for individualizing instruction to meet the student's needs. Teachers also use preassessment for whole class or individual feedback prior to planning instruction.

During instruction, formative assessment offers feedback to the student in order to check his or her understanding. Formative assessment usually occurs through questioning or teacher observation. Sometimes this assessment takes the form of self-monitoring, or metacognition, where the student is involved in self-checking his or her own levels of understanding. Another purpose of formative assessment is to provide direction for planning future instruction.

Summative assessment, on the other hand, follows instruction and typically involves quizzes, chapter tests, or unit tests. Summative assessment may incorporate student presentations, group projects, and written reports. Summative assessment yields important data for teachers to use in determining a student's level of mastery and decisions of promotion. Through interpretation, the data is used to determine the student's level of proficiency. This information is beneficial to both the student and the teacher and is essential in planning future instruction.

Knowing when and how to implement a particular assessment strategy is critical for implementing developmentally appropriate assessment. In fully implemented, developmentally appropriate programs, student learning and assessment are intertwined. Accurate assessment is desired to create meaningful and relevant learning experiences based upon the interests and learning needs of the students. Teachers do not design instruction based upon what they wish their students know or are able to do. Instead, assessment of student learning continues in an ongoing and systematic process as teachers use assessment to inform and improve teaching and learning.

The author of this passage implies that the three stages of assessment are equally important to designing effective instruction.

Questions 21–24 are based on the passage that you have just read. Now you are prepared with information about the context for these three first questions. Read the first question carefully and critically. Think about the question being asked. Eliminate any wrong answers and select the answer choice that best answers the question. Mark the correct answer choice on your answer sheet. Continue until you have answered all of the remaining questions.

Question 21 assesses two INTASC Standards:

INTASC Standard Principle 2: *The teacher understands how children learn and develop and can provide learning opportunities that support their intellectual, social, and personal development, and* INTASC Standard Principle 8: *The teacher understands and uses formal and informal assessment strategies to evaluate and ensure the continuous intellectual, social, and physical development of the learner.*

21. Which of the following assessment strategies would the author most likely recommend that a teacher engage students in beginning a thematic unit of study?
    A. The author would recommend that the teachers facilitate a brainstorming session with students on research topics related to the unit.
    B. The author would recommend that the teacher pretest over the unit's outcomes to assess prior knowledge and student understanding before the unit study.
    C. The author would recommend that the teacher facilitate a K-W-L inquiry session to determine prior knowledge and interest in topics related to the unit.
    D. The author would recommend that the teacher review the previous unit to make connections and assist students in goal setting for the new unit.

Question 22 assesses two INTASC Standards:

INTASC Standard Principle 8: *The teacher understands and uses formal and informal assessment strategies to evaluate and ensure the continuous intellectual, social, and physical development of the learner, and* INTASC Standard Principle 2: *The teacher understands how children learn and develop and can provide learning opportunities that support their intellectual, social, and personal development.*

22. It can be inferred from the passage that the author would find which of the following grading practices LEAST likely to be effective for implementing developmentally appropriate assessment?
    A. Determining semester grades based upon formative and summative assessments.
    B. Using standardized criterion referenced tests for grading student mastery.
    C. Providing opportunities for students to self-assess and make peer assessments for group work.
    D. Grading on a curve so that all students will pass.

Question 23 assesses INTASC Standard Principle 8: *The teacher understands and uses formal and informal assessment strategies to evaluate and ensure the continuous intellectual, social, and physical development of the learner.*

23. The author would regard which of the following teacher behaviors as essential for supporting fair and impartial assessment?
    A. Using checklists or rubrics for evaluating student products and performances.
    B. Using self and peer assessment for evaluating group work.
    C. Asking students' parents to attend a conference for discussing student progress.
    D. Using portfolio assessment to examine student growth over time.

Question 24 assesses two INTASC Standards:

INTASC Standard Principle 8: *The teacher understands and uses formal and informal assessment strategies to evaluate and ensure the continuous intellectual, social, and physical development of the learner,* and INTASC Standard Principle 2: *The teacher understands how children learn and develop and can provide learning opportunities that support their intellectual, social, and personal development.*

24. The passage suggests that which of the following is a critical element in designing appropriate assessment?
    A. Knowing a variety of assessment strategies.
    B. Understanding the function and purpose of various assessment strategies.
    C. Following district mandates for reporting assessment data.
    D. Working with teachers in other grade levels to design assessment strategies.

Congratulations! You have completed the Diagnostic Test for the Principles of Learning and Teaching Test. You may check your answers with the answer explanations and scoring guide provided in Chapter 13. Using the answer explanations and scoring guide, analyze your results, assess your strengths and weaknesses on the test, and design further study using this guide and other resources in preparation for the actual PRAXIS test.

Chapter 13

Answer Explanations

for Principles of Learning and Teaching Diagnostic Test

Two Case Histories and Constructed Response Questions

24 Multiple-Choice Questions

GENERAL SCORING GUIDE

All constructed-response questions will be assessed using a holistic rating scale ranging from 0-2.

Score of 2

The response appropriately answers all parts of the question and demonstrates an understanding of all of the details in the case study and of the principles of learning and teaching as outlined in the content categories covered in the test.

Score of 1

The response appropriately answers only part of the question.

Score of 0

The response does not appropriately answer any part of the question.

Note: Criteria for determining whether an answer is appropriate or not and scoring guides were established through a "model answer" approach, which consisted of the following process:

After the case and questions are written, three of four knowledgeable experts are asked to read the case and answer the questions, addressing each question exactly as it is worded. The experts are selected carefully to represent the diverse perspectives and situations relevant to the testing population.

The case writer uses these model answers to develop a question-specific scoring guide for each question, creating a list of specific examples that c\would receive full credit. The list contains some, but not all, possible correct answers.

These question-specific scoring guides provide a basis for selecting papers to serve as benchmark responses for the purpose of training scorers at the scoring session.

During the scoring sessions, the evaluators may add new answers to the scoring guide if they are considered appropriate responses.

Training at the scoring sessions is aimed to ensure that evaluators score papers based upon carefully established criteria in the scoring guide, not on their own opinions or preferences.

This section presents two case histories with constructed-response questions similar to those asked on the Principles of Learning and Teaching test. The questions are accompanied by sample responses with the standards used in scoring these responses. On the actual exam, your response will be scored by two readers who are practicing teachers. If the scores differ by more than one point, a third reader will be invited to assess your response. Readers assign scores based upon the following criteria. No credit is given for blank or off-topic responses.

Directions: Using your constructed response answers from the Chapter 12 Diagnostic Test, compare your responses to the scoring guide and the answer explanations provided below. The sample constructed response questions illustrate the kinds of questions that will be on the test. They are not, however, representative of the entire scope of the test in terms of content or difficulty. Answers with explanations and a general scoring guide follow the questions.

Case History 1—Ms. Almira
Answer Explanations for Sample Constructed Response Questions

QUESTION 1
Review the initial planning and early implementation phase of the interview research project. Describe two activities that Ms. Almira could have planned and introduced at the beginning of the project to ensure the likelihood of student success on the interviews. Base your response on principles of communication, motivation theory, and planning instruction.

Sample response that would receive a score of 2.
In the initial planning and implementation phase, Ms. Almira provides time for the students as a class to develop their own questions for the interview. However, there is no mention of allowing the students to practice in a mock interview before actually conducting the live interviews with the senior citizens.

Providing this kind of practice will allow the students to practice their communication skills in a risk-free environment and will enable them to attend to the new information during the actual interview. In order to familiarize themselves with the challenges of conducting a live interview, Ms. Almira should suggest that students practice posing questions with a parent or grandparent before conducting the real thing.

Another way that Ms. Almira could ensure student success on the interviews is to have the student groups find a prompt related to the interview topic to "break the ice" at the beginning of the interview. Ms. Almira should help students identify prompts by looking at newspaper clippings or photographs, and/or listening to recordings of music from the Depression era.

Sample response that would receive a score of 1.

Ms. Almira recognizes that student interest is important in planning instruction that is relevant and meaningful to the students and she demonstrates this by having the students brainstorm questions for the interview. One way that Ms. Almira could improve the students' chances for success is having the students conduct a mock interview in class in pairs in order to become comfortable with the questions and to become accustomed to their partner's communication style.

Sample response that would receive a score of 0.

In planning the unit, Ms. Almira has effectively demonstrated the importance of student interest by implementing activities to incorporate local history into each specific unit of study. Interviewing members of the senior center is an effective way to bring in perspectives of the local community and reflect local events. One thing that Ms. Almira could do to strengthen this activity would be to allow the senior citizens to reciprocate with questions for the students on the topic of the Great Depression.

QUESTION 2

Review the minutes from the first partnership meeting (Document 3) and the conversation with the local news editor (Document 4). In addition to publicizing the partnership through the local newspaper, describe two ways that Ms. Almira could strengthen student involvement and extend the activity of the partnership within the school and the community. Base your response on principles of motivation, human development, and behavior.

Sample response that would receive a score of 2.

One way that Ms. Almira can strengthen and sustain student involvement in the partnership is to consider the interests of the students that are expressed in the first partnership meeting and revisit these ideas in later months as the project gets underway and begins to grow. This focus on student interest will allow the partnership activity to develop around the students' pursuit of ideas and center on issues that are relevant to the students. Also, by involving the students in planning and developing the partnership activity as it grows, the students will be more likely to realize that they are making a positive impact on the community and will be more likely to develop social-emotional maturity and interpersonal skills as they participate in the partnership activity.

In addition to writing the articles in the paper, Ms. Almira could involve the students in creating a permanent archive of the interviews through videotaping, which would allow the students to share the project with the community in a tangible way. The video archive could be stored in the school library with access provided to the community citizens. The archive would allow Ms. Almira to share the activity with other teachers in the school and they, in turn, could gain an interest in the partnership as a result of viewing the interviews. As a result, the partnership could grow to include other classes, thus strengthening and extending the students' involvement in the partnership.

Sample response that would receive a score of 1.

Once the project is underway and students are writing news articles about their various interviews, Ms. Almira should ask the students to reflect upon the new information that they have learned in relation to the unit of study on the Great Depression and the activity's impact on themselves. Ms. Almira should then facilitate a discussion with the students to explore ways that they can integrate the partnership within the school's total instructional program. This dialogue will help the students recognize the benefits of the partnership activity to themselves, the school, and the community, and will be more likely to enhance students' perceptions of self-worth and potential by enabling them to make a positive impact on the school and the local community.

Sample response that would receive a score of 0.

Ms. Almira is aware of the importance of organizing the partnership activity around the students' interests. She should focus on student interest in the first partnership meeting and share these ideas with the director of the senior center for approval. This will allow these ideas to be implemented as the project grows over time.

Case History 2—Carl

QUESTION 1

Explain two strengths in Mr. Garrett's instructional approach in this lesson. Base your response on principles of learning theory, instructional design, and communication.

Sample response that would receive a score of 2.

Mr. Garrett's decision to implement the "I Say, You Say" instructional approach was primarily implemented to assist Carl in developing interpersonal communication and better relational skills with his peers. As evidenced in Mr. Garrett's teacher reflection log, this did occur.

One strength of the lesson design is that by allowing students to work in pairs as they read various passages, students are able to monitor and clarify their understanding in a low risk setting. Another strength of the instructional approach is that the "I Say, You Say" technique allows students to reinforce the concepts they are studying by building on one another's knowledge.

Sample response that would receive a score of 1.

The "I Say, You Say" approach has several advantages and disadvantages. One advantage, or strength, is that students develop a strong sense of ownership in the activity as they are responsible for guiding the timing of the reading and creating questions about the passage. By doing this, the students are co-constructors of knowledge. A disadvantage is that the students are responsible for monitoring their reading time and their partner's input so that one person's perspective is not eclipsed by others.

Sample response that would receive a score of 0.

Mr. Garrett recognized Carl's reluctance to work in groups and implemented the "I Say, You Say" activity to foster interaction of Carl among his peers. The activity was not received well at first, but Mr. Garrett adjusted the activity and spoke with Carl to allay his fears about not reading well and not being able to make sense of the text. One strength of the approach is that Mr. Garrett responded admirably to Carl. If he had not, this situation could have resulted in Carl's increased frustration and lower achievement.

QUESTION 2

Review Mr. Garrett's conversations with Carl (Document 2) and the colleague, Ms. Washington. Explain two additional ways that Mr. Garrett might modify the assignment further to better meet the needs of Carl and other students. Base your response on principles of learning theory, human development, and instructional design.

Sample response that would receive a score of 2.

In the conversation with Carl, Mr. Garrett does little to instill confidence in Carl's ability to read. Carl is left feeling frustrated. However, this changes with Ms. Washington's suggestions and Carl seems to become more comfortable working with a peer and setting his own purposes for reading and is on his own timetable. One way that Mr. Garrett could further strengthen Carl's involvement is by allowing the teams to adjust and flex the amount of time for silent reading to suit their preferences and needs. This modification is likely to foster a greater sense of ownership among the students.

A second way that Mr. Garrett could modify the assignment to better meet the needs of the students is to offer a follow-up writing activity by asking students to write a brief description of what they discovered during the activity. This reflective writing prompt will foster student's sense of responsibility for their own learning while making the shared reading purposeful and personally meaningful.

Sample response that would receive a score of 1.

Mr. Garrett is a caring teacher who demonstrates the importance of collaborating and seeking the counsel of colleagues in making instructional decisions. Mr. Garrett realized in his reflection journal that he did not respond to Carl's needs wisely and that he would have to modify the assignment in order to reduce Carl's frustration and raise his chances for success. One suggestion for Mr. Garrett is to solicit student feedback on the modification he provides to the assignment. With this feedback, Mr. Garrett should be able to better determine whether students' needs are being met and to provide additional modifications if necessary to enhance the success of all students in this activity.

Sample response that would receive a score of 0.

Another way that Mr. Garrett might extend the assignment is to build a classroom library with resources that students may use for their research projects. In constructing this library, it is essential that Mr. Garrett use a variety of media and that the library resources be developmentally and age appropriate so students may connect current understanding with new learning. One consideration that Mr. Garrett should address is whether to keep the library open and accessible to other students and teachers.

Principles of Learning and Teaching Test

24 Multiple-Choice Questions

Answer Explanations

1. B. Question 1 assesses the INTASC Standard Principle 7: *The teacher plans instruction based upon knowledge of subject matter, students, the community, and curriculum goals.*

This question asks you to apply your understanding of assessment as it relates to designing effective instruction. Tapping into students' prior knowledge is an important component of designing instruction that is meaningful and relevant to students. Pretests are one way that teachers may determine what students know about a particular topic. Pretests are also for inquiring into students' interests and concerns about areas of study.

None of the other choices address ways to administer pretests for assessing prior knowledge. Students could be grouped by ethnicity and gender by demographic data. Social bias could be identified through interview or a sociogram. Likewise, test data could be used to rank students on the basis of their achievement.

The correct answer, therefore, is B.

2. A. Question 2 assesses the INTASC Standard Principle 5: *The teacher uses an understanding of individual and group motivation and behavior to create a learning environment that encourages positive social interaction, active engagement in learning, and self-motivation.*

This question asks you to apply your knowledge of motivation theory and behavior in relation to cognition and learning. By posing the question about the two weights, the teacher asks the student to make a prediction about a concept that will be explored in the unit. The act of making predictions naturally raises the level of the students' concern in a positive way and should result in heightened interest in the unit of study.

The questioning technique does not pertain to building confidence, nor does it promote an application of knowledge. The students' predictions will not be corrected by the teacher. They are merely stated to raise student interest and ownership in the activity.

The correct answer, therefore, is A.

3. C. The third question assesses the INTASC Standard Principle 6: *The teacher uses knowledge of effective verbal, nonverbal, and media communication techniques to foster active inquiry, collaboration, and supportive interaction in the classroom.*

This question asks you to demonstrate your understanding of human development and the inquiry process. Asking students to explain their reasoning behind their predictions causes them to analyze their response stand. This analysis enhances their sense of responsibility and ownership for the rationale they provide.

None of the other choices foster responsibility and ownership in the learning activity. Through explaining their reasoning, the students are not developing perseverance in critical thinking or settling a dispute. Their explanations will not lead to motivate them to record observations more carefully either.

The correct answer, therefore, is C.

4. A. The fourth question assesses the INTASC Standard Principle 3: *The teacher understands how students differ in their approaches to learning and creates instructional opportunities that are adapted to diverse learners.*

This question asks you to recognize the principle of cooperative learning, which states that students learn and work together most effectively in heterogeneous cooperative groups. This learning principle is based upon empirical studies of cooperative learning that show student achievement is raised when students of mixed ability are placed in cooperative learning groups.

Including students who are culturally different and mixing groups by gender is important to establishing true heterogeneous groups. However, establishing groups according to social patterns outside of school is not advised since groups may develop sibling rivalry or display discrimination. The first factor that should be considered in mixed ability grouping for instruction is academic diversity.

The correct answer, therefore, is A.

5. D. The fifth question assesses the INTASC Standard Principle 5: *The teacher uses an understanding of individual and group motivation and behavior to create a learning environment that encourages positive social interaction, active engagement in learning, and self-motivation.*

This question asks you to demonstrate your understanding of human development in relation to designing developmentally appropriate practice. Creating transitions and dividing long periods of instruction into briefer time intervals help sustain student attention and enhance students' ability to remain engaged and on task during instruction.

Self-evaluation and resistance to authority are not addressed by the item stimulus. Option choice B does address the effect of time on students' attention but does not present a design that will engage students and raise participation.

The correct answer, therefore, is D.

6. C. The sixth question assesses the INTASC Standard Principle 4: *The teacher understands and uses a variety of instructional strategies to encourage students' development of critical thinking, problem-solving, and performance skills.*

This question asks you to apply your knowledge of the lesson cycle in Madeline Hunter's model of direct instruction. This model is recommended for instruction in psychomotor skills or teaching basic concepts. Following modeling and demonstration of the particular skill, students are given the opportunity to practice a new skill with assistance.

Option A is a necessary step in the anticipatory set. Option B is appropriately used for direct instruction and modeling, and Option D may occur at several intervals during the lesson cycle depending on the purpose of the lesson.

The correct answer, therefore, is C.

7. A. The seventh question assesses the INTASC Standard Principle 3: *The teacher understands how students differ in their approaches to learning and creates instructional opportunities that are adapted to diverse learners.*

This question asks you to recognize the tenet of classroom management theory that suggests teachers model respect for diversity within the classroom learning community. By engaging students in class discussions prior to instruction, students are able to hear and respond to divergent perspectives. Option Choice A is the only response that allows the teacher to model respect for diversity and different points of view.

Skepticism (option B), authoritarianism (option D), and monitoring a discussion with strict rigidity (option C) do not lend themselves to promoting autonomy and acceptance of ideas in a class discussion.

The correct answer, therefore, is A.

8. B. Question 8 assesses the INTASC Standard Principle 4: *The teacher understands and uses a variety of instructional strategies to encourage students' development of critical thinking, problem-solving, and performance skills.*

This question asks you to apply your knowledge of the instructional strategy of journaling. Journaling is a self-directed independent writing exercise that encourages students to write for personal expression and with self-guided purpose. Having students journal in response to *metacognitive* prompts will engage students in writing for the purpose of self-monitoring one's own thinking.

Journaling is not instructive for developing communication skills since it usually occurs in isolation. For this reason, it is not used to foster interpersonal skills. Also, journaling is not used to help students develop organizational skills such as time management or study skills.

The correct answer, therefore, is B.

9. D. Question 9 assesses the INTASC Standard Principle 5: *The teacher uses an understanding of individual and group motivation and behavior to create a learning environment that encourages positive social interaction, active engagement in learning, and self-motivation.*

This question asks you to consider the most effective way to involve students in encouraging parent involvement in school activities. Choice (D) expresses the only means of a student-led schoolwide activity that would encourage parents and guardians to become involved and take a more active role in school functions.

Each of the strategies offered has merit in encouraging positive social interaction and involving parents and the community in the students' learning. However, the question asks you to identify which strategy offers the best potential for involving students in this capacity of encouraging and including parents to take a more active role. Option A does not allow the parents choice or input in the affairs of the school. Option B has a more required, less optional approach to parent involvement, and Option C stops short of gathering the parents' ideas about their involvement.

The correct answer, therefore, is D.

10. D. Question 10 assesses the INTASC Standard Principle 10: *The teacher fosters relationships with school colleagues, parents, and agencies in the larger community to support students' learning and well-being.*

This question asks you to apply your understanding of assessment and motivation principles. Utilizing a needs assessment is the first step in designing programs that serve the needs of a given population. In order to optimally involve all families, a needs assessment to identify the interests and needs of the parents and guardians within a school is essential.

Recruiting students to serve as ambassadors or outreach representatives, curriculum enrichment, and hosting schoolwide festivals on multiculturalism may follow the first step to identify interest and need for school involvement according to the parents.

The correct answer, therefore, is D.

11. B. Question 11 assesses the INTASC Standard Principle 3: *The teacher understands how students differ in their approaches to learning and creates instructional opportunities that are adapted to diverse learners.*

This question asks you to recognize the most effective type of professional development for teachers who need to communicate with parents whose home language is not English. Choice (B) is the only choice which offers teachers the opportunity to learn common phrases in the home language and will facilitate the teachers' ability to communicate with the parents more effectively.

None of the other choices address the needs of teachers who wish to communicate with parents and guardians who speak a language at home other than English. Option choice C, understanding effective parent-teacher conference protocols, is important for all teachers. Option A is also helpful for facilitating cross-cultural communication. However, the approach that is most likely to help teachers is Option B: to learn common phrases and basic communication in the students' home languages.

The correct answer, therefore, is B.

12. C. Question 12 assesses the INTASC Standard Principle 3: *The teacher understands how students differ in their approaches to learning and creates instructional opportunities that are adapted to diverse learners.*

This question asks you to demonstrate your understanding of effective ways to support the learning of ESL students. Communicating with parents is an important way to support student learning. For those students whose home language is a language other than English, teachers need to ensure that notes and other school documents to be sent home are translated into the home language of the parents or guardians of the ESL student.

The practice of utilizing students as home interpreters (option A), while common, is not advisable due to miscommunication or misunderstanding which might occur. Posting messages on the school's website (option B) may exclude parents who do not have a computer or access to the Internet. It is not cost-effective to send an interpreter into the homes of all students whose parents or guardians do not speak English at home.

The correct answer, therefore, is C.

13. B. Question 13 assesses the INTASC Standard Principle 8: *The teacher understands and uses formal and informal assessment strategies to evaluate and ensure the continuous intellectual, social, and physical development of the learner.*

This question asks you to demonstrate your understanding of the meaning of percentile ranking. Percentile rank indicates the percentage of students in a norm group whose scores are exceeded by any specific raw score. In other words, only 3% of the students taking the test scored higher than Lisandra.

Option A offers an interpretation of scoring generally found on criterion-referenced tests. Option C is incorrect mathematically for a national percentile rank of 97%. Option D is also incorrect since the test population includes a national sample, not Lisandra's class.

The correct answer, therefore, is B.

14. A. Question 14 assesses the INTASC Standard Principle 8: *The teacher understands and uses formal and informal assessment strategies to evaluate and ensure the continuous intellectual, social, and physical development of the learner.*

This question asks you to apply your understanding of one particular aspect of standardized test score reporting. A grade-equivalent score is a score that compares the raw score attained on a test by an individual student to the raw score attained by the average student in the norm group for the particular test and then reports the grade and month level of that norm group comparison. In this case, Lisandra's raw score was equivalent to the raw score of all fifth graders in the fifth month of school who were part of the norm group.

Option B may be eliminated since Lisandra's grade equivalent suggests that she is already performing at a higher level than fourth grade. Option C may be eliminated since the interpretation is based on a fifth grade test and not a standardized achievement test as described in the item stimulus. Option D is not suggested in the passage.

The correct answer, therefore, is A.

15. D. Question 15 assesses the INTASC Standard Principle 8: *The teacher understands and uses formal and informal assessment strategies to evaluate and ensure the continuous intellectual, social, and physical development of the learner.*

This question asks you to recognize the critical attribute of a criterion-referenced test. Criterion-referenced tests are developed to assess knowledge and understanding of specific standards for learning particular content. They are designed to enable individual students or groups of students who have studied the same material to assess how much they have learned as compared to the criterion, or standard.

None of the other answer choices describe information that can be obtained from a standardized criterion-referenced test. Options A and B offer comparisons which are more likely to be determined by an achievement test.

The correct answer, therefore, is D.

16. B. Question 16 assesses the INTASC Standard Principle 8: *The teacher understands and uses formal and informal assessment strategies to evaluate and ensure the continuous intellectual, social, and physical development of the learner.*

This question asks you to recognize the effective use of a particular strategy, signaling, to informally assess student understanding. Signaling is one way to indirectly monitor students' understanding during instruction. Many different signaling techniques exist, including hand gestures, writing in the air, writing on small wipe-off boards, and/or choral response. Option choice B allows the teacher to informally monitor and check the students' understanding during a particular lesson.

The other option choices do not allow for informal assessment to occur during the lesson. Reflective inquiry teams (option A) foster student participation, ownership, and critical thinking. Journaling at the beginning of the lesson (option C) would encourage setting purposes for learning and offer an opportunity for reflective inquiry. Pop quizzes (option D) also do not offer informal assessment during the lesson since they are administered after the lesson is finished.

The correct answer, therefore, is B.

17. B. Question 17 assesses the INTASC Standard Principle 7: *The teacher plans instruction based upon knowledge of subject matter, students, the community, and curriculum goals.*

This question asks you to apply your knowledge of a particular aspect of the learning process, namely, metacognitive behavior that enables students to guide their own learning and be self-regulating. Metacognition is the cognitive process that allows an individual to step out of a particular learning experience and reflect on his or her thinking and identify preferred ways of learning. The instructional practice of allowing students to add focus questions to facilitate the early stages of their research fosters the potential for students to engage in metacognitive activity.

Adding their own focus questions to the list does not help students determine their own areas of strength (option A), nor does it allow the teacher to assess their achievement (option C) or learning styles (option D). The student-generated questions are best utilized to provide a guide for instruction that is designed around student ownership and interest.

The correct answer, therefore, is B.

18. C. Question 18 assesses the INTASC Standard Principle 10: *The teacher fosters relationships with school colleagues, parents, and agencies in the larger community to support students' learning and well-being.*

This question asks you to recognize the author's opinion of the use of community resources in fostering student growth. By exploring a variety of media externships for students, Mr. DeLeon shows his appreciation for the use of community of resources to meet the students' expressed interest in serving as interns in different kinds of media externships.

None of the other option choices address the function of community internships and their relationship to the students' learning. Internships might reveal teen problems to the educational community (option A), and they could also help students become more aware of local issues (option B). However, neither revealing need, nor raising awareness, nor understanding the community's need for a well-educated workforce is the central purpose for arranging the student internships.

The correct answer, therefore, is C.

19. A. Question 19 assesses the INTASC Standard Principle 8: *The teacher understands and uses formal and informal assessment strategies to evaluate and ensure the continuous intellectual, social, and physical development of the learner.*

This question asks you to demonstrate your understanding of the use of multiple measures of assessment for evaluating student performance during an interdisciplinary unit. All of the options describe various assessment strategies, but answer choice (A) is the only one that offers a combination of assessment techniques.

None of the other option choices offer the teacher multiple measures for accurate and holistic assessment of the students' learning during the interdisciplinary unit. The standardized test is a decontextualized assessment (option B). Teacher observation is usually reserved for assessing performance and process skills rather than product assessment, such as assessing a group project (option C). Also, the concept mapping is one technique that is helpful for review but would not be valuable for assessing the learning of the group in a project.

The correct answer, therefore, is A.

20. D. Question 20 assesses the INTASC Standard Principle 5: *The teacher uses an understanding of individual and group motivation and behavior to create a learning environment that encourages positive social interaction, active engagement in learning, and self-motivation.*

This question asks you to demonstrate your understanding of effective practices for classroom management. Offering students choices for structuring their own learning and breaking the time spent on direct instruction into shorter time segments demonstrate the learning principle that pacing during instruction should be varied to meet the needs of all students.

While several of the option choices are based upon principles of effective classroom management, this question does not address the use of student routines in classroom management (option A) nor does it examine adjusting the physical setting according to different educational goals (option C). Moreover, the item stimulus does not address the role of teacher expectations and standards setting (option B) in classroom management.

The correct answer, therefore, is D.

21. C. Question 21 assesses two INTASC Standards:

INTASC Standard Principle 2: *The teacher understands how children learn and develop and can provide learning opportunities that support their intellectual, social, and personal development, and*

INTASC Standard Principle 8: *The teacher understands and uses formal and informal assessment strategies to evaluate and ensure the continuous intellectual, social, and physical development of the learner.*

This question asks you to recognize a particular assessment strategy that may be used to effectively introduce a unit of study. The K-W-L strategy is an inquiry technique used to facilitate the discovery of what students know about a particular topic in relation to what they wish to find out. Designed to introduce a unit of study, the K-W-L allows teachers to activate prior knowledge and promote interest in the new topic or area of study while assessing what students know about the subject.

The purpose of the brainstorming session (option A) is described as allowing the teacher to identify and branch into other related areas of study, but this technique will expand the list of ideas for study and not necessarily promote interest in the new unit of study. The pretest (option B) may allow the teacher to assess previous learning in relation to the new unit, but will not serve to foster interest or promote purpose setting. Option D, reviewing the previous unit to set goals for the new unit, will neither allow the teacher to activate prior knowledge, nor foster interest, nor allow the teacher to assess the level of student interest in the new unit of study.

The correct answer, therefore, is C.

22. D. Question 22 assesses two INTASC Standards:

INTASC Standard Principle 8: *The teacher understands and uses formal and informal assessment strategies to evaluate and ensure the continuous intellectual, social, and physical development of the learner, and*

INTASC Standard Principle 2: *The teacher understands how children learn and develop and can provide learning opportunities that support their intellectual, social, and personal development.*

This question asks you to make an inference based upon the author's argument regarding developmentally appropriate assessment. Options A, B, and C all reflect the use of various appropriate assessment strategies. Each is important in accurate assessment of student learning using multiple measures.

The question asks you to determine the LEAST effective practice. Option D reflects the use of a grading technique that allows grades to be statistically raised or lowered in relation to a curve equivalence scale in order to meet a particular passing standard. This is not a direct assessment of a student's ability or understanding, but offers a comparison of the student in relation to the performance of the rest of the class.

The correct answer, therefore, is D.

23. A. Question 23 assesses INTASC Standard Principle 8: *The teacher understands and uses formal and informal assessment strategies to evaluate and ensure the continuous intellectual, social, and physical development of the learner.*

This question asks you to consider a professional question relevant to fair and impartial assessment. Performance-based assessment relies on observation and is often considered subjective and influenced by the attitudes and opinions of the person conducting the assessment. The use of checklists or rubrics for evaluating student performance and products is one way to minimize bias and enhance objective evaluation.

The use of self-assessment and peer assessment in Option B does not ensure fair and impartial assessment. Likewise, student portfolios assessed without the use of checklists or rating scales (option D) may be subjective and reflect partiality. Option C, which addresses parent conferences for progress updates, does not pertain to the item stimulus and question.

The correct answer, therefore, is A.

24. B. Question 24 assesses two INTASC Standards:

INTASC Standard Principle 8: *The teacher understands and uses formal and informal assessment strategies to evaluate and ensure the continuous intellectual, social, and physical development of the learner, and*

INTASC Standard Principle 2: *The teacher understands how children learn and develop and can provide learning opportunities that support their intellectual, social, and personal development.*

This question asks you to identify a critical element in designing appropriate assessment. The passage says, "Knowing when and how to implement a particular assessment strategy is critical for implementing appropriate assessment." In other words, understanding the function and purpose of various assessment strategies is essential to the appropriate implementation of assessment.

Variety (option A) does not guarantee accuracy in designing developmentally appropriate assessments. Working with teachers (option D) may help broaden ideas for assessment strategies and may ease the time constraints for designing contextualized, local assessments, but does not ensure that the assessments will be developmentally appropriate. Reporting assessment data according to district protocols (option C) does not pertain to the item stimulus and question.

The correct answer, therefore, is B.

Chapter 14

Review for the Principles of Learning and Teaching Test

The Principles of Learning and Teaching test is designed to assess the professional knowledge of beginning teachers. The test is closely aligned with the Interstate New Teacher Assessment and Support Consortium (INTASC) standards. The INTASC standards are national standards used in states within the consortium that specify what teachers should know and be able to do. This chapter describes the major sections of the Principles of Learning and Teaching test, provides a comprehensive listing of central concepts organized in a test study guide, and shows the alignment of each subsection of the test in the study guide with the relevant INTASC standards.

The Principles of Learning and Teaching test requires two different types of responses. The constructed-response questions ask you to analyze and respond in writing to questions concerning a case study. The other type of question is multiple-choice, which requires you to select an answer from a set of four possible responses. Using this chapter, you will be able to prepare yourself for the actual test by familiarizing yourself with the key concepts and principles assessed on the Principles of Learning and Teaching test. There are two practice tests in this book (see Chapter 12 and Chapter 15) that will allow you to practice types of questions similar to those you will be asked on the actual Principles of Learning and Teaching test. Scoring guides with answer explanations accompany each of the practice tests in this text. These scoring guides may be used to diagnose your areas of strength and weakness in order to better prepare yourself for the actual test.

Test at a Glance

Students as Learners

This section accounts for approximately 35 percent of the total score and covers the following areas:

- Student development and the learning process
- Students as diverse learners
- Student motivation and the learning environment

Instruction and Assessment

This section accounts for approximately 35 percent of the total score and covers the following areas:

- Instructional strategies
- Planning strategies
- Assessment strategies

Communication Techniques

This section accounts for approximately 15 percent of the total score and covers the following areas:

- Effective verbal and nonverbal communication
- Cultural and gender differences in communication
- Stimulating discussion and responses in the classroom

Profession and the Community

This section accounts for approximately 15 percent of the total score and covers the following areas:

- The reflective practitioner
- The larger community

The next section of the chapter contains a study guide to be used for the Principles of Learning and Teaching test. The guide is divided into four sections that list the important terminology, major learning theories, and concepts that may be used in questions on the Principles of Learning and Teaching test. Each subsection is aligned with the INTASC principle(s) that pertains to the concepts addressed. The INTASC principles are listed and fully described within this chapter following the next section.

Principles of Learning and Teaching Study Guide

I. Students as Learners (approximately 35% of the total score)

Student Development and the Learning Process (INTASC Principle 2)

Terms to know:
Constructivism
Metacognition
Readiness
Schemata
Transfer
Scaffolding

Bloom's taxonomy
Zone of proximal development
Intrinsic and extrinsic motivation

Important theorists:
Albert Bandura
Jerome Bruner
John Dewey
Jean Piaget
Lev Vygotsky
Howard Gardner
Abraham Maslow
B. F. Skinner

Theoretical foundations about how learning occurs:
How students construct knowledge
How students acquire skills
How students develop habits of mind

Students as Diverse Learners (INTASC Principle 3)

Differences in the ways students learn and perform:
Learning styles
Multiple intelligences
Performance modes
Concrete operational thinkers
Visual and aural learners
Gender differences
Cultural expectations and styles

Areas of exceptionality in students' learning:
Visual and perceptual difficulties
Special physical or sensory challenges
Learning disabilities
Attention deficit disorder (ADD); attention deficit-hyperactivity disorder
    (ADHD)
Functional mental retardation

Legislation and institutional responsibilities relating to exceptional students:
Americans with Disabilities Act (ADA)
Individuals with Disabilities Education Act (IDEA)
Inclusion, mainstreaming, and "least restrictive environment"
IEP (individualized education plan), including the elements that, by law, must
    be included in each IEP

Approaches for accommodating various learning styles, intelligences, or exceptionalities:
Differentiated instruction
Alternative assessments
Testing modifications

Process of second-language acquisition and strategies to support the learning of students for whom English is not a first language:
Understanding of influences of individual experiences, talents, and prior learning, as well as language, culture, family, and community values on students' learning
Multicultural backgrounds
Age-appropriate knowledge and behavior
The student culture at the school
Family backgrounds
Linguistic patterns and differences
Cognitive patterns and differences
Social and emotional issues

Student Motivation and the Learning Environment (INTASC Principle 5)

Theoretical foundations about human motivation and behavior:
Abraham Maslow
Albert Bandura
B. F. Skinner
W. Glasser

Terms to know:
Hierarchy of needs
Intrinsic motivation
Extrinsic motivation
Learned helplessness
Self-efficacy
Operant conditioning
Reinforcement
Positive reinforcement
Negative reinforcement
Shaping successive approximations
Prevention
Extinction
Punishment
Continuous reinforcement
Intermittent reinforcement

*Principles of effective classroom management and strategies to promote a
positive learning environment:*
Establishing daily procedures and routines
Establishing classroom rules, punishments, and rewards
Giving timely feedback
Maintaining accurate records
Communicating with parents and caregivers
Using objective behavior descriptions
Response to student misbehavior
Arrangement of classroom space
Pacing and structure of the lesson

II. Instruction and Assessment (approximately 35% of the total score)

Instructional Strategies (INTASC Principles 1 and 4)

Major cognitive processes associated with student learning:
Critical thinking
Creative thinking
Higher-order thinking
Inductive and deductive thinking
Problem structuring and problem solving
Invention
Memorization and recall

Major categories, advantages, and appropriate uses of instructional strategies:
Cooperative learning
Direct instruction
Discovery learning
Whole-group discussion
Independent study
Interdisciplinary instruction
Concept mapping
Inquiry method
Questioning

Principles, techniques, and methods associated with major instructional strategies:
Direct instruction
Madeline Hunter's model of direct instruction, sometimes referred to as
    "effective teaching model"
Mastery learning
Demonstrations

Mnemonics

Note taking

Graphic organizers

Outlining

Use of visual or tactile aids

Student-centered models

Inquiry model

Discovery learning

Cooperative learning (think-pair-share, jigsaw, teams, games)

Collaborative learning

Concept models (concept development, concept attainment, concept mapping)

Laboratories

Project-based learning

Simulations

Methods for enhancing student learning through the use of a variety of resources and materials:

Computers, Internet resources, Web pages, e-mail

Audiovisual technologies, such as videotapes and compact disks

Local experts

Primary documents and artifacts

Field trips

Libraries

Service learning

Planning Instruction (INTASC Principle 7)

Techniques for planning instruction to meet curriculum goals, including the incorporation of learning theory, subject matter, curriculum development, and student development:

National and state learning standards

State and local curriculum frameworks

State and local curriculum guides

Scope and sequence in specific disciplines

Units and lessons

Behavioral objectives: affective, cognitive, psychomotor

Learner objectives and outcomes

Techniques for creating effective bridges between curriculum goals and students' experiences:

Modeling

Guided practice

Independent practice, including homework

Transitions

Activating students' prior knowledge
Anticipating preconceptions
Encouraging exploration and problem solving
Building new skills on those previously acquired

Assessment Strategies (INTASC Principle 8)

Understanding of measurement theory and uses of assessments:
Standardized tests, norm-referenced or criterion-referenced
Achievement tests
Aptitude tests
Structured observations
Anecdotal records
Assessments of prior knowledge
Student responses during a lesson
Portfolios
Essays written to prompts
Journals
Self-evaluations
Performance-based assessments

Characteristics of assessments:
Validity
Reliability
Norm-referenced
Criterion-referenced
Mean, median, mode
Sampling strategy

Assessment issues related to scoring and interpreting assessments:
Analytical scoring
Holistic scoring
Rubrics
Checklists
Rating scales
Reporting assessment results
Stanine
Mastery levels
Percentile rank
Raw score
Scaled score
Grade-equivalent score
Standard deviations
Standard error of measurement

III. Communication (approximately 15% of the total score)

Communication Techniques (INTASC Principle 6)

Basic, effective verbal and nonverbal communication techniques:
Effect of cultural and gender differences on communication in the classroom
Types of questions that can stimulate discussion in different ways for
    particular purposes
Probing for learner understanding
Helping students articulate their ideas and thinking processes
Promoting risk taking and problem solving
Facilitating factual recall
Encouraging convergent and divergent thinking
Stimulating curiosity
Helping students to question

IV. Profession and Community (approximately 15% of the total score)

The Reflective Practitioner (INTASC Principle 9)

Types of resources available for professional development and learning:
Professional literature
Colleagues
Professional associations
Professional development activities

Ability to read and understand articles and books about current views, ideas, and debates regarding best teaching practices:
Why personal reflection on teaching practices is critical, and approaches that
    can be used to achieve this

The Larger Community (INTASC Principle 10)

Role of the school as a resource to the larger community:
Factors in the students' environment outside of school (family circumstances,
    community environments, health and economic conditions) that may
    influence students' life and learning
Basic strategies for involving parents/guardians and leaders in the community
    in the educational process

Major laws related to students' rights and teacher responsibilities

Equal education

Appropriate education for handicapped students

Confidentiality and privacy

Appropriate treatment of students

Reporting situations related to possible child abuse

The following section contains the descriptions of the INTASC standards upon which the Principles of Learning and Teaching test is based.

INTASC Standards

Principle 1: The teacher understands the central concepts, tools of inquiry, and structures of the discipline(s) he or she teaches and can create learning experiences that make these aspects of subject matter meaningful for students.

Knowledge

- The teacher understands major concepts, assumptions, debates, processes of inquiry, and ways of knowing that are central to the discipline(s) he or she teaches.
- The teacher understands how students' conceptual frameworks and their misconceptions for an area of knowledge can influence their learning.
- The teacher can relate his or her disciplinary knowledge to other subject areas.

Dispositions

- The teacher realizes that subject-matter knowledge is not a fixed body of facts but is complex and ever-evolving. He or she seeks to keep abreast of new ideas and understandings in the field.
- The teacher appreciates multiple perspectives and conveys to learners how knowledge is developed from the vantage point of the knower.
- The teacher has enthusiasm for the discipline(s) he or she teaches and sees connections to everyday life.
- The teacher is committed to continuous learning and engages in professional discourse about subject matter knowledge and children's learning of the discipline.

Performances

- The teacher effectively uses multiple representations and explanations of disciplinary concepts that capture key ideas and links them to students' prior understandings.

- The teacher can represent and use differing viewpoints, theories, "ways of knowing," and methods of inquiry in his or her teaching of subject-matter concepts.
- The teacher can evaluate teaching resources and curriculum materials for their comprehensiveness, accuracy, and usefulness for representing particular ideas and concepts.
- The teacher engages students in generating knowledge and testing hypotheses according to the methods of inquiry and standards of evidence used in the discipline.
- The teacher develops and uses curricula that encourage students to see, question, and interpret ideas from diverse perspectives.
- The teacher can create interdisciplinary learning experiences that allow students to integrate knowledge, skills, and methods of inquiry from several subject areas.

Principle 2: The teacher understands how children learn and develop and can provide learning opportunities that support their intellectual, social, and personal development.

Knowledge
- The teacher understands how learning occurs—how students construct knowledge, acquire skills, and develop habits of mind—and knows how to use instructional strategies that promote student learning.
- The teacher understands that students' physical, social, emotional, moral, and cognitive development influences learning and knows how to address these factors when making instructional decisions.
- The teacher is aware of expected developmental progressions and ranges of individual variation within each domain (physical, social, emotional, moral, and cognitive), can identify levels of readiness in learning, and understands how development in any one domain may affect performance in others.

Dispositions
- The teacher appreciates individual variation within each area of development, shows respect for the diverse talents of all learners, and is committed to help them develop self-confidence and competence.
- The teacher is disposed to use students' strengths as a basis for growth and their errors as an opportunity for learning.

Performances
- The teacher assesses individual and group performance in order to design instruction that meets learners' current needs in each domain (cognitive, social, emotional, moral, and physical) and that leads to the next level of development.

- The teacher stimulates student reflection on prior knowledge and links new ideas to already-familiar ideas, making connections to students' experiences, providing opportunities for active engagement, manipulation, and testing of ideas and materials, and encouraging students to assume responsibility for shaping their learning tasks.
- The teacher accesses students' thinking and experiences as a basis for instructional activities by, for example, encouraging discussion, listening and responding to group interaction, and eliciting oral and written samples of student thinking.

Principle 3: The teacher understands how students differ in their approaches to learning and creates instructional opportunities that are adapted to diverse learners.

Knowledge

- The teacher understands and can identify differences in approaches to learning and performance, including different learning styles, multiple intelligences, and performance modes, and can design instruction that helps use students' strengths as the basis for growth.
- The teacher knows about areas of exceptionality in learning—including learning disabilities, visual and perceptual difficulties, and special physical or mental challenges.
- The teacher knows about the process of second-language acquisition and about strategies to support the learning of students whose first language is not English.
- The teacher understands how students' learning is influenced by individual experiences, talents, and prior learning, as well as language, culture, and family and community values.
- The teacher has a well-grounded framework for understanding cultural and community diversity and knows how to learn about and incorporate students' experiences, cultures, and community resources into instruction.

Dispositions

- The teacher believes that all children can learn at high levels and perseveres in helping all children achieve success.
- The teacher appreciates and values human diversity, shows respect for students' varied talents and perspectives, and is committed to the pursuit of "individually configured excellence."
- The teacher respects students as individuals with differing personal and family backgrounds and various skills, talents, and interests.
- The teacher is sensitive to community and cultural norms.
- The teacher makes students feel valued for their potential as people and helps them learn to value each other.

Performances

- The teacher identifies and designs instruction appropriate to students' stages of development, learning styles, strengths, and needs.
- The teacher uses teaching approaches that are sensitive to the multiple experiences of learners and that address different learning and performance modes.
- The teacher makes appropriate provisions (in terms of time and circumstances for work, tasks assigned, and communication and response modes) for individual students who have particular learning differences or needs.
- The teacher can identify when and how to access appropriate services or resources to meet exceptional learning needs.
- The teacher seeks to understand students' families, cultures, and communities, and uses this information as a basis for connecting instruction to students' experiences (for instance, drawing explicit connections between subject matter and community matters, making assignments that can be related to students' experiences and cultures).
- The teacher brings multiple perspectives to the discussion of subject matter, including attention to students' personal, family, and community experiences and cultural norms.
- The teacher creates a learning community in which individual differences are respected.

Principle 4: The teacher understands and uses a variety of instructional strategies to encourage students' development of critical thinking, problem-solving, and performance skills.

Knowledge

- The teacher understands the cognitive processes associated with various kinds of learning (such as critical and creative thinking, problem structuring and problem solving, invention, and memorization and recall) and how these processes can be stimulated.
- The teacher understands principles and techniques, along with advantages and limitations, associated with various instructional strategies (such as cooperative learning, direct instruction, discovery learning, whole-group discussion, independent study, and interdisciplinary instruction).
- The teacher knows how to enhance learning through the use of a wide variety of materials as well as human and technological resources (including computers, audio-visual technologies, videotapes and disks, local experts, primary documents and artifacts, texts, reference books, literature, and other print resources).

Dispositions

- The teacher values the development of students' critical thinking, independent problem solving, and performance capabilities.
- The teacher values flexibility and reciprocity in the teaching process as necessary for adapting instruction to student responses, ideas, and needs.

Performances

- The teacher carefully evaluates how to achieve learning goals, choosing alternative teaching strategies and materials to achieve different instructional purposes and to meet student needs (such as developmental stages, prior knowledge, learning styles, and interests).
- The teacher uses multiple teaching and learning strategies to engage students in active learning opportunities that promote the development of critical thinking, problem solving, and performance capabilities and that help students assume responsibility for identifying and using learning resources.
- The teacher constantly monitors and adjusts strategies in response to learner feedback.
- The teacher varies his or her role in the instructional process (including that of instructor, facilitator, coach, and audience) in relation to the content and purposes of instruction and the needs of students.
- The teacher develops a variety of clear, accurate presentations and representations of concepts, using alternative explanations to assist students' understanding, and presenting diverse perspectives to encourage critical thinking.

Principle 5: The teacher uses an understanding of individual and group motivation and behavior to create a learning environment that encourages positive social interaction, active engagement in learning, and self-motivation.

Knowledge

- The teacher can use knowledge about human motivation and behavior drawn from the foundational sciences of psychology, anthropology, and sociology to develop strategies for organizing and supporting individual and group work.
- The teacher understands how social groups function and influence people and how people influence groups.
- The teacher knows how to help people work productively and cooperatively with each other in complex social settings.
- The teacher understands the principles of effective classroom management and can use a range of strategies to promote positive relationships, cooperation, and purposeful learning in the classroom.

- The teacher recognizes factors and situations that are likely to promote or discourage intrinsic motivation and knows how to help students become self-motivated.

Dispositions

- The teacher takes responsibility for establishing a positive climate in the classroom and participates in maintaining such a climate in the school as a whole.
- The teacher understands how participation supports commitment and is committed to the expression and use of democratic values in the classroom.
- The teacher values the role of students in promoting each other's learning and recognizes the importance of peer relationships in establishing a climate of learning.
- The teacher recognizes the value of intrinsic motivation to students' lifelong growth and learning.
- The teacher is committed to the continuous development of individual students' abilities and considers how different motivational strategies are likely to encourage this development for each student.

Performances

- The teacher creates a smoothly functioning learning community in which students assume responsibility for themselves and one another, participate in decision making, work collaboratively and independently, and engage in purposeful learning activities.
- The teacher engages students in individual and cooperative learning activities that help them develop the motivation to achieve, by, for example, relating lessons to students' personal interests, allowing students to have choices in their learning, and leading students to ask questions and pursue problems that are meaningful to them.
- The teacher organizes, allocates, and manages the resources of time, space, activities, and attention to provide active and equitable engagement of students in productive tasks.
- The teacher maximizes the amount of class time spent in learning by creating expectations and processes for communication and behavior along with a physical setting conducive to classroom goals.
- The teacher helps the group to develop shared values and expectations for student interactions, academic discussions, and individual and group responsibility that create a positive classroom climate of openness, mutual respect, support, and inquiry.
- The teacher analyzes the classroom environment and makes decisions and adjustments to enhance social relationships, student motivation and engagement, and productive work.
- The teacher organizes, prepares students for, and monitors independent and group work that allows for full and varied participation of all individuals.

Principle 6: The teacher uses knowledge of effective verbal, non-verbal, and media communication techniques to foster active inquiry, collaboration, and supportive interaction in the classroom.

Knowledge

- The teacher understands communication theory, language development, and the role of language in learning.
- The teacher understands how cultural and gender differences can affect communication in the classroom.
- The teacher recognizes the importance of nonverbal as well as verbal communication.
- The teacher knows about and can use effective verbal, nonverbal, and media communication techniques.

Dispositions

- The teacher recognizes the power of language for fostering self-expression, identity development, and learning.
- The teacher values the many ways in which people seek to communicate and encourages many modes of communication in the classroom.
- The teacher is a thoughtful and responsive listener.
- The teacher appreciates the cultural dimensions of communication, responds appropriately, and seeks to foster culturally sensitive communication by and among all students in the class.

Performances

- The teacher models effective communication strategies in conveying ideas and information and in asking questions (that is, by monitoring the effects of messages, restating ideas and drawing connections, using visual, aural, and kinesthetic cues, or being sensitive to nonverbal cues given and received).
- The teacher supports and expands learner expression in speaking, writing, and other media.
- The teacher knows how to ask questions and stimulate discussion in different ways for particular purposes, for example, probing for learner understanding, helping students articulate their ideas and thinking processes, promoting risk taking and problem solving, facilitating factual recall, encouraging convergent and divergent thinking, stimulating curiosity, and helping students to question.
- The teacher communicates in ways that demonstrate a sensitivity to cultural and gender differences (such as appropriate use of eye contact, interpretation of body language and verbal statements, and acknowledgment of and responsiveness to different modes of communication and participation).
- The teacher knows how to use a variety of media communication tools, including audio-visual aids and computers, to enrich learning opportunities.

Principle 7: The teacher plans instruction based upon knowledge of subject matter, students, the community, and curriculum goals.

Knowledge
- The teacher understands learning theory, subject matter, curriculum development, and student development and knows how to use this knowledge in planning instruction to meet curriculum goals.
- The teacher knows how to take contextual considerations (instructional materials; individual student interests, needs, and aptitudes; and community resources) into account in planning instruction that creates an effective bridge between curriculum goals and students' experiences.
- The teacher knows when and how to adjust plans based on student responses and other contingencies.

Dispositions
- The teacher values both long-term and short-term planning.
- The teacher believes that plans must always be open to adjustment and revision based on student needs and changing circumstances.
- The teacher values planning as a collegial activity.

Performances
- As an individual and a member of a team, the teacher selects and creates learning experiences that are appropriate for curriculum goals, relevant to learners, and based upon principles of effective instruction (such as those that activate students' prior knowledge, anticipate preconceptions, encourage exploration and problem solving, and build new skills on those previously acquired).
- The teacher plans for learning opportunities that recognize and address variation in learning styles and performance modes.
- The teacher creates lessons and activities that operate at multiple levels to meet the developmental and individual needs of diverse learners and to help each progress.
- The teacher creates short-range and long-term plans that are linked to student needs and performance and adapts the plans to ensure and capitalize on student progress and motivation.
- The teacher responds to unanticipated sources of input, evaluates plans in relation to short- and long-range goals, and systematically adjusts plans to meet student needs and enhance learning.

Principle 8: The teacher understands and uses formal and informal assessment strategies to evaluate and ensure the continuous intellectual, social, and physical development of the learner.

Knowledge

- The teacher understands the characteristics, uses, advantages, and limitations of different types of assessments (such as criterion-referenced and norm-referenced instruments, traditional standardized and performance-based tests, observation systems, and assessments of student work) for evaluating how students learn, what they know and are able to do, and what kinds of experiences will support their further growth and development.
- The teacher knows how to select, construct, and use assessment strategies and instruments appropriate to the learning outcomes being evaluated and to other diagnostic purposes.
- The teacher understands measurement theory and assessment-related issues, such as validity, reliability, bias, and scoring concerns.

Dispositions

- The teacher values ongoing assessment as essential to the instructional process and recognizes that many different assessment strategies, accurately and systematically used, are necessary for monitoring and promoting student learning.
- The teacher is committed to using assessment to identify student strengths and promote student growth rather than to deny students access to learning opportunities.

Performances

- The teacher appropriately uses a variety of formal and informal assessment techniques (for example, observation, portfolios of student work, teacher-made tests, performance tasks, projects, student self-assessments, peer assessment, and standardized tests) to enhance her or his knowledge of learners, evaluate students' progress and performances, and modify teaching and learning strategies.
- The teacher solicits and uses information about students' experiences, learning behavior, needs, and progress from parents, other colleagues, and the students themselves.
- The teacher uses assessment strategies to involve learners in self-assessment activities, to help them become aware of their strengths and needs, and to encourage them to set personal goals for learning.
- The teacher evaluates the effect of class activities on both individuals and the class as a whole, collecting information through observation of classroom interactions, questioning, and analysis of student work.

- The teacher monitors his or her own teaching strategies and behavior in relation to student success, modifying plans and instructional approaches accordingly.
- The teacher maintains useful records of student work and performance and can communicate student progress knowledgeably and responsibly, based on appropriate indicators, to students, parents, and other colleagues.

Principle 9: The teacher is a reflective practitioner who continually evaluates the effects of his or her choices and actions on others (students, parents, and other professionals in the learning community) and who actively seeks out opportunities to grow professionally.

Knowledge
- The teacher understands methods of inquiry that provide him or her with a variety of self-assessment and problem-solving strategies for reflecting on his or her practice, its influences on students' growth and learning, and the complex interactions between them.
- The teacher is aware of major areas of research on teaching and of resources available for professional learning (including professional literature, colleagues, professional associations, and professional development activities).

Dispositions
- The teacher values critical thinking and self-directed learning as habits of mind.
- The teacher is committed to reflection, assessment, and learning as an ongoing process.
- The teacher is willing to give and receive help.
- The teacher is committed to seeking out, developing, and continually refining practices that address the individual needs of students.
- The teacher recognizes his or her professional responsibility for engaging in and supporting appropriate professional practices for self and colleagues.

Performances
- The teacher uses classroom observation, information about students, and research as sources for evaluating the outcomes of teaching and learning and as a basis for experimenting with, reflecting on, and revising practice.
- The teacher seeks out professional literature, colleagues, and other resources to support his or her own development as a learner and a teacher.
- The teacher draws upon professional colleagues within the school and other professional arenas as supports for reflection, problem solving, and new ideas, actively sharing experiences and seeking and giving feedback.

Principle 10: The teacher fosters relationships with school colleagues, parents, and agencies in the larger community to support students' learning and well-being.

Knowledge

- The teacher understands schools as organizations within the larger community context and understands the operations of the relevant aspects of the system(s) within which he or she works.
- The teacher understands how factors in the students' environment outside of school (such as family circumstances, community environments, or health and economic conditions) may influence students' lives and learning.
- The teacher understands and implements laws related to students' rights and teacher responsibilities (including those for equal education, appropriate education for handicapped students, confidentiality, privacy, appropriate treatment of students, and reporting in situations related to possible child abuse).

Dispositions

- The teacher values and appreciates the importance of all aspects of a child's experience.
- The teacher is concerned about all aspects of a child's well-being (cognitive, emotional, social, and physical), and is alert to signs of difficulties.
- The teacher is willing to consult with other adults regarding the education and well-being of his or her students.
- The teacher respects the privacy of students and confidentiality of information.
- The teacher is willing to work with other professionals to improve the overall learning environment for students.

Performances

- The teacher participates in collegial activities designed to make the entire school a productive learning environment.
- The teacher makes links with the learners' other environments on behalf of students by consulting with parents, counselors, teachers of other classes and activities within the schools, and professionals in other community agencies.
- The teacher can identify and use community resources to foster student learning.
- The teacher establishes respectful and productive relationships with parents and guardians from diverse home and community situations and seeks to develop cooperative partnerships in support of student learning and well-being.
- The teacher talks with and listens to the student, is sensitive and responsive to clues of distress, investigates situations, and seeks outside help as needed and appropriate to remedy problems.
- The teacher acts as an advocate for students.

Helpful Terms to Know

A

Achievement test: A standardized test that measures academic skills or knowledge.

Active listening: Active listening is a learned skill that teaches you to fully listen and respond to others in the most effective manner possible.

ADA: American with Disabilities Act. This act prohibits discrimination based on disability.

ADD/ADHD: Attention deficit disorder or attention deficit hyperactivity disorder. ADD/ADHD is a treatable medical condition that results in a combination of distractibility, impulsivity, and hyperactive behavior.

Advanced Placement: A program run by the College Board whereby high school students complete a rigorous course of study and are then tested on their knowledge. Many colleges award credit to students for passing scores .

Advocate: An individual working for parents of students with disabilities to ensure their child receives an appropriate education.

Affective objectives: A lesson objective that involves feelings and dispositions.

Alternative assessments: Nontraditional assessments, such as checklists, peer-assessment, and self-assessment, that are different from traditional teacher-made tests, such as multiple-choice and matching.

Auditory learner: a learner who learns best through listening.

B

Behavioral learning theory: a theory of learning based on changing observable behavior through reinforcement.

Block schedule: A system whereby a school restructures the school day or week so that students are in classes for longer stretches of time.

Bloom, Benjamin: American educator who developed a hierarchical classification of cognitive levels known today as Bloom's taxonomy.

Bloom's taxonomy: A hierarchical system created by Benjamin Bloom that classifies the level of abstraction associated with a learning task. The six levels of Bloom's taxonomy in increasing order are the following: knowledge, comprehension, application, analysis, synthesis, and evaluation.

Bodily kinesthetic intelligence: The ability to control one's body and skillfully handle objects.

Brain hemisphericity: The concept that the brain has a right and left hemisphere and that individuals have a tendency toward having either right-brained or left-brained dominance.

Brown v. Board of Education: 1954 case in which the U.S. Supreme Court decided that "separate educational facilities are inherently unequal," which resulted in the desegregation of schools.

Busing: A transportation solution implemented to institute the changes brought about by desegregation. Students are bused from neighborhood schools in an effort to level racial percentages in a district.

C

Charter schools: Special public schools that have specific missions and goals not subject to many of the regulations that traditional public schools must follow. They are generally awarded a charter for a certain number of years with opportunities for renewal.

Cognitive objective: A lesson objective that involves thinking capabilities, from recalling facts to judging the quality of an argument.

Constructed-response or essay question: A type of test question that requires the respondent to create a written response.

Convergent question: A question that is closed-ended and has one correct answer.

Cooperative learning: An instructional strategy that involves students working together in small groups to complete an academic task.

Co-teaching: A system in which two certified teachers teach in a room at the same time. This is typically used to accommodate the needs of students with disabilities within the mainstreamed classroom.

Constructivism: This is a theory about how students learn based on the principle that students must construct their own understandings by connecting new knowledge to prior knowledge and through active experience with concepts.

Criterion-referenced test: A test in which questions are written according to specific predetermined criteria. A student knows what the standards are for passing and only competes against himself.

Critical thinking: Thinking in ways that draws conclusions and makes analyses using facts and information. This type of thinking is typically associated with the upper level of Bloom's taxonomy.

D

Deductive thinking: A type of thinking that uses one or more general rules to reach a conclusion about a specific case.

Distance learning: Education that is received at a geographical location separate from that of the educational institution providing the curriculum and material.

Divergent question: A question that is open-ended and has multiple correct responses.

Double sessions: A situation that typically occurs when schools are overcrowded. The school is divided in half. Half of the students attend classes in the morning, and the other half attend them in the afternoon or evening.

E

ESL: English as a second language. ESL classes are designed for individuals whose primary language is other than English.

Existential intelligence: The ability and desire to ask and search for answers to questions concerning human existence.

Extrinsic motivation: Incentives that are external to a student, such as tangible rewards or recognition.

F

FAPE: Free and Appropriate Public Education. FAPE is available to students with special needs under the Individuals with Disabilities Education Act (IDEA).

Field experience: In teacher preparation programs, this is a teaching experience in a real school setting.

Fill-in-the-blank or completion question: A type of question that requires students to fill in a blank with one word or a brief answer.

Formative evaluation: Evaluation that is ongoing during a program so that changes or modification can be made, if needed.

4 x 4 plan: A system whereby a school reorganizes its class time and structure so that students only have four courses per semester and courses are completed in half the "normal" time.

Full inclusion: The idea that a student with a disability should be placed in a classroom with non-disabled classmates and should only be removed from the regular classroom if the disability is so severe that, even with extra aid and help, the student cannot learn in that environment.

G

Gardner, Howard: A leading developmental psychologist who devised the influential theory of multiple intelligences.

Gifted: A term used by schools to define students who have high intelligence and/or who show creativity or talent at a level more advanced than their peers.

H

High-stakes testing: A practice that relates success on a standardized test to recognition or rewards of one kind or another.

Holistic grading: A method of grading in which a teacher grades a student's work as a whole, based on established criteria. In some cases, a group of teachers get together, decide on criteria for grading, and then quickly grade a set of papers based on these criteria.

I

IDEA: Individuals with Disabilities Education Act. This act requires that students who have disabilities be given the same opportunities to acquire the same level of education as students without disabilities. The main tool for implementing IDEA is the IEP.

IEP: Individualized Education Plan. This is an accountability measure that must be followed by the school, special education teachers, and regular education teachers. If accommodations are not made according to the IEP, the school can be liable for disciplinary and legal actions.

Inductive thinking: A type of thinking that proceeds from particular examples to reach a general conclusion.

Instructional strategies: The strategies a teacher uses to deliver instruction.

INTASC: the Interstate New Teacher Assessment and Support Consortium. This is a national consortium of higher education institutions, state agencies, and organizations formed for the purpose of reforming teacher certification and professional development.

INTASC standards: These are national standards used in states within the consortium that specify what teachers should know and be able to do.

Intrinsic motivation: Motivation that comes from the student's own internal incentives.

Interpersonal intelligence: Ability to relate well with others and to respond appropriately.

Intrapersonal intelligence: Having a strong sense of self-awareness and the ability to understand one's own feelings, values, and beliefs.

K, L

Kinesthetic learner: A learner who learns best through physical interaction.

LD: Learning disabled. Individuals with learning disabilities often have difficulty interpreting what they see and/or hear or have problems linking information from different parts of the brain.

Learning communities: A system that places students into "schools within schools" based on their abilities or career goals.

Learning style: The preferred way an individual processes information. One system classifies learners into three major types: visual, auditory and tactile/kinesthetic. Each person has a learning style by which they learn the best.

Left-brain learner: A learner whose learning approach is analytical, logical, and sequential.

Lesson objective: The instructional purpose of a lesson.

Linguistic intelligence: Having well-developed verbal skills and the ability to recognize the difference between sounds and rhythms of speech.

Logical-mathematical intelligence: The ability to see patterns and think in logical sequences.

LRE: Least restrictive environment. The provision under IDEA that a special education student should receive educational services in the regular education classroom to the maximum extent possible.

M

Magnet schools: Special schools that focus on a specific interest and use different types of organization for students with similar interests. For example, a performing arts magnet school offers and requires more performing arts courses than are available in a traditional school.

Manipulative: A physical object that can be used to model a concept.

Matching question: A type of test question that requires students to match a list of items with a set of answer choices based on a relationship between the items listed and their matching answer choices (e.g., countries with their capitals, terms with their characteristics).

Mean: The arithmetic average of a set of scores.

Median: The middle score or the average of the two middle scores when a set of scores is placed in order from least to greatest.

Mode: The score that occurs most often in a set of scores.

Motivation: A drive or incentive to do something.

Multiple intelligences: Howard Gardner devised this theory, which proposes that the traditional intelligence quotient (IQ) measure of intelligence does not show the whole or even part of the picture. He proposed that instead there are eight multiple intelligences and each person has his or her *own* strengths and weaknesses: linguistic, logical-mathematical, spatial, bodily kinesthetic, musical, interpersonal, intrapersonal, and naturalistic. Recently, Gardner also added a ninth intelligence—existential intelligence.

Multiple-choice question: A type of test question that requires students to select the correct or best answer from a number of possible options.

Musical intelligence: The ability to recognize musical patterns and discern rhythm and pitch.

N

National certification: A rigorous program in which teachers create a portfolio and take an exam in order to become nationally certified.

Naturalistic intelligence: A strong affinity with nature and ability to classify plants, animals, and other natural objects.

Negative reinforcement: Withdrawing unpleasant experiences as a means to increase correct behavior.

No Child Left Behind Act of 2001: This act signed into law by President George W. Bush has the goal of reducing the achievement gap between at-risk students and those that are traditionally successful in the classroom environment.

Norm-referenced test: A test that determines a student's placement on a normal distribution curve. On this type of assessment, students are compared to a norm group of test takers.

O

Objective test question: A test question (e.g., multiple-choice) that depends less on teacher judgment in the scoring process.

Online learning: Education that is delivered through the Internet. The Florida Virtual School is one example of an online learning school.

Operant conditioning: A system of discipline and behavior modification whereby an association is created between an action and a consequence.

P

Paradigm: A community's shared set of assumptions, values, and practices that shapes their reality. When major changes occur in education and life, it is sometimes said that a paradigm has shifted.

Pedagogy: The profession of teaching.

Portfolio: A collection of a student's work used to help determine progress and grade.

Positive reinforcement: Praising and rewarding students for correct behavior.

Psychomotor objective: A lesson objective that involves physical skills and coordination.

R

Range: The difference between the greatest score and the least score in a set of scores.

Reliability: In terms of assessments, a test is considered reliable if it allows for stable estimates of student ability. In other words, it achieves similar results for students who have similar ability and knowledge levels.

Right-brain learner: A learner whose learning style is holistic and global.

Rubric: A grading tool that defines the requirements each part of an assignment must meet to receive full or partial credit.

S

Scaffolding: Providing a student with assistance in completing a task that is just above the student's level of competence by building on what the student can already do.

Senior project: Typically, a portfolio or project created during a student's senior year in high school.

Skinner, B. F.: The psychologist who studied reinforcement and operant conditioning. His studies led to the development of programmed instruction.

Social promotion: The practice of promoting students to the next grade even though their progress doe not merit such promotion.

Spatial intelligence: The ability to perceive things visually. This type of learner typically thinks in pictures and needs to create mental images to retain information.

Standard deviation: A measure of the variability of a data set from its mean.

Subjective test question: A test question (e.g., essay) that requires more teacher judgment in the scoring process.

Summative evaluation: Evaluation that is used to assess the quality of a program.

T

Test bias: A preference for a certain group of test takers shown in compiling a test, so that results of the test vary based on group membership.

True-false question: A type of test question that requires students to decide whether a statement is true or false.

V

Validity: In terms of assessments, validity refers to the extent to which a test's content is representative of the actual skills learned and whether the test can provide accurate conclusions concerning achievement.

Varying exceptionalities: The idea that students of diverse needs following an IEP can be serviced effectively by being placed in a traditional classroom with a single certified education specialist.

Visual learner: A learner who learns best though seeing or reading.

Vouchers: A type of reform through which student or their parents/guardians receive the money that would have been used for their education in the public school system to help finance private school tuition.

Y, Z

Year-round education: A system in which students do not have a long summer break during the school year. Instead, they take a few weeks off periodically throughout the year. The most common method for doing this is the 45-15 Plan, which has students going to school for nine weeks and then taking three weeks of vacation.

Zone of proximal development: The gap between the level of performance or ability that a student can attain competently and the level of performance or ability immediately above that level.

Chapter 15

Principles of Learning and Teaching Practice Test

Two Case Histories and Constructed Response Questions

GENERAL SCORING GUIDE

All constructed-response questions will be assessed using a holistic rating scale ranging from 0-2.

Score of 2

The response appropriately answers all parts of the question and demonstrates an understanding of all of the details in the case study and of the principles of learning and teaching as outlined in the content categories covered in the test.

Score of 1

The response appropriately answers only part of the question.

Score of 0

The response does not appropriately answer any part of the question.

Note: Criteria for determining whether an answer is appropriate or not and scoring guides were established through a "model answer" approach, which consisted of the following process:

After the case and questions are written, three of four knowledgeable experts are asked to read the case and answer the questions, addressing each question exactly as it is worded. The experts are selected carefully to represent the diverse perspectives and situations relevant to the testing population.

The case writer uses these model answers to develop a question-specific scoring guide for each question, creating a list of specific examples that c\would receive full credit. The list contains some, but not all, possible correct answers.

These question-specific scoring guides provide a basis for selecting papers to serve as benchmark responses for the purpose of training scorers at the scoring session.

During the scoring sessions, the evaluators may add new answers to the scoring guide if they are considered appropriate responses.

Training at the scoring sessions is aimed to ensure that evaluators score papers based upon carefully established criteria in the scoring guide, not on their own opinions or preferences.

This section presents two case histories with constructed-response questions similar to those asked on the Principles of Learning and Teaching test. The questions are accompanied by sample responses with the standards used in scoring these responses. On the actual exam, your response will be scored by two readers who are practicing teachers. If the scores differ by more than one point, a third reader will be invited to assess your response. Readers assign scores based upon the following criteria. No credit is given for blank or off-topic responses.

Directions: The following case history is accompanied by two short answer questions. You should allow yourself approximately twenty minutes to read the case history and create a constructed response for both questions. The sample questions that follow illustrate the kinds of questions on the test. They are not, however, representative of the entire scope of the test in terms of content or difficulty. Answers with explanations and a general scoring guide follow the questions.

Case History 1—Ms. Lee
Scenario

Michele Lee, a middle school math teacher, observed that a number of students in her eighth-grade classes were having difficulty using and interpreting graphs, charts, and tables. As a result, she planned to offer a short unit of study on this topic.

Document 1: Initial Planning and Early Stages of the Unit

To begin the unit, Ms. Lee gave students a number of diagnostic problems, which she called "challenge problems." Enrichment activities were offered to students who could already solve the challenge problems. Students who were unable to solve the challenge problems received additional instruction for reinforcement. During the course of the unit, students were regularly allowed to attempt to solve the challenge problems that they were unable to solve at the outset. When a student was able to solve the challenge problems, he or she moved on to the enrichment activities. Ms. Lee planned to continue to offer the supplementary instruction periodically throughout the semester until every student in the class could solve all the challenge problems.

Document 2: Phone Conference with Parent—November 5

Shortly after beginning the unit, Ms. Lee received a telephone call from Mr. Wetzel, the parent of one of her eighth-grade students. The parent was concerned that too much emphasis was being given to graphic representations of information in

Ms. Lee's class and that students were not learning what they would need to know to pass the end-of-course district math test for eighth graders. Here is an excerpt from their conversation.

Mr. Wetzel: When I was in school, we learned how to calculate and solve the math problems. Now, when I offer to help Jacob with his homework, he tells me that he has to draw a graph or create a chart. What does this have to do with math? It sounds like science to me! Jacob is going to have to learn how to calculate and solve equations to pass the course exam, but I don't see anything about graphs, charts, or tables listed in the objectives I received for the eighth-grade math test.

Ms. Lee: I understand your concern Mr. Wetzel, but many students have difficulty learning how to create and read graphs and charts. Since these skills are needed in science and other classes besides math, we want to ensure that each student masters them, no matter how long it takes. It has always been against my educational philosophy to "teach to the test." More importantly, on the Algebra I end-of-course test, which your son will be taking next year or the year after, an entire domain is devoted to graphing.

Mr. Wetzel: That may be true, but right now what I'm most concerned about is the test Jacob will be taking at the end of this year, not the year after.

Document 3: Interdisciplinary Planning with the Science Teacher— November 10

The students in Ms. Lee's eighth-grade class are also students of Mr. Castillo, the science teacher on Ms. Lee's team. During the course of the unit, Ms. Lee met with Mr. Castillo to discuss ways of coordinating their instructional plans to help students who were having difficulty using and interpreting graphic representations. At the meeting, Ms. Lee showed Mr. Castillo her plans for the additional lessons for reinforcement. She asked him about the feasibility of basing some of the challenge problems on data that students gathered from experiments in science class. Ms. Lee felt that students related much better to data that they collected themselves than to data given in a textbook.

Document 3, continued

Mr. Castillo was enthusiastic about Ms. Lee's idea. He showed her his instructional plans for some upcoming experiments and described the learning objectives that they addressed. Mr. Castillo also offered to work with Ms. Lee to develop interesting and accessible scientific examples to illustrate key math concepts she would be teaching.

The following two questions address **Case History 2—*Ms. Lee***. Use the information presented in the case history to analyze and following the questions. Base your answers on your understanding of basic principles of teaching and learning.

Read the question carefully and make sure to answer all parts of the question. Write your constructed response answers on the lined pages indicated on the pages that follow.

QUESTION 1
Review the initial planning and early implementation phase of the unit. Describe two ways that Ms. Lee could strengthen the use of "challenge problems" and encourage students to persevere in working on the challenge problems that they find difficult. Base your response on principles of learning theory, motivation, and effective instruction.
Stop for a moment. Reflect on what is being asked in this question.
In the space below, write, in your own words, what you think is being asked in this Question 1.

_____

_____

_____

_____

Compare your description with the following explanation of the question in the space below.
The question asks you to assess the planning and implementation of an instructional unit and identify two ways that Ms. Lee could strengthen the strategy and use of "challenge problems."

QUESTION 2
Review the parent conversation with Mr. Wetzel in which Ms. Lee states the purpose for the emphasis on graphic representation of answers for math equations. What could Ms. Lee have done differently to improve the communication with this parent? Base your response on principles for effective communication and appropriate uses of instructional strategies.
Stop for a moment. Reflect on what is being asked in this question.
In the space below, write, in your own words, what you think is being asked in this Question 2.

_____

_____

_____

_____

Compare your description with the following explanation of the question in the space below.
The question asks you to evaluate the parent-teacher conference and make suggestions to improve Ms. Lee's communication with Mr. Wetzel to improve the outcome of the conference.

Principles of Learning and Teaching Practice Test

Write your response to Question 1 here.

_____
_____
_____
_____
_____
_____
_____
_____
_____
_____
_____
_____
_____
_____
_____
_____
_____
_____
_____
_____
_____
_____
_____
_____
_____
_____
_____

Principles of Learning and Teaching Practice Test
Write your response to Question 2 here.

Directions: The following case history is accompanied by two short answer questions. You should allow yourself approximately twenty minutes to read the case history and create a constructed response for both questions. The sample questions that follow illustrate the kinds of questions on the test. They are not, however, representative of the entire scope of the test in terms of content or difficulty. Answers with explanations and a general scoring guide follow the questions.

Case History 2—Mr. Weaver

Scenario

Chet Weaver, a new seventh-grade English teacher, is concerned about his last-period class. It is now the second month of the school year, and he has been having ongoing problems with the students in this class being inattentive, restless, loud, and interrupting each other and himself.

Document 1: Conversation with Mentor during Planning Period– October 7

Mr. Weaver describes the problems to his mentor, Ms. Preston, and she asks him to explain what he thinks may be causing the problems. Following is an excerpt from their conversation.

Mr. Weaver: You know, I don't have problems like this with my other classes, so I really think a big part of the problem is simply that this class meets the last period of the day. I think the kids are just tired and hungry and burned out.

Ms. Preston: I know what you mean. But you still have to find ways to help them settle down and pay attention.

Mr. Weaver: Don't you know that I realize that? I'm really quite concerned because they'll be giving oral reports soon, and I'm afraid that at this point they'd be really rude to one another and not pay attention.

Ms. Preston: So, what do you think might help the situation the most?

Mr. Weaver: Well, it's clear to me that I'm not the only one who is concerned about the noise level in the class. Some of the students have complained and have even told their friends to knock it off. I was actually thinking of using that and encouraging the students to try to solve the problem themselves—have *them* focus on the problem. And then encourage them to work out guidelines for class behavior that'll address everyone's concerns and that they all will have to follow.

Ms. Preston: I think that's a very good idea. That approach has worked well for me. To help you facilitate their discussion, I'd be happy to show you some examples of guidelines for talking and listening that my students have come up with in the past.

Mr. Weaver: I'd appreciate that. I'm also thinking of ways to harness all that unfocused energy. Maybe if the students were actively engaged in group activities more of the time . . .

Document 2: Class Assignment—October 8

Based upon his discussion with his mentor, Mr. Weaver decides to help the students develop and adopt their own guidelines for behavior in large group activities. Mr. Weaver approaches the lesson in the following way.

Mr. Weaver: I want to get your ideas about a class problem. The behavior of most of our students during the large group's activities is not acceptable in here. Please tell me:

>What do you think the causes of the problem are?
>
>How has the problem affected you?
>
>What solutions do you think might work?

Document 3: Teacher Reflection Log—October 13

I think that today's activity went really well. Already I am seeing a difference in the students' behavior. I asked the students to engage in a creative role play before presenting their oral reports. After the role play, I asked the students who were playing the role of the speaker to describe how the various audience reactions, body language, gestures, etc. made them feel. As a result, the students decided to add a new section to their class behavior guidelines that includes "do's and don'ts" for good listening. Wow! Ms. Preston was right. I could not believe it—they actually came up with suggestions to help each other listen better. I am worried about Mary Grace, however. She seems listless and tired. Her participation has dropped off and her homework has been missing or incomplete lately. I think I'll ask Ms. Preston to watch her behavior when she comes to observe me later in the week and see if she can help me find out what is wrong.

Document 4: Mentor Anecdotal Record of Class Observation— October 17

Mr. Weaver's classroom management difficulties have improved significantly. Students came in quieter and were easily focused on the topic of today's lesson. They are generally more attentive and less disruptive. Mr. Weaver asked me to pay close attention to one student in particular, Mary Grace, whose class participation and homework have dropped off since the beginning of the year. Today, the student seemed tired and drained of energy. She did not participate and started to fall asleep during the period, but one of her classmates prodded her before Mr. Weaver saw her nodding off.

QUESTION 3

Review the conversation with the mentor, the class assignment, and the teacher reflection log. Describe two strengths that explain the success of the mentor teacher's suggestions and Mr. Weaver's follow-up lesson in which the students adopted their own guidelines for their behavior. Base your response on principles of effective classroom management, motivation, and human development.

Stop for a moment. Reflect on what is being asked in this question.

In the space below, write, in your own words, what you think is being asked in this Question 3.

_____

_____

_____

_____

_____

Compare your description with the following explanation of the question in the space below.

The question asks you to review the archival documents and assess the mentor teacher's suggestions to Mr. Weaver by identifying and describing two strengths that explain the follow-up lesson's success.

QUESTION 4

Review the mentor teacher's observation notes from the class meeting on October 20. Explain two actions that Ms. Preston might suggest to Mr. Weaver to help determine the change in Mary Grace's behavior and to foster improvement in her class participation and homework. Base your response on principles of human development, motivation, and the learning environment.

Stop for a moment. Reflect on what is being asked in this question.

In the space below, write, in your own words, what you think is being asked in this Question 4.

_____

_____

_____

_____

_____

Compare your description with the following explanation of the question in the space below.

The question asks you to interpret anecdotal records of a student's behavior and make recommendations of two actions that the mentor teacher might suggest to facilitate a positive change in the student's class participation and completion of homework.

Principles of Learning and Teaching Practice Test

Write your response to Question 3 here.

Principles of Learning and Teaching Practice Test

Write your response to Question 4 here.

_____

_____

_____

_____

_____

_____

_____

_____

_____

_____

_____

_____

_____

_____

_____

_____

_____

_____

_____

_____

_____

_____

_____

Principles of Learning and Teaching Practice Test
Multiple-Choice Questions Answer Sheet for Practice Test

1. Ⓐ Ⓑ Ⓒ Ⓓ Ⓔ
2. Ⓐ Ⓑ Ⓒ Ⓓ Ⓔ
3. Ⓐ Ⓑ Ⓒ Ⓓ Ⓔ
4. Ⓐ Ⓑ Ⓒ Ⓓ Ⓔ
5. Ⓐ Ⓑ Ⓒ Ⓓ Ⓔ
6. Ⓐ Ⓑ Ⓒ Ⓓ Ⓔ
7. Ⓐ Ⓑ Ⓒ Ⓓ Ⓔ
8. Ⓐ Ⓑ Ⓒ Ⓓ Ⓔ

9. Ⓐ Ⓑ Ⓒ Ⓓ Ⓔ
10. Ⓐ Ⓑ Ⓒ Ⓓ Ⓔ
11. Ⓐ Ⓑ Ⓒ Ⓓ Ⓔ
12. Ⓐ Ⓑ Ⓒ Ⓓ Ⓔ
13. Ⓐ Ⓑ Ⓒ Ⓓ Ⓔ
14. Ⓐ Ⓑ Ⓒ Ⓓ Ⓔ
15. Ⓐ Ⓑ Ⓒ Ⓓ Ⓔ
16. Ⓐ Ⓑ Ⓒ Ⓓ Ⓔ

17. Ⓐ Ⓑ Ⓒ Ⓓ Ⓔ
18. Ⓐ Ⓑ Ⓒ Ⓓ Ⓔ
19. Ⓐ Ⓑ Ⓒ Ⓓ Ⓔ
20. Ⓐ Ⓑ Ⓒ Ⓓ Ⓔ
21. Ⓐ Ⓑ Ⓒ Ⓓ Ⓔ
22. Ⓐ Ⓑ Ⓒ Ⓓ Ⓔ
23. Ⓐ Ⓑ Ⓒ Ⓓ Ⓔ
24. Ⓐ Ⓑ Ⓒ Ⓓ Ⓔ

Principles of Learning and Teaching Practice Test

Practice Multiple-Choice Questions

24 Multiple-Choice Questions
Time: 25 minutes

Directions: This practice test offers you the opportunity to simulate the actual Principles of Learning and Teaching test in terms of length, time, and questions. Use the suggested approaches and test taking strategies introduced in Chapter 12 to assist you in answering the multiple choice questions that follow.

Read each question carefully and critically. Think about the question being asked. Eliminate any wrong answers and select the answer choice that best answers the question. Mark the correct answer choice on your answer sheet.

The following multiple choice questions are not related to the previous case. For each question, select the best answer and mark the corresponding space on your answer sheet.

1. A team of middle school teachers is working to develop an interdisciplinary unit for their fifth grade students. These teachers realize that an important advantage of using interdisciplinary instruction rather than single-subject instruction is that interdisciplinary instruction is more likely to help students:
   A. develop the social and emotional competence to work effectively in different content areas.
   B. acquire the ability to reflect on and evaluate their own learning strategies.
   C. recognize and take advantage of significant connections among the content areas.
   D. take greater responsibility for their own learning and develop a lifelong love of learning.

2. When grouping students for small-group activities, Mr. Rose tries to ensure that each group is heterogeneous in terms of students' backgrounds and achievement levels. This grouping practice is most likely to benefit students by helping them:
   A. learn at a pace that is better adjusted to their individual abilities and needs.
   B. reach the same level of achievement as their classmates in about the same amount of time.
   C. experience working with a team that has members who are skilled in more than one subject.
   D. work more productively with students whose backgrounds differ from their own.

3. Ms. Burke, a fourth grade science teacher, realizes that an important benefit to students of having them complete self-assessment tasks is that the tasks are likely to:

    A. encourage students to evaluate their performance relative to other students.

    B. give students a sense of ownership in their fitness plans.

    C. help students identify incentives for attaining acceptable levels of performance.

    D. motivate students to work cooperatively on their fitness plans.

4. This year, Ms. Burke's classes include several students with mild to severe physical disabilities. Ms. Burke can best fulfill her legal and professional responsibilities to these students by:

    A. modifying the students' individual educational plans to include planned class activities.

    B. designing alternative, less-demanding instructional activities for the students.

    C. exempting the students as much as possible from participating in competitive activities.

    D. adapting instruction to comply with the students' individual educational plans.

5. Mr. Larkin, a ninth grade history teacher, realizes that engaging students in a role-playing activity and follow-up discussion is most likely to improve their conduct in class by:

    A. improving their oral communication skills.

    B. creating a classroom climate of mutual respect.

    C. encouraging them to correct one another's behavior.

    D. encouraging them to explore a variety of communication styles.

6. Which of the following approaches would be best for Ms. Weaver, a sixth grade math teacher, to use in beginning her conversation in a parent-teacher conference concerning Link, a student in Ms. Weaver's classroom?

    A. Describe positive aspects of Link's performance in the classroom.

    B. Emphasize the need for the parents to work closely with teachers to ensure that Link completes his work on time.

    C. Impress upon the parents the negative consequences of failing to deal with Link's problems at an early stage.

    D. Allow the parents to guide the conversation in the direction that is most comfortable for them.

7. Mr. Jackson is a seventh grade P.E. teacher who decides to consult the ESL teacher about Maricela's performance in his class. This decision most clearly demonstrates Mr. Jackson's awareness that:
   A. student diversity in the classroom creates unique learning opportunities.
   B. a student's level of development in one area may affect performance in other areas.
   C. student performance is often enhanced when clear goals for learning are identified.
   D. a student's learning style can play an important role in academic achievement.

8. In working with her seventh and eighth graders, Ms. DeLeon discovers that one group is having difficulty agreeing on a media topic to investigate. The most effective way for her to help the group members work out their difficulty is to:
   A. offer to make the decision for them if agreement cannot be reached.
   B. talk to each member individually to assess the social dynamics involved in the conflict.
   C. suggest they take a vote and abide by the wish of the majority.
   D. ask questions designed to prompt them to weigh different perspectives and reach consensus.

9. One of Mr. Jackson's ninth-grade students, Addie, is new to the school this year. Mr. Jackson observes:
   Addie seems bright and motivated, but appears physically restless and easily distracted in class.
   Addie demonstrates an ability to understand and apply mathematical concepts, but her homework is often missing or incomplete.
   Addie is eager to participate in class discussions, but she tends to interrupt the teacher or other students and has difficulty working in small groups.

   Over the next few weeks, Mr. Jackson works closely with Addie, varying her opportunities to interact with other students, helping her use computer tutorials, and arranging additional support through the school's peer mentoring program. Addie's performance, however, shows no improvement.

   As Mr. Jackson explores additional ways to help Addie, which of the following steps would be best for him to take *next*?
   A. Provide Addie with direct teacher support through individual coaching sessions.
   B. Contact Addie's other teachers to see if she is experiencing similar difficulties in their classes.
   C. Provide Addie with peer feedback by pairing her with a high-ability study partner.
   D. Contact other English teachers to discuss alternative instructional strategies.

10. When Addie's performance continues to show no improvement, Mr. Jackson examines records from her previous school and informally consults with Ms. Greer, the school's special education teacher. After listening to Mr. Jackson's description of Addie's behavior and observing her in class, Ms. Greer suggests that Addie may have a learning disability and recommends further evaluation.

    The series of actions taken by Mr. Jackson with regard to Addie best demonstrates his understanding that teachers should:
    A. collaborate with special education staff to develop individual educational plans for students with special needs.
    B. initiate special education referrals as soon as possible if they suspect that students may need special education services.
    C. work with special education staff when necessary to provide transition services for students with special needs.
    D. initiate special education referrals only when other classroom strategies fail to enhance student learning.

11. Mr. Jackson and Ms. Green decide to discuss with Addie's parents the possibility of screening Addie for a learning disability. When Mr. Jackson speaks with Addie's parents, they initially react with alarm to the possibility of special education services for Addie. "She's just now getting used to your class," they tell Mr. Jackson. "Wouldn't switching her to a special education class just make matters worse?" Mr. Jackson can best respond to the parents' concern by pointing out that:
    A. the potential benefits of special education services for students with special needs outweigh the possible drawbacks.
    B. special education services can often be provided within the context of the regular education classroom.
    C. the school is legally obligated to provide special education services to students with disabilities.
    D. the school's special education staff conduct a thorough evaluation before recommending a student for special education services.

12. Addie's parents question Mr. Jackson about the role of admission, review, and dismissal (ARD) committees. The parents say that they are worried about surrendering control of their daughter's education to an ARD committee. Mr. Jackson can best reassure Addie's parents on this point by explaining that parents of students referred for special education services:
    A. may discuss their concerns outside of the ARD committee meeting at any time.
    B. are full participants in all meetings and they may request a meeting of the ARD committee at any time.
    C. are allowed to attend ARD committee meetings as observers.
    D. may select the members of the ARD committee.

13. For each work sample that students include in their portfolios, Ms. Hanson, a fourth grade teacher, asks her students to write a one- to two-paragraph explanation of why they consider the work sample to be among their best work. The most important benefit to students of preparing these written self-evaluations is that it is likely to encourage students to:
    A. manage their workload more effectively.
    B. learn more about other ways in which they can express themselves.
    C. develop a reflective and critical attitude toward their own work.
    D. compare their own progress with that of their peers.

14. Ms. Hanson can most effectively avoid any appearance of bias or arbitrariness in her evaluation of students' portfolios by:
    A. using evaluative criteria that students understand and agree on.
    B. establishing a minimum number of items for students to include in the portfolios.
    C. evaluating portfolios on a credit/no credit or pass/fail basis.
    D. providing a written evaluation to each student.

15. Taking students on a field trip associated with an instructional unit is likely to benefit students most by:
    A. exposing them to more complex and challenging cognitive tasks than in the classroom.
    B. providing them with opportunities to interact with their peers.
    C. helping them develop an awareness that learning takes place both inside and outside the classroom.
    D. providing them with opportunities for first-hand experiences related to subject matter they are studying.

16. The science teacher, Ms. Winn, is a new teacher and has limited experience with classroom management. The first time she brings a large group of students to the pond to collect samples, a number of them have difficulty staying focused. Though the teacher repeatedly instructs students to stay out of the water, some students begin to splash and wade into the pond. One piece of equipment is dropped into the water and lost. Which of the following would be the most appropriate and effective way for Ms. Winn to prevent such behavior problems from happening in the future during outdoor activities?
    A. Significantly reduce the number of outdoor activities associated with the unit and make it clear to students that they have lost that privilege.
    B. Inform students that their behavior will be counted as a factor when calculating grades for the outdoor activity.
    C. Clarify her expectations for student behavior during outdoor activities and outline the consequences for individuals who misbehave.
    D. Formulate detailed written directions about the activity to hand out to students as soon as they leave the building for an outdoor activity.

17. Students have varying degrees of experience with computer technology. Some students are well versed in the use of computer technology, while others have little or no experience with computers. Which of the following activities is the most appropriate way for teachers to try to increase students' motivation to improve their computer skills?

    A. Foster work partnerships between students with strong computer skills and students whose skills are more limited.

    B. Grant students extra credit for turning in assignments that were completed on the computer.

    C. Require after-school tutorials for students who cannot perform at a certain level of proficiency on the computer.

    D. Praise in front of their peers those students who are highly skilled in using computers.

18. A middle school has recently completed the construction of a new library media center that offers students and teachers the benefits of state-of-the-art technology equipment and high-speed Internet access, in addition to a wide variety of multimedia and software editing equipment. How can teachers best promote positive interactions between students and members of the community using the new media center's resources?

    A. Use word processing software to produce a newsletter of school activities for distribution to parents and guardians.

    B. Videotape a simulated news broadcast on a local community issue and make copies available for parents and guardians to borrow from the school's library media center.

    C. Use spreadsheet software to graph trends and patterns in local community growth and send the results to relevant officials in the town government.

    D. Use the Internet to exchange information and establish contacts with others in the community who are involved and interested in local issues.

19. Before taking students on a field trip to the Art Museum, Mr. Geisel plans to engage students in a discussion in which they explore textiles, listen to music, and examine photographs of architecture from the time period of the exhibit that they will visit at the Museum. This discussion is most likely to facilitate student learning during the field trip by:

    A. encouraging students to make predictions they can test during the trip.

    B. supplying students with background information about the trip.

    C. increasing students awareness and exposure to concepts that will be explored on the trip.

    D. helping students understand how their participation in the trip will be assessed.

20. Ms. Stephen's principal is encouraging teachers to use discovery learning as an alternative to direct instruction approaches. Discovery learning is most appropriately used to help students:
    A. memorize the rules of subject-verb agreement.
    B. learn the process for finding the least common denominator.
    C. understand the concept of decomposition.
    D. learn the functions of the major systems in the body.

21. Mr. Jenlink asks his students to use a graphic organizer in conjunction with the assigned reading. This strategy best demonstrates Mr. Jenlink's understanding of the importance of:
    A. selecting appropriate resources to address individual student needs.
    B. helping students process and assimilate new information.
    C. evaluating the effectiveness of instructional techniques.
    D. managing collective student use of limited materials and resources.

22. Mr. Jenlink then asks students to use the information they have collected on their graphic organizers to try to explain in their own words what they think a certain phrase means. This activity is likely to benefit students most by:
    A. testing their ability to remember factual information contained in the text.
    B. accommodating their individual learning styles.
    C. engaging them in higher-order thinking about information in the text.
    D. rewarding them for completing their reading of the text.

23. Ms. Townes has her students keep reflection logs to evaluate their learning and identify the strategies they feel help them learn best. Which of the following principles of learning is Ms. Townes helping her students to develop with this strategy?
    A. metacognition
    B. social learning
    C. schema theory
    D. transfer

24. Mr. Ross, a social studies teacher, suggests that students consider studying a culture from their own family background in an upcoming unit. This suggestion demonstrates that Mr. Ross understands the principle that teachers should try to:
    A. work cooperatively with families in addressing students' needs.
    B. establish regular communication between the school and the home.
    C. create contexts that foster family involvement in students' learning.
    D. devise study strategies that can be used in the home.

Answer Explanations for
Sample Constructed Response Questions

Case History 1—Ms. Lee

QUESTION 1

Review the initial planning and early implementation phase of the unit. Describe two ways that Ms. Lee could strengthen the use of "challenge problems" and encourage students to persevere in working on the challenge problems that they find difficult. Base your response on principles of learning theory, motivation, and effective instruction.

Sample response that would receive a score of 2.

One way that Ms. Lee can strengthen use of the challenge problems, and at the same time encourage students to persevere in working on challenge problems, is to provide regular constructive feedback to the students about their responses to the questions. To raise student motivation, Ms. Lee can weight the students' effort higher than their performance when assessing the challenge problems. Furthermore, she can weight improvement higher than performance when evaluating students. Helping the students understand the purpose for challenge problems and using the challenge problems as a diagnostic self-assessment tool to identify the students' strengths and needs will increase the likelihood that students will persevere in solving the challenge problems without becoming discouraged.

Sample response that would receive a score of 1.

Ms. Lee can do a number of things in order to help her students stay motivated to solve challenge problems. The most important thing for her to do is to award students partial credit for partially correct answers and weight improvement higher than performance. This will keep students motivated because they receive some credit for their work.

Sample response that would receive a score of 0.

Although challenge problems sound like a good idea, Ms. Lee probably should not use them in her classroom. Since this is early in the teaching unit, this strategy is not appropriate for reinforcement. Furthermore, this technique makes students who cannot complete the problem feel inferior to their classmates.

QUESTION 2

Review the parent conversation with Mr. Wetzel in which Ms. Lee states the purpose for the emphasis on graphic representation of answers for math equations. What could Ms. Lee have done differently to improve the communication with this parent? Base your response on principles for effective communication and appropriate uses of instructional strategies.

Sample response that would receive a score of 2.

To begin with, Ms. Lee needed to address the parent's concern more directly. Mr. Wetzel was concerned that his son, Jacob, would not be prepared for the end-of-course exam because Ms. Lee was spending time teaching a math concept that was not on the test. Ms. Lee needed to explain and reassure Mr. Wetzel that all of the concepts on the end-of-course exam were given equal consideration while other concepts were being reinforced that would be needed later.

Ms. Lee needed to gain the parent's confidence in her abilities to plan instruction that would promote the success of every student in the course. In order to improve her communication with Mr. Wetzel, Ms. Lee should have examined whether any cultural or linguistic factors were present that may have inhibited her understanding of the parent's concern. An example of one such factor is that sometimes a person's action, speech, or behavior may send a different message to a person from a different culture.

Sample response that would receive a score of 1.

Ms. Lee needed to address the parent's concern about not preparing his son, Jacob, for the test. Ms. Lee should schedule a conference with the parent so she can talk with him face-to-face and share some of Jacob's work on other math objectives that will be tested. Also, Ms. Lee may want to show Mr. Wetzel the course outline and course objectives in comparison with the end-of-course exam in order to reassure him that his son will be adequately prepared.

Sample response that would receive a score of 0.

Ms. Lee should not have to defend her position to the parent. She is doing an excellent job of teaching the skills that the students need while covering others which they do not yet grasp, but will need later. Mr. Wetzel appears to be a hostile parent and Ms. Lee should have the assistant principal for instruction talk with the parent.

Case History 2—Mr. Weaver

QUESTION 3

Review the conversation with the mentor, the class assignment, and the teacher reflection log. Describe two strengths that explain the success of the mentor teacher's suggestions and Mr. Weaver's follow-up lesson in which the students adopted their own guidelines for their behavior. Base your response on principles of effective classroom management, motivation, and human development

Sample response that would receive a score of 2.

There are several reasons for the success of the mentor teacher's recommendation to ask students to develop their own guidelines for improving behavior in class. First, by drafting and adopting their own guidelines, the students were more likely to be self-motivated to improve their behavior. Also, the class assignment made the students more aware of the need for rules for appropriate behavior. Finally, the role-playing activity and follow-up discussion promoted a view of the class as a community of learners and helped the students recognize more of their strengths and needs in serving as a good audience for each other.

Sample response that would receive a score of 1.

The lesson and the follow-up activity promoted self-responsibility among the students. Through class discussion, they became aware of the problems and possible solutions for improving their behavior in Mr. Weaver's class. The role playing also gave them an opportunity to act responsibly and set up consequences for their behavior.

Sample response that would receive a score of 0.

One can easily tell that the mentor teacher gave Mr. Weaver a good suggestion because the students responded well. Mr. Weaver followed Ms. Preston's suggestion closely and the success naturally followed. Mr. Weaver is fortunate to have such a mentor to guide his developing classroom management skills.

QUESTION 4

Review the mentor teacher's observation notes from the class meeting on October 20. Explain two actions that Ms. Preston might suggest to Mr. Weaver to help determine the change in Mary Grace's behavior and to foster improvement in her class participation and homework. Base your response on principles of human development, motivation, and the learning environment.

Sample response that would receive a score of 2.

First, Ms. Preston should suggest that Mr. Weaver talk with Mary Grace about the changes that he has seen in her behavior in the class and to ask her how she is doing in her other classes. The mentor should explain to Mr. Weaver that he begin the conference by describing positive aspects of Mary Grace's performance in the classroom. He then should describe the changes in her behavior and ask Mary Grace to reflect and explain if she has noticed any changes in the way she feels in class or to explain why she thinks her participation level and grades have dropped. Following the discussion with Mary Grace, Ms. Preston should also suggest that Mr. Weaver call her parents or caregivers to schedule an appointment for a three way parent-student-teacher conference.

Sample response that would receive a score of 1.

One recommendation that Ms. Preston should suggest is that Mr. Weaver talk with the other teachers on the team to see if Mary Grace's participation has also dropped in their classes. If so, the teachers should contact Mary Grace individually to discuss her participation and performance in each of their respective classes. The teachers might discuss setting up a contingency plan, or contract, for Mary Grace and offer her an incentive to increase her participation in their classes.

Sample response that would receive a score of 0.

Ms. Preston should recommend that Mr. Weaver schedule an appointment with Mary Grace's parents or caregivers to inquire about changes at home that may have influenced Mary Grace's performance in school. Making Mary Grace's parents aware of the changes is the first step to helping her improve her participation and raise her grades. Ms. Preston should emphasize the need for Mr. Weaver to work closely with Mary Grace's parents to ensure that she completes her work on time.

Principles of Learning and Teaching Practice Test

Answer Explanations of Correct and Incorrect Answers

1. C. Question 1 assesses the INTASC Standard Principle 4: *The teacher understands and uses a variety of instructional strategies to encourage students' development of critical thinking, problem-solving, and performance skills.*

This question asks you to show your understanding of instructional strategies and the cognitive processes associated with student learning. A major advantage of interdisciplinary instruction is that subject matter is taught in relation to a common concept or theme, which allows students to make connections across the disciplines.

An interdisciplinary unit is unlikely to develop social and emotional competence (option A). The unit also does not ensure that students will take greater responsibility for their own learning (option D) nor reflect on and evaluate their own learning strategies (option B).

Therefore, the right answer choice is C.

2. D. Question 2 assesses the INTASC Standard Principle 5: *The teacher uses an understanding of individual and group motivation and behavior to create a learning environment that encourages positive social interaction, active engagement in learning, and self-motivation.*

This question asks you to demonstrate your understanding of methods for enhancing student learning. Research on cooperative learning clearly shows that students in mixed-ability groups reach higher learning gains than students placed in homogenous groups.

None of the other options pertains to best practices for grouping students. Grouping will not alter the pace at which a student learns (option A). Also, grouping will not assist students in reaching achievement levels simultaneously (option B). While heterogeneous groups may allow some members to work with diverse members (option C), the grouping practice is most likely to benefit students by facilitating group productivity.

Since these groups are mixed in terms of their abilities and backgrounds, answer choice D is the correct answer.

3. B. Question 3 assesses the INTASC Standard Principle 8: *The teacher understands and uses formal and informal assessment strategies to evaluate and ensure the continuous intellectual, social, and physical development of the learner.*

This question asks you to demonstrate your understanding of assessment theory and recognize appropriate use of a specific assessment strategy. Fostering the use of self-assessment promotes autonomy in learners and gives students a sense of ownership in their plans.

This question does not relate to evaluation in relation to others (Option A) or motivating students to work cooperatively (option D). Self-assessment does not lend itself to helping students identify incentives for acceptable levels of performance.

Thus, the correct answer is B.

4. D. The fourth question assesses the INTASC Standard Principle 3: *The teacher understands how students differ in their approaches to learning and creates instructional opportunities that are adapted to diverse learners.*

This question asks you to consider a professional question related to the rights of students with disabilities and teacher responsibilities. According to IDEA, the Individuals with Disabilities Education Act, students with disabilities must be served in the least restrictive environment. Students who are identified should receive instruction that is modified to best meet their learning needs. These modifications are prescribed on an Individualized Education Plan (IEP).

Modifying the students' individual educational plan (option A) will not fulfill the teacher's responsibilities regarding the rights of special education students. Designing modified assignments that are less rigorous than those in the regular classroom (option B) and exempting students from compliance requirements (option C) are also not in the best interest of students with mild to severe disabilities.

Thus, answer choice D is the right answer.

5. B. Question 5 assesses the INTASC Standard Principle 6: *The teacher uses knowledge of effective verbal, nonverbal, and media communication techniques to foster active inquiry, collaboration, and supportive interaction in the classroom.*

This question asks you to apply your understanding of instructional approaches that are used to foster classroom management and promote cooperation and positive relationships. Role playing and discussion engage students in a medium-risk environment that will allow them to develop trust.

Improving oral communication skills (option A) and encouraging a variety of communication styles will help facilitate communication in the classroom, but not necessarily improve class conduct. Also, having students correct one another could be detrimental to their class behavior and conduct (option C).

Answer choice B is the right answer.

6. A. Question 6 assesses the INTASC Standard Principle 6: *The teacher uses knowledge of effective verbal, nonverbal, and media communication techniques to foster active inquiry, collaboration, and supportive interaction in the classroom.*

This question asks you to apply principles of effective communication and identify an appropriate communication technique when communicating with parents and caregivers. Teachers should begin and end parent conferences on a positive note about the student. This action will promote a positive relationship between the teacher and the parent(s).

Item choices C and D offer two strategies that are based on best practices for facilitating positive parent-teacher conferences. Emphasizing the more negative aspects of consequences for failing to attend to the student's problems (option C) is most likely to be a deterrent to positive relations in the conference. The correct answer choice is A.

7. B. Question 7 assesses the INTASC Standard Principle 2: *The teacher understands how children learn and develop and can provide learning opportunities that support their intellectual, social, and personal development.*

This question asks you to show your understanding of human development and its relationship to the effects of cultural, gender, and linguistic differences on communication in the classroom. The teacher recognizes that development is interrelated and that language differences may influence a student's understanding and performance in more than one class.

Teacher-to-teacher consultation for understanding student performance is not addressed in the general statements about learning opportunity and diversity (option A), performance and goal setting (option C), or the relationship of learning style and academic achievement.

Answer choice B is the right answer.

8. D. Question 8 assesses the INTASC Standard Principle 6: *The teacher uses knowledge of effective verbal, nonverbal, and media communication techniques to foster active inquiry, collaboration, and supportive interaction in the classroom.*

This question asks you to demonstrate your understanding of instructional strategies and apply principles of effective classroom management to identify a strategy that would be appropriate for resolving group conflict in a small cooperative learning group. A general principle of cooperative learning is that students, when placed in cooperative groups to learn, should resolve their conflicts as a group. The teacher acts as a facilitator and helps the group to realize its differences of opinion and resolve conflicts (Option D) in order to reach a common goal.

In conflict resolution, the teacher should not offer to make the decision for the students (option A). A majority rule vote (option C) is an inappropriate way to help the group members resolve their difficulties in the role of problem solver. Also, assessing the individual and group social dynamic (option B) will not lead to conflict resolution.

Answer choice D, therefore, is the right answer.

9. B. Question 9 assesses the INTASC Standard Principle 10: *The teacher fosters relationships with school colleagues, parents, and agencies in the larger community to support students' learning and well-being.*

This question asks you to extend your understanding of differentiating instruction to meet students' different learning needs. In this case, the teacher implements several approaches to assist the student, including computer-assisted tutorials and peer mentoring. When the student does not respond, the next logical step is for the teacher to consult with the other teachers to see if the student is having similar difficulties in her other classes in order to determine what approach might best serve the student's needs.

The teacher has already varied the instructional opportunities for Addie including working with peers, using computer tutorials, and assigning a peer mentor. The next logical step in improving the student's achievement is seeking input from the other teachers (option B), yet there is no indication in the item stimulus that Addie is a second language learner.

The correct answer choice is B.

10. D. Question 10 assesses the INTASC Standard Principle 10: *The teacher fosters relationships with school colleagues, parents, and agencies in the larger community to support students' learning and well-being.*

This question asks you to demonstrate your understanding of human development, exceptionality in student's learning, and the teacher's responsibilities relating to exceptional students. When the student in this case does not respond to various intervention strategies, the teacher should consult with the appropriate school personnel to initiate a referral for testing and evaluation.

The teacher's responsibility to the special needs student is to work with other teachers and support staff according to the legal guidelines to meet the student's learning needs. In this case, referrals should be issued after strategy adaptation has failed to enhance the student's ability to learn (option D), not as a short-term fix or immediate response to student difficulty.

Answer choice D is the right answer.

11. B. Question 11 assesses the INTASC Standard Principle 10: *The teacher fosters relationships with school colleagues, parents, and agencies in the larger community to support students' learning and well-being.*

This question asks you to consider a professional question relevant to the learning environment and institutional responsibilities relating to exceptional students' rights. Initiating a referral in this case does not automatically place the student in a different classroom. The teacher can best respond to the parents' concern by sharing information about the referral process and key points of IDEA, the Individuals with Disabilities Education Act, such as the least restrictive environment. The student may not necessarily be removed from the teacher's classroom.

The parents' concerns and fears are unlikely to be relieved by knowing about the benefits of special education (option A) or the rights of the parents to testing and evaluation for referral of students with disabilities (option C and D).

Answer choice B is the right answer.

12. B. Question 12 assesses the INTASC Standard Principle 10: *The teacher fosters relationships with school colleagues, parents, and agencies in the larger community to support students' learning and well-being.*

This question asks you to identify the role of parents in the admission, review, and dismissal committee. To answer this question, you need to be familiar with major legislation and institutional responsibilities relating to exceptional students. According to IDEA, parents are full participants in the committee review process and must be notified and invited to attend all ARD committee meetings. Furthermore, the parents may request a meeting of the ARD committee at any time.

Since the parents are concerned about losing the control of their daughter's education to the ARD committee, attending as an observer (option C) and discussing their concerns outside of the meeting (option A) are unlikely to foster reassurance and confidence in the school's special education services. Also, allowing the parents to select members of the committee does not guarantee that the parents will have more confidence in the ARD process.

Answer choice B is the right answer.

13. C. Question 13 assesses the INTASC Standard Principle 8: *The teacher understands and uses formal and informal assessment strategies to evaluate and ensure the continuous intellectual, social, and physical development of the learner.*

This question asks you to demonstrate your understanding of the purposes and advantages of different types of assessment strategies. In portfolio assessment, students are asked to evaluate and select examples of their best work to represent their understanding and growth in a particular subject. This activity is valuable to students because it helps promote self-reflection and critique.

Managing the workload, learning about how to express themselves, and self-assessment for the sake of comparison do not contribute to the reflective and critical thinking inspired by this prompt.

Answer choice C is the right answer.

14. A. Question 14 assesses the INTASC Standard Principle 8: *The teacher understands and uses formal and informal assessment strategies to evaluate and ensure the continuous intellectual, social, and physical development of the learner.*

This question asks you to identify appropriate implementation of a particular type of assessment strategy: portfolio assessment. By establishing a rubric or checklist with the students in advance, the teacher can minimize bias in the evaluation of the student portfolios.

Establishing a minimum number of items (option A) does not address bias or subjectivity. Likewise, a pass-fail or written portfolio evaluation (option B and

C) defeats the purpose and does not lend itself to eliminating bias in the student chapter.

Answer choice A is the right answer.

15. D. Question 15 assesses the INTASC Standard Principle 4: *The teacher understands and uses a variety of instructional strategies to encourage students' development of critical thinking, problem-solving, and performance skills.*

This question asks you to show your understanding of instructional strategies and the cognitive processes associated with student learning. First-hand experience provides students with opportunities to construct knowledge based upon interaction with the environment and concrete experiences. First-hand experience offers a broad spectrum of sensory stimuli and is more likely to create permanent records that are stored in students' long-term memory. Field trips offer first-hand experiences that support and extend instruction in the classroom.

Answer choice D is the right answer.

16. C. Question 16 assesses the INTASC Standard Principle 5: *The teacher uses an understanding of individual and group motivation and behavior to create a learning environment that encourages positive social interaction, active engagement in learning, and self-motivation.*

This question asks you apply your understanding of human motivation and the learning environment in order to determine the most appropriate strategy for classroom management in an outdoor setting. Taking students outdoors safely is very motivational and often provides meaningful first-hand experience. However, students who are not used to learning outdoors can become disruptive and inattentive in a different, more spacious setting. In this case, the teacher needs to establish clear routines and expectations for behavior before going outdoors with her students in order to prevent the same types of behavior problems from occurring in the future.

Reducing the number of learning opportunities outdoors (option A) and threatening the students with lowering their grades as a result of the behavior (option B) will lessen student motivation and not prevent such behavior from recurring. Formulating detailed written activity directions (option D) also diminishes student autonomy and will not ensure improvement in self-regulating behavior during outdoor activity.

Answer choice C is the correct answer.

17. A. Question 17 assesses the INTASC Standard Principle 5: *The teacher uses an understanding of individual and group motivation and behavior to create a learning environment that encourages positive social interaction, active engagement in learning, and self-motivation.*

This question addresses the selection of methods for enhancing student learning through a variety of resources and instructional strategies. The question specifically asks you to demonstrate your understanding of various instructional strategies for affecting student motivation when learning new technology. This question enables the teacher to act as a facilitator.

Students possess varying levels of understanding and exposure to different types of technology. Based upon principles of motivation, the teacher should promote cooperation and foster positive learning experiences with the new technology by encouraging students with more advanced computer skills to partner with less advanced students.

Requiring after-school remediation (option C) is more likely to diminish student motivation since it will be perceived as punishment. False praise (option D) and giving extra credit for completing work on the computer (option B) are strategies that are based on extrinsic motivation through token reinforcement. The most appropriate way for the teacher to foster student motivation that is intrinsic, genuine, and self-reinforcing is by promoting collaborative pairs to form among students of varying ability.

Answer choice A is the right answer.

18. D. Question 18 assesses the INTASC Standard Principle 10: *The teacher fosters relationships with school colleagues, parents, and agencies in the larger community to support students' learning and well-being.*

This question asks you to evaluate methods for enhancing student learning and identify appropriate ways to involve parents/guardians and leaders in the educational community. In order to promote positive interaction between the students and members of the community using the school's new media library, the teachers should encourage student use of the Internet as a research and communication tool with parents and the community.

The first three options seem fairly rigid and lead to static sharing.

Answer choice D is the right answer.

19. C. Question 19 assesses the INTASC Standard Principle 7: *The teacher plans instruction based upon knowledge of subject matter, students, the community, and curriculum goals.*

This question asks you to demonstrate your understanding of effective planning techniques for creating bridges between curriculum goals and the students' experiences. Activating students prior knowledge is essential to help students connect the known with the unknown before beginning a new topic of study and to accommodate new experiences into existing schema. An important part of instruction in planning any first-hand experience is to acquaint the students with the materials, concepts, and environment that will be explored in the new area of study.

There is no link that establishes the pre-field trip activities with encouraging students to make predictions to test on the field trip (option A) or supplying background information (option B) as possible strategies to facilitate their learning on the field trip. Also, discussing how participation will be assessed is not known to enhance student learning (option D).

Answer choice C is the right answer.

20. C. Question 20 assesses the INTASC Standard Principle 4: *The teacher understands and uses a variety of instructional strategies to encourage students' development of critical thinking, problem-solving, and performance skills.*

This question asks you to identify an appropriate use of discovery learning. In discovery learning, students utilize inquiry to induce or generalize a principle based upon a series of guided experiences. Discovery learning is especially useful for introducing new concepts, asking students to find patterns, and for solving problems that have more than one right answer.

The other option choices do not suggest appropriate uses of discovery learning as a strategy for content instruction. The other options utilize other strategies such as rote memorization (option A), applying mathematical processes (option B), and understanding micro-systems (option D).

Thus, the correct answer choice is C.

21. B. Question 21 assesses the INTASC Standard Principle 4: *The teacher understands and uses a variety of instructional strategies to encourage students' development of critical thinking, problem-solving, and performance skills.*

Question 21 asks you to demonstrate your understanding of advantages and appropriate uses of instructional strategies. The use of concept maps or graphic organizers for note taking in content area reading is an excellent tool to help students organize and assimilate information. The map provides a visual display of the important information and may be used to show relationships among ideas in the spoken or written text.

The selection of appropriate resources for student needs (option A) or evaluation of the effectiveness of instructional techniques (option C) are not functions of graphic organizers. Also, graphic organizers are not utilized to manage student use of resources (option D).

Answer choice B is the right answer.

22. C. Question 22 assesses the INTASC Standard Principle 4: *The teacher understands and uses a variety of instructional strategies to encourage students' development of critical thinking, problem-solving, and performance skills.*

This question asks you to show your understanding of major cognitive processes associated with student learning. As described in the answer explanation for Question 21, graphic organizers are excellent tools for selecting and categorizing information from a reading passage or a lecture. The use of graphic organizers in this manner encourages students to engage in critical and higher-order thinking about the written or spoken text.

Collecting and organizing information on a graphic organizer does not serve as a study aid for memorization (option A). To accommodate different learning styles (option B), the teacher would need to modify instruction and present several alternative approaches for engaging students in higher-order thinking. Also, the use of graphic organizers does not involve extrinsic motivation as a token reinforcer (option D).

Thus, answer choice C is the correct answer.

23. A. Question 20 assesses the INTASC Standard Principle 4: *The teacher understands and uses a variety of instructional strategies to encourage students' development of critical thinking, problem-solving, and performance skills.*

This question asks you to demonstrate your understanding of major cognitive processes and instructional strategies that promote student learning. Reflection logs are commonly used to allow students to reflect and deconstruct a particular learning experience. In reflection logs, students record their thoughts, feelings, and attitudes toward a particular learning experience. By asking students to evaluate the strategies that they feel help them learn best, the teacher is fostering metacognition, the act of thinking about one's thinking. Metacognition is an important cognitive process that is associated with self-regulation and self-efficacy in learning.

Social learning theory (option B) is associated with Vygotskian approaches to fostering meaning through dialogue and social construction. Schema theory (option C) pertains to Piagetian theory of concept attainment through experiential learning. Transfer theory (option D) refers to the ability of the brain to utilize and apply previously learned information to new performance skills and for problem-solving applications.

Answer choice A is the right answer.

24. C. Question 24 assesses the INTASC Standard Principle 3: *The teacher understands how students differ in their approaches to learning and creates instructional opportunities that are adapted to diverse learners.*

This question asks you to demonstrate your understanding of students as diverse learners. Individual experiences, talent, language, culture, family and community values influence students' learning. Utilizing the students' diverse backgrounds as their individual areas of study in the upcoming unit creates a context that celebrates diversity and is more likely to promote family involvement in the students' learning.

Working cooperatively with parents and caregivers (option A) and establishing regular communication between school and home (option B) are important to involving parents and the students' families in the learning process. Devising study strategies to be used in the home (option D) is important for academic success for many students. However, these strategies are not designed to specifically promote greater understanding of diversity among students as suggested by including those cultures represented in the students' family backgrounds in a unit of study.

Answer choice C is the right answer.

Part 6

Elementary Education

Chapter 16

Overview for the Elementary Education: Content Knowledge Test
(Test Code 10014)

The Elementary Education: Content Knowledge Test consists of 120 multiple-choice questions with a two-hour time limit. Examinees are allowed to use a scientific or four-function calculator for the test. The test covers the content taught in the elementary school curriculum and is arranged in four major areas: language arts, mathematics, social studies, and science. The test consists of thirty questions from each subject area, and each area counts for 25 percent of the test's total score.

According to Tests at a Glance on the ETS Web site (*www.ets.org/praxis*), the test assesses knowledge of the following areas:

- Language arts—includes literary genres, reading and writing, research methods, literacy and reading instruction, children's literature, grammar and punctuation, and listening and speaking.
- Mathematics—includes numbers and numeration; operations and their properties; estimation and reasonableness of answers; problem-solving strategies; patterns; place value; factors, prime, and composite; ratio, proportion, and percent; using calculators; number line and comparison of numbers; elementary algebraic concepts; functions, relationships, and algebraic reasoning; informal geometric concepts; measurement; congruence, similarity, and symmetry; Pythagorean theorem; geometric transformations; nets and surface area; coordinate grids and graphing; perimeter, area, volume; angles; perpendicular and parallel lines; organizing data; and mean, median, and mode.
- Social studies—includes geography topics such as human/environment interaction; regions and location; latitude and longitude; and erosion and deposition; world history topics such as prehistoric, early, and classical civilizations; European history; twentieth century; U.S. history topics such as early exploration and colonization in the United States, the American Revolution, the U.S. Constitution, and the Civil War; political science topics such as types of government, the structure of government in the United States; civil rights; responsibilities of citizenship; state and local governments; social science topics such as cultural and social structures, stereotypes and prejudices,

human growth and development; diversity; economics topics such as economic markets, supply and demand, opportunity costs, and technology and economics.

- Science—includes the scientific method, systems, and models; earth science topics such as earth history and the earth system; life science topics such as living organisms, reproduction, and heredity, regulation of the body, evolution, symbiosis and interdependence; physical science topics such as matter and energy, light, and simple machines; topics associated with science and personal health; topics related to science history and science as a career.

Sample Test Questions:

1. A punch recipe mixes 2 quarts of orange juice with 5 quarts of soda. How many quarts of orange juice will be needed to make 10 gallons of punch using this recipe?
   A. 4 quarts
   B. 8 quarts
   C. 16 quarts
   D. 40 quarts
   E. 100 quarts

2. Structural analysis would be especially useful for helping students decode which of the following words?
   A. superb
   B. hypothesize
   C. rattlesnakes
   D. misstep
   E. confuse

3. Women were granted the right to vote through the:
   A. Bill of Rights
   B. Declaration of Independence
   C. *Brown v. Board of Education*
   D. Nineteenth Amendment
   E. Articles of Confederation

4. Which of the following planets has the longest year?
   A. Jupiter
   B. Neptune
   C. Saturn
   D. Uranus
   E. Pluto

5. In a scientific experiment, which variable does the researcher manipulate?
    A. independent variable
    B. dependent variable
    C. responding variable
    D. observed variable
    E. outcome variable

Answers

1. D

2. D

3. D

4. E

5. A

For a detailed list of the topics, additional information about the Elementary Education: Content Knowledge Test (Test Code 10014), and more sample questions, view or download the printable version of Test at a Glance for this test available on the ETS Web site at *www.ets.org/praxis.*

Chapter 17

Overview for Elementary Education: Curriculum, Instruction, and Assessment (K–5)
(Test Code 10016)

The PRAXIS certification test for Elementary Education: Curriculum, Instruction, and Assessment (K–5) (Test Code 10016) is designed to assess the knowledge and pedagogical skills for prospective teachers of students in prekindergarten through fifth grade. According to Tests at a Glance on the ETS Web site (*www.ets.org/praxis*), the test consists of 120 multiple-choice questions that address curriculum, instruction, and assessment divided across six primary areas: reading and language arts (35 percent), mathematics (20 percent), science (10 percent), social studies (10 percent), arts and physical education (10 percent), and general pedagogical knowledge related to these subject areas (15 percent). The time limit for completing the test is two hours.

The Elementary Education: Curriculum, Instruction, and Assessment test is designed to assess your understanding of content knowledge and process skills related to curriculum and lesson planning, instruction, and assessment of student learning for elementary-age students. Some questions are related to general curriculum and implementing developmentally appropriate practices. Others present specific problems that teachers may encounter in the classroom and may include real-life examples of student work.

According to Tests at a Glance (*www.ets.org/praxis*), the test assesses knowledge of curriculum, instruction, and assessment in the six areas on topics such as the following:

- Reading and language arts—includes scope and sequence; literacy and reading instruction; balanced programs; basals and tradebooks; children's literature, literary genres; reading levels and readability; language acquisition and readiness; beginning reading instruction; concepts of print; alphabet principle; phonological and phonemic awareness; comprehension instruction; K-W-L charts; phonics and word recognition strategies (such as structural analysis, decoding, syntactic cues); content-area reading; vocabulary development;

reading fluency; speaking and listening; invented spelling; stages of spelling; writing process (prewriting, drafting, revising, editing, publishing); assessment strategies (such as miscue analysis, Cloze procedure, running record, Frye readability index); technology; and content-specific pedagogy (such as flexible reading groups, cooperative learning groups, guided oral reading and silent sustained reading, interdisciplinary instruction, use of technology and the Internet).

- Mathematics—includes scope and sequence; number and numeration; sets; whole numbers to rationals; number patterns; classifying objects, base ten; place value; operations and their relationships; invented computation strategies; estimation and reasonableness of answers; problem-solving strategies; concepts of number theory (such as factors, prime, and composite); ratio, proportion, and percent; using calculators; number line and comparison of numbers; informal geometric concepts; metric and nonmetric measurement; congruence, similarity, and symmetry; Pythagorean theorem; geometric transformations; perimeter and area; angles; perpendicular and parallel lines; organizing data and mean, median, and mode; and content-specific pedagogy (such as NCTM standards, problem-based learning, cooperative learning).

- Science—includes scope and sequence; the scientific method; systems and models; the earth, sun, and the solar system; living organisms; herbivores, carnivores, omnivores; adaptation; matter and energy; light; magnetism; gravity; simple machines; chemical and physical changes; atoms and molecules; topics associated with science and personal health; technology; and content-specific pedagogy (such as inquiry-based learning, discovery learning, computer simulation, interdisciplinary instruction, use of technology and the Internet).

- Social studies—includes scope and sequence, the self, family, and community; human/environment interaction, regions and location, latitude and longitude, and erosion and deposition; early civilizations, early exploration and colonization in the United States; the American Revolution; the U.S. Constitution; the Civil War; the structure of government in the United States; civil rights; responsibilities of citizenship; state and local governments; cultural and social structures; stereotypes and prejudices; human growth and development; diversity; economic markets, supply and demand, opportunity costs; technology, and content-specific pedagogy (such as inquiry-based learning, constructivist approach, role-playing and simulations, interdisciplinary instruction, use of technology and the Internet).

- Art, music, and physical education—includes scope and sequence; topics from art such as line, texture, hue (color), form (three-dimensional), shape (two-dimensional), value, and space, design, technique, repetition, balance, emphasis, contrast, and unity; topics from music such as pitch, rhythm, harmony, dynamics, timbre, texture, form; topics from physical education such as agility, body awareness, static and dynamic balance, equilibrium, endurance, aerobic and anaerobic exercise, locomotor and manipulative skills, gross motor skills, fine motor skills, physical fitness and health; games and sportsmanship; technology; and content-specific pedagogy (such as questioning and problem-solving, interdisciplinary instruction, use of technology and the Internet).

- General—includes knowledge and understandings related to children's social, emotional, cognitive, and physical development; learning theories (such as behaviorism, constructivism); components of curriculum (including scope and sequence); instructional strategies; classroom management; assessment; professional growth and development.

Sample Test Questions:

Directions: Each of the questions or statements below is followed by four suggested answers or statements. Select the one that is best in each case.

1. Writing in learning logs about independent and self-designed projects is most likely to benefit students by:
   A. Prompting them to visit a specific learning center more frequently.
   B. Encouraging them to reflect on their own learning strategies.
   C. Providing feedback to the teacher on learning center use.
   D. Helping them establish personal learning goals.

Questions 2–4 are based on the following scenario:

Ms. Gomez is a new third-grade teacher at Forest Park Elementary School. Her class includes a wide range of ability levels and cultural backgrounds. Ms. Gomez uses a mixed approach for instruction that incorporates direct instruction and cooperative learning projects in small groups. Ms. Gomez would like for her students to have the opportunity to apply mathematical concepts during their problem solving and cooperative group discussions. Some of the activities she selects for group problem solving include estimating the number of objects in a collection, such as beans in a jar, creating a budget for a class field trip, and making predictions of weather based on data from the Internet.

2. Ms. Gomez' selection of activities for cooperative learning support her understanding that children at this level of development learn best when they are given:
   A. classroom experiences that build on the personal interests of individual students.
   B. a clear understanding of teacher expectations regarding student work.
   C. instructional activities that are modified for individual learning style.
   D. concrete classroom experiences in which they can practice and extend understanding of concepts and skills.

3. By having cooperative learning groups work on open-ended mathematical questions, as opposed to working on problems with only one right answer, Ms. Gomez is promoting the students' ability to:

    A. evaluate the reasonableness of their investigations.

    B. relate personal experience to instructional concepts.

    C. communicate thinking and provide reasons for conclusions.

    D. select questions that are worth investigating.

4. In setting up the cooperative learning groups, Ms. Gomez includes students with different levels of mathematical ability and experience. Which of the following is an important advantage of this method of grouping?

    A. Each student learns at a pace that is adjusted to his/her own level of ability.

    B. Students learn to appreciate the special talents and unique skills of the other students in their group.

    C. Students are able to be assessed on individual effort and on their level of academic performance.

    D. Only high-achieving students may deepen their understanding by explaining difficult material to their peers.

5. Which of the following theories supports most directly the use of rewards for classroom management?

    A. Social constructivism

    B. Operant conditioning

    C. Cognitive field-interaction

    D. Classical conditioning

Answers:

1. B

2. D

3. C

4. B

5. B

For a detailed list of the topics, additional information about the Elementary Education: Content Knowledge Test (Test Code 10016), and more sample questions, view or download the printable version of Test at a Glance for this test available on the ETS Web site at *www.ets.org/praxis.*

Chapter 18

Overview for the Elementary Education: Content Area Exercises
(Test Code 20012)

The Elementary Education: Content Area Exercises requires the examinee to write four essays in response to a teaching situation. The test has a two-hour time limit, and each response counts for 25 percent of the total test score. The test is designed to measure how well candidates for elementary certification can write thoughtful, well-written, and scholarly responses to a problem posed. The problems are challenging and complex and require an in-depth understanding of subject-specific pedagogy in elementary education.

Each of the four essay prompts is set in the context of a subject area (or integrated subject areas) and a classroom situation. The subject areas covered are reading and language arts, mathematics, science, and social studies.

According to Tests at a Glance (*www.ets.org/praxis*), the test assesses knowledge of curriculum, instruction, and assessment in the content areas on topics such as:

- Reading and language arts—includes scope and sequence, literacy and reading instruction, balanced programs, basals and tradebooks, children's literature, literary genres, reading levels and readability, language acquisition and readiness, beginning reading instruction, concepts of print, alphabet principle, phonological and phonemic awareness, comprehension instruction, K-W-L charts, phonics and word recognition strategies (such as structural analysis, decoding, syntactic cues), content-area reading, vocabulary development, reading fluency, speaking and listening, invented spelling, stages of spelling, writing process (prewriting, drafting, revising, editing, publishing), assessment strategies (such as miscue analysis, Cloze procedure, running record, Frye readability index), technology, and content-specific pedagogy (such as flexible reading groups, cooperative learning groups, guided oral reading and silent sustained reading, interdisciplinary instruction, use of technology and the Internet).
- Mathematics—includes scope and sequence; number and numeration; sets; whole numbers to rationals: number patterns; classifying objects; base ten; place value; operations and their relationships; invented computation strategies;

estimation and reasonableness of answers; problem-solving strategies; concepts of number theory (such as factors, prime, and composite); ratio, proportion, and percent; using calculators; number line and comparison of numbers; informal geometric concepts; metric and nonmetric measurement; congruence, similarity, and symmetry; Pythagorean theorem; geometric transformations; perimeter and area; angles; perpendicular and parallel lines; organizing data and mean, median, and mode; and content-specific pedagogy (such as NCTM standards, problem-based learning, cooperative learning).

- Science—includes scope and sequence; the scientific method; systems and models; the earth, sun, and the solar system; living organisms; herbivores, carnivores, omnivores; adaptation; matter and energy; light; magnetism; gravity; simple machines; chemical and physical changes; atoms and molecules; topics associated with science and personal health; technology; and content-specific pedagogy (such as inquiry-based learning, discovery learning, computer simulation, interdisciplinary instruction, use of technology and the Internet).

- Social studies—includes scope and sequence, the self, family, and community; human/environment interaction, regions and location, latitude and longitude, and erosion and deposition; early civilizations, early exploration and colonization in the United States; the American Revolution; the U.S. Constitution; the Civil War; the structure of government in the United States; civil rights; responsibilities of citizenship; state and local governments; cultural and social structures, stereotypes and prejudices; human growth and development; diversity; economic markets, supply and demand, opportunity costs; technology, and content-specific pedagogy (such as inquiry-based learning, constructivist approach, role-playing and simulations, interdisciplinary instruction, use of technology and the Internet).

- General—includes knowledge and understandings related to children's social, emotional, cognitive, and physical development; learning theories (such as behaviorism, constructivism); components of curriculum (including scope and sequence); instructional strategies; classroom management; assessment; professional growth and development.

Sample Question

As part of the writing activities in a first grade classroom's Writing Workshop, children are encouraged to write in their journals. In the following example, the children were instructed to write about something of interest to them. The question below refers to the following journal entry produced by a first-grade boy.

My dad pold my tuth last nit and put it ondr my pelr. And I wet to sleep and wen I wok up I fid it desg perd but I fid a to dilrbel to. The End.

My dad pulled my tooth last night and put it under my pillow. And I went to sleep and when I woke up I find it disappeared but I find a two-dollar bill too.

QUESTION: Children problem-solve and apply what they know about writing as they produce text. In the sample above, describe at least four (4) aspects of writing that the child is capable of controlling.

Sample Response That Received a Score of 5

The student seems to be writing about a personal experience as he writes about losing a tooth. His story follows a logical pattern that has a beginning, middle, and end, and includes details (put it under my pillow and found a two-dollar bill). The story is also focused on meaning. He uses transitional words (but, and, when) and complex structural patterns. The child is hearing and recording sounds in words (nit for night, wok for woke) by listening to the sounds of words in sequence and finding letters to represent these sounds, showing evidence of letter/sound knowledge. Although he does not hear the sounds buried within some words (went, find), he has a nice store of high-frequency words (my, it, up, and, but). The use of capital letters at the beginning of the sentences and periods at the end reflects an awareness of punctuation to communicate meaning. As he tries to analyze the sounds in vowels, he makes certain substitutions that are readable (pelr for pillow, ondr for under, dilr for dollar). There are no omissions of sounds and partially correct attempts at other words (tuth for tooth, fid for find).

Sample Response That Received a Score of 2

The student uses complete sentences and correct punctuation marks. The story is focused on meaning as it includes a beginning, middle, and end. He appears to be able to sound out words and match sounds with letters. The child seems to enjoy writing and is excited about finding the money under the pillow.

For a detailed list of the topics, additional information about the Elementary Education: Content Area Exercises (Test Code 20012) and a sample question, view or download the printable version of Test at a Glance for this test available on the ETS Web site at *www.ets.org/praxis*.

Part 7

Specialty Areas

Chapter 19

Overview for the Fundamental Subjects: Content Knowledge Test
(Test Code 30511)

The Fundamental Subjects: Content Knowledge Test consists of 100 multiple-choice questions with a two-hour time limit. Examinees are allowed to use a nonprogrammable, four-function calculator for the test.

According to Tests at a Glance on the ETS Web site (*www.ets.org/praxis*), the test assesses general knowledge of the content from four broad areas: English language arts, mathematics, citizenship and social science, and science. The test consists of twenty-five questions from each subject area, and each area counts for 25 percent of the test. Topics assessed from these four areas are the following:

- English language—includes themes, author's purpose, audience, point of view, character, setting, tone and mood, imagery and figurative language to reading, main idea and supporting details, organization, fact versus opinion, literal and inferential meaning, and drawing conclusions.
- Mathematics—includes topics from arithmetic and basic algebra such as number concepts and computation skills using rational numbers, base ten and place value, comparing and ordering rational numbers; equivalent representations of rational numbers, problem-solving strategies, estimation; ratios and proportions, percents, problem-solving using basic algebraic methods; topics from geometry and measurement, such as converting in metric and customary systems, using scale factors, area, perimeter and circumference, volume, congruence and similarity, symmetry, Pythagorean theorem, geometric transformations; nets and surface area, perpendicular and parallel lines, coordinate grids and graphing; topics from elementary probability and statistics such as tables, charts, and graphs, mean, median, mode, and range, and simple probabilities.
- Citizenship and social science—includes fact versus opinion; multiple points of view; primary and secondary sources; artifacts and historical places; human/environment interaction; impact of social movements on history; analysis of historical events; basic geographic concepts (e.g., latitude and longitude);

types of government; the structure of government in the United States; the Constitution; civil rights; responsibilities of citizenship; state and local governments; cultural and social structures; stereotypes and prejudices; human growth and development; diversity; economic markets; supply and demand; opportunity costs; and interdependence.

- Science—includes history of science, the scientific method, systems, and models; earth history and the earth system; living organisms and diversity, reproduction and heredity, regulation of the body, evolution, symbiosis and interdependence; matter and energy, light, and simple machines; science and personal health, science and society, politics, and technology.

Sample Test Questions

1. Which of the following genres best describes a humorous, exaggerated story like "Paul Bunyan" that has a larger-than-life main character who does unbelievable things?
   A. tall tale
   B. fable
   C. legend
   D. myth
   E. historical fiction

2. A scientist is conducting an experiment to investigate the effect of using different colors of light on the growth of 40 plants. Ten plants are growing under red light, 10 plants are growing under blue light, 10 plants are growing under purple light, and 10 plants are growing under green light. All other growing conditions are identical. All the plants used in the experiment are from the same parent plant. Which of the following would be most advisable?
   A. The scientist should use plants that come from different parent plants.
   B. The scientists should have a group of 10 plants that are growing under white light.
   C. The scientist should reduce the number of plants in the experiment.
   D. The scientist should perform the identical experiment on a different type of plant.
   E. The scientist should keep the experiment exactly as it is.

3. A shopper finds a CD player on sale for 20% off the original price of $179. The next week, the CD player has been reduced another 15% off the sale price. If there is an 8% sales tax rate, how much (rounded to the nearest cent) would the shopper pay for the CD player?
   A. $116.35
   B. $121.72
   C. $131.46
   D. $143.20
   E. $144.00

4. Which of the following illustrates the operation of the system of checks and balances established by the U.S. Constitution?
   A. The Supreme Court declares a law unconstitutional.
   B. The President appoints members of his Cabinet.
   C. Congressional members of both Houses meet to work out a compromise on a bill.
   D. Congress controls foreign and interstate commerce.
   E. The President delivers the State of the Union Address.

Answers:

1. A

2. B

3. C

4. A

For additional information about the Fundamental Subjects: Content Knowledge Test (Test Code 30511) and more sample questions, view or download the printable version of Test at a Glance for this test available on the ETS Web site at *www.ets.org/praxis.*

Chapter 20

Overview for the English Language, Literature, and Composition: Content Knowledge Test

The English Language, Literature, and Composition: Content Knowledge test is designed to assess whether an examinee has the broad base of knowledge and competencies necessary to be licensed as a beginning teacher of English in a secondary school. The 120 multiple-choice questions are based on the material typically covered in a bachelor's degree program in English and English education. Features of the test and the approximate percentage of the examination are as follows:

Reading and understanding text—approximately 55% of the test
Language and Linguistics—approximately 15% of the test
Composition and Rhetoric—approximately 30% of the test

The topics covered in the test include the following categories.

I. Reading and Understanding Text

- Paraphrasing, comparing, and interpreting (literally and inferentially) various types of texts, including fiction, poetry, essays, and other nonfiction
- Identifying and interpreting figurative language and other literary elements, such as metaphor, simile, voice, point of view, tone, style, setting, diction, mood, allusions, irony, clichés, analogy, hyperbole, personification, alliteration, and foreshadowing
- Identifying patterns, structures, and characteristics of literary forms and genres, such as elements of fiction and features of different poetic and prose forms and understanding how these patterns, structures, and characteristics may influence the meaning and effect of a work

- Identifying major works and authors of American, British, and world literature from various cultures, genres, and periods, including literature for young adults
- Situating and interpreting texts within their historical and cultural contexts
- Recognizing and identifying various instructional approaches to and elements of teaching reading and textual interpretation, such as cueing systems, activating prior knowledge, constructing meaning through context, and metacognitive strategies

II. Language and Linguistics

- Understanding the principles of language acquisition and development, including social, cultural, and historical influences and the role and nature of dialects
- Understanding elements of the history and development of the English language and American English, including linguistic change, etymology, and processes of word formation
- Understanding and applying the elements of traditional grammar, such as syntax, sentence types, sentence structure, parts of speech, modifiers, sentence combining, phrases and clauses, capitalization, and punctuation
- Understanding the elements of semantics, including ambiguity, euphemism, doublespeak, connotation, and jargon, and how these elements affect meaning

III. Composition and Rhetoric

- Understanding and applying elements of teaching writing, including the following:
  1. Individual and collaborative approaches to teaching writing, such as stages of the writing process (prewriting, drafting, revising, editing, publishing, evaluating) and how those stages work recursively
  2. Tools and response strategies for assessing student writing, such as peer review, portfolios, holistic scoring, scoring rubrics, self-assessment, and conferencing
  3. Common research and documentation techniques, such as gathering and evaluating data and using electronic and print media
- Understanding and evaluating rhetorical features in writing, including the following:
  1. Purposes for writing and speaking and the role of the audience within varying contexts
  2. Organization in a piece of writing and the creation and preservation of coherence
  3. Strategies for the organization, development, and presentation of print and visual media

4. Discourse aims, for example, creative, expository, persuasive
5. Methods of argument and types of appeals, such as argumentative, analogy, extended metaphor, allusion
6. Style, tone, voice, and point of view as part of rhetorical strategy
7. Recognition of bias, distinguishing between fact and opinion, and identifying stereotypes, inferences, and assumptions

Sample Questions

Below are questions that illustrate the kinds of questions in the test. Since the entire breadth and scope of the content and difficulty of the test cannot be represented in this preparation manual, the questions are to be used as sample questions.

Directions: Read the passage. Select the best answer to each question.

Questions 1–2

"The Twins"
One is Billy.
One is Willy.
Sister Lilly
Thinks they're silly.
The twins, Billy and Willy.

1. Poets use certain devices to create medleys of sound, suggest visual interpretations, and communicate messages. In the poem "The Twins," which poetic element is the poet using?
   A. hyperbole
   B. rhyme
   C. metaphors
   D. rhythm

2. The mood of the poem is:
   A. dreamlike and happy
   B. happy and humorous
   C. angry and frightening
   D. poignant and melancholy

Questions 3–5

The book explores both the subtle and explicit racial prejudice that many white Americans expressed toward African-Americans in the early twentieth century. Cassie and her brother, who live in rural Mississippi, excitedly await their new schoolbooks, only to receive badly worn, dirty castoffs from the white elementary school.

3. The passage above discusses:
   A. Gary Paulsen's *Nightjohn*
   B. Mildred Ames's *Grandpa Jake and the Grand Christmas*
   C. Mildred Taylor's *Roll of Thunder, Hear My Cry*
   D. William Armstrong's *Sounder*

4. What is the genre of the book to which the passage refers?
   A. historical fiction
   B. contemporary fiction
   C. biography
   D. traditional literature

5. Which of the following is the best description of a child using the semantic aspect of the cueing system?
   A. The child uses information from the meaning of the message and what he or she reads makes sense.
   B. The child uses visual information from the letters and words or the layout of print.
   C. The child reads word by word as if recalling each word from a memory bank.
   D. The child uses information from the structure of the sentence.

Answer Key

1. B

2. B

3. C

4. A

5. D

For additional information about the English Language, Literature, and Composition: Content Knowledge Test (Test Code 0041), view or download the printable version of Test at a Glance for this test available at *www.ets.org/praxis* on the ETS Web site.

Chapter 21

Overview for the Mathematics: Content Knowledge Test
(Test Code 10061)

The Mathematics: Content Knowledge test consists of fifty multiple-choice questions with a two-hour time limit. Examinees are required to use a graphing calculator for the exam. Examinees can program formulas into the calculator before the exam because calculator memories will not be cleared. According to Tests at a Glance on the ETS Web site (*www.ets.org/praxis*), the test assesses knowledge of mathematics content from the following areas:

- Arithmetic and algebra—includes number and numeration concepts for rational, real, and complex numbers; field properties; ratios, proportions, and percents; simplifying algebraic expressions; solving equations and inequalities; and the binomial theorem.
- Geometry—includes properties of two-dimensional and three-dimensional figures; congruence, similarity, and symmetry, the Pythagorean theorem; perimeter, area, and volume; and geometric transformations.
- Trigonometry—includes properties of the six basic trigonometric functions; special angles; law of sines and cosines; half-angle, double-angle, and sum and difference formulas; identities; trigonometric equations and inequalities; rectangular and polar coordinates; and complex numbers.
- Analytic geometry—includes equations of lines and planes, distance and midpoint formulas, and conic sections.
- Functions—includes types of functions and their graphs; domain, range, intercepts, asymptotes; graphing equations; solving equations involving functions; one-to-one functions and inverses of functions.
- Calculus—includes limits, continuity and differentiability, derivatives and integrals, numerical approximations of derivatives and integrals, minima-maxima, mean value theorem and fundamental theorem of calculus, areas of regions in the plane and volume of rotated solids, and sequences and series.
- Probability and statistics—includes data organization; central tendency and dispersion; discrete and joint probability; binomial distribution; random variables; normal, uniform, and chi-square distributions; hypothesis testing.

- Discrete mathematics—includes symbolic logic, set operations, permutations and combinations, base-n arithmetic, equivalence relations, and linear programming.
- Linear algebra—includes scalars, vectors, and matrices; inverses of matrices; linear transformations; and systems of linear equations.
- Computer science—includes hardware and software, terminology, and algorithms.
- Mathematical reasoning—includes mathematical models, problem-solving strategies, reasonableness of answers, estimation, axioms, and unsolved problems.

Sample Test Questions

1. Which of the following expressions is another way to write $(3x^2 - 6)^{-\frac{1}{3}}$?

   A. $-x^2 + 2$

   B. $\dfrac{1}{\sqrt[3]{3x^2 - 6}}$

   C. $\dfrac{-1}{\sqrt[3]{3x^2 - 6}}$

   D. $\dfrac{1}{3\sqrt[3]{x^2 - 2}}$

   E. $-\sqrt[3]{3x^2 - 6}$

2. Which property of the real numbers is illustrated below?
   $(10 + 14)(a + b) = 10(a + b) + 14(a + b)$
   A. Distributive property
   B. Commutative property for addition
   C. Associative property for addition
   D. Commutative property for multiplication
   E. Associative property for multiplication

3. Which of the following sets of ordered pairs is NOT a function?
   A. $\{(1, 5), (7, -2), (3, -2), (4, 5)\}$
   B. $\{(2, 6), (-7, 10), (5, -8), (3, 4)\}$
   C. $\{(1, 1), (2, 2), (3, 3), (4, 4)\}$
   D. $\{(1, 0), (7, 0), (3, 0), (4, 0)\}$
   E. $\{(10, 5), (4, -3), (10, 2), (9, -5)\}$

4. Find the length of side AC in the figure given:

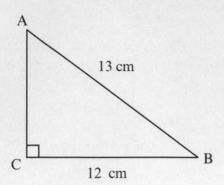

A. 1 cm
B. 5 cm
C. 25 cm
D. 156 cm
E. 313 cm

5. Find the median for the following data set:
50, 42, 34, 76, 68, 10, 10, 10
A. 10
B. 37.5
C. 38
D. 72
E. 76

Answers:

1. B

2. A

3. E

4. B

5. C

For a detailed list of the topics covered, additional information about the Mathematics: Content Knowledge test (Test Code 10061), and more sample questions, view or download the printable version of Test at a Glance for this test available on the ETS Web site at *www.ets.org/praxis.*

Appendix: Tips for New Teachers

After you pass your PRAXIS tests and obtain your license or certification, you are ready to go into the classroom. How will your first year go? Veteran teachers will tell you that you will learn more that first year of teaching than you learned in all your years of coursework preparing for it. That is a disconcerting notion, but it's also one that should be very exciting to you. You've finally made it, and now you're ready to jump in and go it on your own! In this Appendix, you'll find some tips to help make your first year and subsequent years a successful experience for you. We wish you good luck as you step into your own classroom!

TIP 1: Plan Every Lesson

Perhaps, when you were completing your field experience as a preservice teacher, you were told something similar to the following, "When you start teaching, you won't be writing those long, detailed lesson plans. That's a waste of time." The truth is, to be an effective teacher you should plan deliberately and thoughtfully. Of course, you don't have to write out "model" lesson plans, but you do need to write out what you are planning to do, how you are going to do it, and how you will determine that it worked.

Step 1. Your *first* step in planning is to define your goals and objectives. Nowadays, most states have curriculum standards. Use these to decide what your students should know and be able to do as a result of participation in learning opportunities in your classrooms. As you write your objectives keep the following in mind: Objectives (as classified by Benjamin S. Bloom) can be cognitive, affective, or pychomotor. Don't just stick to one type. Try to write objectives that address all three categories for learning.

Cognitive objectives involve thinking capabilities, from recalling facts to judging the quality of an argument. Here is an example: "At the end of the lesson, the students will be able to solve right triangles using the Pythagorean Theorem."

Affective objectives involve feelings and dispositions. Don't overlook this category! Too many teachers fail to think about the importance of promoting positive dispositions toward their subject matter. Just because a student can read, doesn't mean the student *likes* to read or *wants* to read. In reality, affective objectives may be the *most* important because they ultimately determine whether the student values the learning and finds it meaningful. Here is an example: "At the end of the lesson, the students will show awareness of the importance of laws in a free society."

Psychomotor objectives, as you might expect, involve physical activity on the part of the student. In teaching sports, psychomotor objectives deal with physical skills and coordination (e.g., running, hitting, balancing, jumping, etc.). Here is an example. "At the end of the lesson, the student will be able to catch a softball." If you are planning a subject area lesson, your pychomotor objectives are the physical skills the students have to perform during the lesson. Here is an example. "At the end of the lesson, the students will be able to walk heel-to-toe to measure distance."

Step 2. Your second step in planning a lesson is to decide on your assessment strategies. How are you going to determine that the students "got it"? Keep in mind that good assessment reflects what is taught— it's aligned with the curriculum and how it is taught. It matches the method of instruction. This is why you decide on how you will assess *before* you plan how you will teach. You want to make sure that you are not going to teach one way and test another. Plan to use multiple assessment approaches in your lessons. There are many ways to find out how well students know, understand, and are able to apply the curriculum. One very effective way to do that is to use informal observation and questioning. In other words, watch the students when they are working to see if they are "getting it." Ask them questions about what they are doing and what they are thinking as they work. This approach will give you much insight into the effectiveness of your lesson. Other assessment strategies include formal interviews, collections of students' work over time (portfolios), self-assessment, peer assessment, formal performance assessments, and traditional tests. You assessment strategies will be most useful when they aim to help the students by identifying their unique strengths and needs so as to inform your planning. You also want to make sure that your assessment strategies are appropriate for the students you are teaching—especially for ethnically, culturally, and linguistically diverse students and students with special needs—and that your tests are developmentally appropriate. Your assessment strategies for younger students (early childhood to grade 3) will be different from those you might use for older learners.

Traditional teacher-made tests, in combination with less-formal methods, can be useful tools to help you determine what older students have learned. When you are designing a test, an important decision you need to make is to decide on the form that the test questions will take. In selecting a format for your test, think about the degree of *objectivity* of the test questions. *Objective* questions depend less on teacher judgment when grading, while *subjective* questions require more teacher judgment in the scoring process. In general, multiple-choice questions, matching, fill-in-the blank, and true-false questions are considered objective. Short response and essay questions fall into the subjective category. To reduce inconsistency in your grading, you should try to design your teacher-made tests so that subjectivity in grading is reduced. Following are some guidelines for writing the various test question types to help you with your test construction.

Multiple-Choice Questions

A multiple-choice question requires students to select the correct or best answer from a number of possible options.

Here is an example.

Directions: Read each question and select the best response. Write the letter corresponding to your answer in the blank provided.

What is the perimeter of a square that measures 6 meters on a side?

A. 12 meters
B. 24 meters
C. 36 meters
D. 60 meters
(Correct answer is B.)

Advantages: Multiple-choice questions can be used to test at lower and higher cognitive levels, can be used for diagnostic purposes, and are easy to grade.

Disadvantages: Preparing a well-written multiple-choice question is time-consuming. Coming up with plausible distractors (incorrect answer choices) is difficult. Writing stems that present situations briefly is challenging.

Here are some guidelines for construction.

DO:

Write questions based on the significant ideas you've presented—important facts, principles, and concepts.

Make sure each question tests one, and only one, main idea.

Use no more than five answer choices.

Put the answer choices in a logical order (e.g., alphabetically, from smallest to largest)

Use simple easy-to-understand language.

Write brief, concise stems.

Make sure all answer choices agree grammatically with the stem.

Make sure all answer choices are parallel in construction.

Write question stems that have sufficient information to clearly indicate the correct answer.

Write distractors that make sense and are plausible to students.

Write distractors that are based on common misconceptions or errors.

Make sure the distractors are clearly wrong or inadequate.

Make sure one question does not help in answering another question.

Cite the source when the question contains material based on opinion.

Include questions that test higher levels of thinking.

Write directions that are clear and specific.

AVOID:

Using statements copied from the book.

Using ambiguous language.

Stating questions negatively.

Using "giveaway" words like *always* or *never* that help students eliminate incorrect answer choices.

Using "none of the above," "none of these," "not given," or "all of the above" as a final answer choice.

Falling into a pattern when placing the correct answer choice in the questions.

True-False Questions

A true-false question requires students to decide whether a statement is true or false. Here is an example.

Directions: Read each question and decide whether it is true or false. Write the letter corresponding to your answer in the blank provided.

Abraham Lincoln was the 16th president of the United States.

A. True
B. False
(Correct answer is A.)

Advantages: True-false questions are easy to write, can be used to test a lot of content efficiently, and are easy to grade.

Disadvantages: Writing nontrivial questions is a challenge. Most often true-false questions test at lower cognitive levels. Student guessing is a problem. True-false tests have little diagnostic value.

Here are some guidelines for construction.

DO:

Write questions based on the significant ideas you've presented—important facts, principles, and concepts.

Make sure each question tests one, and only one, main idea.

Write questions so that the main idea in the statement is readily apparent to the student.

Write questions that deal with one and only one idea, not a combination of several ideas.

Use simple, easy-to-understand language.

Write simple and clear statements.

Write statements that have sufficient information to clearly indicate whether the statement is true or false.

Write questions that are completely true or completely false, not partially true or partially false.

Make the length of the question, whether true or false, about the same.

Cite the source when the question contains material based on opinion.

Try to include questions that test beyond lower levels of thinking.

Write directions that are clear and specific.

Include about the same numbers of true and false questions on a test.

AVOID:

Using statements copied from the book.

Using ambiguous language.

Stating questions negatively.

Using "giveaway" words like *always* or *never* that help students decide the correctness or incorrectness of the statement.

Using tricky questions or questions for which the correct answer relies on a trivial detail.

Using statements that could be read in more than one way.

Falling into a pattern for the correct answer.

Matching Questions

A matching question requires students to match a list of items with a set of answer choices based on a relationship between the items listed and their matching answer choices (e.g., countries with their capitals, terms with their characteristics).

Here is an example.

Directions: Match the country with its capital. Write the letter corresponding to your answer in the blank provided.

_____	1. Egypt	A.	Berlin
_____	2. Germany	B.	Rome
_____	3. Afghanistan	C.	Canberra
_____	4. Ecuador	D.	Ottawa
_____	5. Canada	E.	Cairo
_____	6. El Salvador	F.	Quito
_____	7. Sweden	G.	Kabul
_____	8. Turkey	H.	San Salvador
_____	9. Australia	I.	Stockholm
_____	10. Switzerland	J.	Ankara
_____	11. Argentina	K.	Bern
_____	12. Italy	L.	Buenos Aires

(Correct answers are 1-E; 2-A; 3-G; 4-F; 5-D, 6-H, 7-I, 8-J, 9-C, 10-K, 12-B.)

Advantages: Matching questions are easy to write, can be used to test a lot of content efficiently, are easy to grade, and are a quick way to check students' recognition of relationships.

Disadvantages: Most often matching questions test at the recall level of thinking. Writing short, succinct answer choices is sometimes challenging. Coming up with plausible extra incorrect choices is sometimes difficult. As students complete the matching, guessing can enter into selecting answer choices.

Here are some guidelines for construction.

DO:

Write questions based on the significant ideas you've presented—important
   facts, principles, and concepts.

Use list items that are similar in content.

Write matching answer choices that are short in length.

Put both the list of items and the answer choices on the same page in two columns.

Use numbers to identify the items in the first column and uppercase letters to
   identify the answer choices in the second column.

Use no more than 10 to 12 answer choices.

Include 1 or 2 extra answer choices that do not match up or let answer choices
   be used more than once.

Write directions that are clear and specific (e.g. "Write the letter corresponding
   to your answer in the blank provided."). Indicate whether answer choices
   may be used more than once.

AVOID:

Listing item in the two columns so that they match up in a predictable manner.

Avoid writing questions that rely on recall of trivial or insignificant details.

Fill-in-the-Blank or Completion Questions

Fill-in-the-blank or completion questions require students to fill in a blank with one word or a brief answer. Here is an example.

Directions: Fill in the blank with a correct response.
The force that causes an object to fall toward Earth is called _____.
(Answer is *gravity*.)

Advantages: Fill-in-the-blank questions are fairly easy to write, can be used to test a lot of content efficiently, and reduce the opportunity for students to guess correctly.

Disadvantages: Most fill-in-the-blank questions test at lower cognitive levels. Writing questions that elicit only the desired correct answer is challenging. Deciphering students' writing can be a problem. Subjectivity may enter into the scoring of responses. How to score unanticipated correct answers has to be dealt with.

Here are some guidelines for construction.

DO:

Write questions based on the significant ideas you've presented—important facts, principles, and concepts.

Make sure each question tests one, and only one, main idea.

Write questions for which only key words or important concepts, rather than trivial words, should be placed in the blanks.

Use simple easy-to-understand language.

Write question that have sufficient information to indicate one correct answer.

Write questions that have one word or a short phrase as the correct answer.

Make sure one question does not help in answering another question.

Cite the source when the question contains material based on opinion.

Include questions that test higher levels of thinking.

Try to put the question blank at or near the end of the question.

Make all blanks the same length.

Use no more than two blanks in a question.

Leave ample space for writing the answer.

Write directions that are clear and specific.

AVOID:

Using statements copied from the book.

Using ambiguous language.

Stating questions negatively.

Using tricky questions or questions for which the correct response relies on recall of a trivial detail.

Using statements that could be read in more than one way.

Constructed Response (or Essay) Questions

Constructed response questions require the students to write an extended response to a question or prompt.

Here is an example.

Directions: In the space provided, write a well-organized 100–150 word response addressing the following prompt:

In your own words, explain the process of photosynthesis.

Advantages: Constructed response questions are fairly easy to write, allow the teacher to test at higher cognitive levels of thinking, allow students more opportunity to express themselves in their own way, and eliminate student guessing.

Disadvantages: Constructed response questions are time-consuming for the student to answer, thus limiting the number per test. Not as much content can be assessed with this type of question. Deciphering students' writing can be a problem. Grading students' responses is time-consuming and difficult to do fairly and reliably.

DO:

Write questions/prompts based on the significant principles and concepts you've presented.

Write clear, specific, and unambiguous questions/prompts.

Use introductory phrases such as *explain in your own words, describe the similarities and differences between, compare and contrast, present an argument for or against, list and describe the major causes of,* and similar phrases.

Write questions/prompts that address higher levels of thinking.

Write questions/prompts that students can reasonably answer in the time allotted.

Write directions that are clear and specific.

Allow students to use word-processing to construct responses, if feasible.

Use a scoring rubric (See below).

Give a separate grade for mechanical skills.

AVOID:

Using broad questions/prompts.

Grading when you are tired or sleepy.

Sample Scoring Rubric

Constructed Response Scoring Rubric

All constructed-response questions will be assessed using a holistic rating scale ranging from 0-2.

Score of 2

The response appropriately answers the question and demonstrates a complete understanding of the principles and concepts.

Score of 1

The response appropriately answers the question and demonstrates a partial understanding of the principles and concepts.

Score of 0

The response does not appropriately answer any part of the question.

Step 3. The final step in planning your lesson is deciding on the instructional strategies that will address your goals and objectives. As you plan what you will do in your lesson to engage students in learning, keep the following points in mind.

DO:

Involve the students in choosing and planning their own learning activities.

Activate the students' prior knowledge related to the concepts to be learned.

Provide challenging experiences that actively engage students.

Provide experiences that reflect the students' own interests and experiences.

Use hands-on, minds-on activities.

Use activities that are developmentally appropriate.

Use activities that address students' individual needs and abilities.

Provide opportunities for both individual and group work.

Allow opportunities for students to talk and discuss their learning among themselves and with you.

Make the learning student-centered, not teacher-centered.

Make sure special-needs students (e.g., special education students or English language learners) will be full participants in the lesson.

AVOID:

Using worksheets or workbooks.

Isolated drill and practice.

Solely relying on the textbook for planning your lesson.

Providing limited options for the students (i.e., everyone doing the same thing the same way).

Using a teacher-center, teacher-dominated format.

TIP 2: Address Learning Styles

Use instructional approaches that promote understanding and are inviting to all the students in your classroom. Students demonstrate different ways of acquiring and processing information. Provide opportunities for your students to learn in ways that are congruent with their preferred modes of learning. Here is some information that will help you design optimum learning opportunities for auditory, kinesthetic, and visual learners.

Auditory Learner

Typical Characteristics

Likes listening activities

Follows oral directions easily

Has trouble following written directions

Understands what is heard better than what is read

Can distinguish sounds

Likes verbal word games

Is good at retelling stories

Can memorize easily

Good at remembering names of people and places

Likes to deliver messages

Tends to talk a lot

Has good speaking vocabulary, but may spell words incorrectly

Wants to be in charge

Likes to make others laugh

May be hyperactive

Makes excuses for misbehavior

Ways to Accommodate

Read directions orally.

Have learner repeat what was said.

Have learner read aloud.

Use music activities.

Use oral discussions.

Read stories aloud to learner.

Have learner verbalize while reading.

Use peer tutoring.

Use taped lessons.

Kinesthetic Learner

Typical Characteristics

Has good motor skills

Needs freedom to move

Wants to smell, taste, and touch everything

Likes hands-on activities and working with concrete objects

Likes to take things apart and put them back together

Often touching others

Gestures with hands when speaking

Prefers physical activity to listening and reading

Likes to do things manually

Good at imitating others

Likes to explore the environment

Seems immature

Appears to be hyperactive

Ways to Accommodate

Use hands-on activities.

Use manipulatives and other tactile materials.

Keep learner actively engaged.

Use outdoor activities.

Use role play and simulations.

Use puppetry and dramatic play.

Use musical instruments.

Associate concepts with movement activities.

Use creative writing.

Use hand gestures and facial expressions when speaking to learner.

Allow learner to stand beside desk or chair.

Allow learner frequent opportunities to move around the classroom.

Visual Learner

Typical Characteristics
Needs to see what is being learned
Wants to be able to see the teacher
Notices small details
Has mental picture where things are
Has trouble understanding oral directions
Prefers written instructions
Likes graphic aids (charts, graphs, diagrams)
Likes drawing pictures
Enjoys looking at books
Likes to watch videos
Watches mouth of speaker and facial expressions
Avoids joining in class discussions
May drift off during class discussions
Often able to learn independently
May have difficulty pronouncing words that he/she can read silently
Has good reading vocabulary
Likes puzzles
Good at finding patterns
Dislikes speaking in public

Ways to Accommodate
Use visual aids (pictures, charts, diagrams, etc.).
Use videos.
Use models and demonstrations.
Encourage learner to draw or illustrate concepts.
Use memory and concentration games.
Play "What's missing?" games.

TIP 3: Use Cooperative Learning

To maximize your students' potential for success, emphasize collaboration and supportive interactions in your classroom. Use cooperative learning, a strategy that builds on students' innate desire to communicate with their peers and work together. Cooperative learning involves students working together in small groups to complete a task, such as the completion of an activity sheet, an exploratory activity, or a project. The responsibility for learning in the classroom is shifted to the students, with the teacher facilitating the process by providing support and guidance when needed. Here are some guidelines for using cooperative learning groups.

DO:
Arrange the furniture (desks, tables, chairs) in your classroom to support
    group interaction (e.g. put desks in clusters of four facing each other).

Schedule sufficient time for the group activity.

Assign students to groups consisting of three to five students.

Form mixed-ability and culturally diverse groups.

Assign a role or job to each student (e.g. group leader, recorder).

Select interesting and challenging tasks.

Present the task as a group task.

Make individual and group behavior expectations clear.

Practice social skills beforehand to foster smoothly functioning groups.

Make sure the group understands what to do and how to do it.

Provide appropriate materials and manipulatives.

Monitor group processes and behaviors during activities.

Prompt or question group members if the group gets "stuck."

Encourage an atmosphere of mutual helpfulness within each group.

Encourage students to talk to each other and exchange viewpoints and ideas.

Prompt students to exhibit encouraging and reinforcing behavior toward one another.

Follow up with informal processing of the learning gained during the group task.

Build both individual accountability (e.g. group members assess each other's participation) and group accountability (e.g., teacher assesses a group presentation) into the assessment process.

AVOID:

Letting students determine group membership (although you can allow them to have input) to avoid discipline problems and ostracism of students who are "not popular."

Using groups consisting of more than five members.

Taking over the task when helping a group.

Rushing students through the group task.

Sitting at your desk while groups are working.

TIP 4: Be a Skilled Questioner

Good teachers are skilled questioners. Questioning plays a critical role in fostering students' critical and higher-order thinking, in promoting understanding of concepts and construction of meaning, and in extending students' knowledge. To be an effective questioner, you need to know how to use different questioning methods to achieve specific purposes (e.g., to facilitate factual recall, to encourage divergent thinking, to foster risk taking, to promote problem solving, to rouse curiosity). Here are some guidelines for using questioning in your classroom.

DO:

Establish a climate of trust and risk taking in your classroom.

Use questioning to help students clarify their thinking.

Ask questions that are simple, clear, and direct.

Evaluate the level of difficulty of your questions.

Make an effort to ask open-ended, divergent questions rather than lower-level questions.

Ask questions appropriate to your students' ability levels.

Call on students in an equitable manner.

Ask the question before calling a student by name for a response.

Give sufficient "wait time" (at least five seconds) after asking a question—do not hurry students into replying to questions.

Model courtesy and kindness.

Listen carefully to students' responses.

Use questioning to assist students in modifying their responses.

Encourage students to ask questions that challenge you or other students.

Use students' questions as launching pads for elaboration and further discussion.

Redirect trivial or irrelevant questions adroitly.

Ask questions that challenge students to justify their thinking and problem solving.

Aim for 100 percent involvement of students in classroom discussions.

AVOID:

Using sarcasm or making fun of incorrect responses.

Asking nonspecific questions like, "Does everyone understand?" or "Are there any questions?"

Asking questions that give away answers.

Answering your own questions.

Using facial expressions that show judgmental reactions to students' responses.

TIP 5: Motivate Your Students

Teachers often become frustrated because their students do not seem interested in learning. Especially if you will have older learners, students' lack of interest may be a problem when you start teaching. What can you do to create a classroom climate that support intellectual risk taking and fosters intrinsic motivation? Here are some ways to enhance motivation in your classroom.

DO:

Learn your students' names right away and use them at every opportunity.

Make sure your students know that you care about them and respect them.

Learn about each student's needs, interests, and desires and use this information to "hook" the student into engaging in learning opportunities.

Be warm and friendly toward your students.

Let your students know that you expect the best from them.

Provide a warm and supportive atmosphere in your classroom.

Recognize and reinforce students' efforts.

Use a variety of instructional strategies.

Involve the students in choosing and planning their own learning activities.

Relate lesson content to students' interests and experiences.

Make an effort (e.g., by using real-world examples) to show students the value and importance of the content to be learned.

Model enthusiasm and interest in the topic to be learned.

Build student choice into lessons.

Make sure students know what to do and how to do it.

Keep students actively engaged and involved.

Provide challenging activities in your lessons.

Make sure students have opportunities for success.

Capitalize on students' expressed interest or curiosity about a topic.

Appeal to your students' desire for fun and social interaction.

Use friendly competition when appropriate.

AVOID:

Giving up on reluctant or slow learners.

Betraying students' trust in you.

Overusing competition.

TIP 6: Praise Effectively

Many teachers automatically assume that praising students is always a good practice. While it is true that praise, if used appropriately, can be an effective tool for eliciting positive student behavior, critics maintain that indiscriminant praise can have undesirable effects in the classroom. They assert that many teachers overuse praise to the point that it becomes meaningless to students. Here are some guidelines for effectively using praise in your classroom.

DO:

Praise honestly and genuinely.

Praise in a natural, not an exaggerated, voice.

Praise privately, rather than publicly in front of the whole class.

State the specific behavior or effort that you are praising (e.g., "That is a clear explanation of how you worked the problem.")

Help students understand why the specific behavior or effort is deserving of praise (e.g., relating it to improvement).

Praise students' efforts, thereby encouraging them to persist at tasks.

Praise in a way that implies that students are intrinsically motivated (e.g., "You must feel good that you were able to work such a hard problem.")

AVOID:

Overusing praise or praising randomly.

Praising students with little thought to meaning.

Using general comments such as "Good job," "Terrific work," which make it difficult for students to determine the specific behavior or effort that is being praised.

Setting students up for failure (e.g., "You're my best-behaved student.").

Using public praise as a control technique (e.g., "I like the way the students at this table are being quiet and well-behaved.")

Suggesting that the praise is deserved because the behavior or effort pleases you.

TIP 7: Use Effective Classroom Management

Make your classroom a place where students feel safe, relaxed, and comfortable. Value and accept all students and treat them with dignity and respect at all times. Your classroom environment needs to be organized and predictable, providing an overall secure structure in which learning takes place. Creating and managing a smoothly functioning learning community is central to your success as a teacher. Here are some guidelines for effective classroom management.

DO:

Learn your students' names right away and use them often.

Be warm and caring toward your students.

Encourage your students to respect others and themselves.

Make sure your classroom is physically comfortable (e.g., not too hot or too cold, sufficient light).

Welcome your students' participation in developing classroom rules and procedures at the beginning of the year.

Involve students in establishing clear, logical consequences for inappropriate behavior.

Work with the students to establish a climate of trust, courtesy, and respect in your classroom.

Make sure the acceptable standards for behavior and the consequences in your classroom are age-appropriate.

Convey to students your expectation that they will accept responsibility for their own behavior.

Practice classroom procedures (e.g., how to transition from whole-group to small-group activities.)

Delay group activities until classroom rules and procedures have been established.

Use simple, easy-to-follow activities in the first few lessons of the school year.

Thoroughly plan lessons that keep students actively engaged.

Make sure you have worked through a lesson at least once before teaching it.

Make sure you have all your materials and supplies for each lesson.

Plan lessons that fit the allowable class time—not too long or too short.

Plan lessons that connect to students' interests and experiences.

Begin lessons promptly and keep a steady pace.

Manage transitions to maximize learning time for the students.

Limit the time students spend working alone at their seats.

Make sure students know they are accountable for doing their work.

Be proactive, anticipating when misbehavior is likely to occur and taking action *beforehand* to prevent or limit its occurrence.

Be quick to stop misbehavior or redirect students to more acceptable behavior with a minimum of disturbance to the learning process.

Be fair and consistent in applying classroom rules.

Use students' mistakes as opportunities to help them learn appropriate behavior.

Listen to and acknowledge students' feelings and frustrations and respond with respect when conflicts arise.

Guide students to resolve conflicts and model skills that encourage them to solve problems constructively.

Elicit the students' help in resolving problems and conflicts in the classroom (e.g., through class meetings).

Start with the least intrusive intervention (e.g., a serious gaze, rather than a verbal warning) when discouraging inappropriate behavior.

Be careful to preserve the student's dignity when using an intervention technique.

Ask students who misbehave to tell you what they did wrong, why the behavior is unacceptable, and what is acceptable behavior.

Focus on the unacceptable behavior, not on the student, when dealing with a student that has misbehaved.

Encourage acceptable behavior with appropriate praise.

Show that you have a sense of humor.

Be a role model for your students.

Continuously monitor your classroom.

AVOID:

Threatening students.

Humiliating students.

Bribing or coaxing students to behave appropriately.

Using punishments (e.g., being put a student in "time-out") rather than applying logical consequences (e.g., having the student clean up a mess the student made deliberately).

Giving students long corrective lectures for inappropriate behavior.

Getting into arguments with students.

Losing your temper and showing anger toward students.